the encyclopedia of cursed objects,

Artifacts of Misfortune, Folklore, and True-Case Hauntings

lorelai hamilton

contents

part three
religious & sacred artifacts

part four
art, writing & media objects

part five
domestic objects (mirrors, furniture, toys)

introduction

Objects are not inert.

They absorb use, belief, intention, memory. They pass through hands, homes, rituals, and moments of crisis, collecting meaning long after their original purpose has faded. Most objects do this quietly. Some do it violently.

The Encyclopedia of Cursed Objects is not a catalog of superstition in the dismissive sense, nor is it an argument for the supernatural as spectacle. It is a study of material folklore—the point at which human fear, grief, devotion, obsession, and belief attach themselves to things, and refuse to let go.

Across cultures and centuries, people have recorded the same unsettling pattern: certain objects become focal points for repeated misfortune. Illness clusters around them. Relationships fracture. Accidents recur. Owners report disturbances that escalate in recognizable stages. The language used to describe these experiences changes with time and place, but the structure of the stories does not.

This book treats cursed objects as phenomena, not props.

Each entry examines what is known—or claimed—about an object's origin, physical construction, cultural context, and documented history. Wherever possible, folklore is placed alongside archival records, museum documentation, oral history, and modern reporting. Skepticism and belief are treated not as opposing forces, but as parallel responses to the same human need: to explain why some things feel wrong to keep.

The objects collected here fall into recurring categories, each reflecting a different way meaning attaches itself to matter.

Ritual Objects & Tools are shaped by intention. Created to channel power, protection, or transformation, they are often cursed not through failure, but through overuse—or use that outlives the knowledge required to contain them.

Jewelry and Clothing & Personal Items cling to the body and the self. These objects absorb identity, intimacy, and loss. Rings remember promises. Veils remember endings. What is worn closest often leaves the deepest imprint.

Religious & Sacred Artifacts occupy a complicated space between devotion and fear. Revered objects can become dangerous when belief fractures, doctrine shifts, or reverence turns into obsession.

Art, Writing & Media Objects demonstrate that curses are not limited to the tactile. Words, images, and recorded stories can behave like vessels, carrying meaning that spreads, replicates, and resurfaces long after creation.

Finally, Domestic Objects—mirrors, furniture, toys, and other items meant to anchor safety and routine—are among the most unsettling. When the familiar turns hostile, the sense of violation is profound. These objects do not need ritual to function. They only need proximity.

A curse, as treated in this volume, is not always a deliberate act. It may arise through unresolved grief, repeated trauma, collective belief, or the simple insistence that an object *means something terrible*. Whether the force at work is psychological, cultural, or something less easily named is left deliberately open. What matters is that the effect persists.

This encyclopedia does not ask you to believe.

It asks you to notice patterns. To recognize how stories accumulate.

To understand why certain objects are locked away, buried, destroyed, or carefully displayed behind glass.

And if, while reading, you recognize something you own—

That is between you and the object.

part one
ritual objects & tools

1
the dybbuk box

T he listing went live in February of 2003.

It appeared on eBay, of all places, posted by a man named Kevin Mannis, an antiques dealer from Portland, Oregon. The description was odd but not sensational—curious, even restrained. Mannis explained that he had acquired a small wooden wine cabinet at an estate sale and that strange things had begun to happen afterward. He believed the box might be haunted. He did not recommend keeping it.

He was not selling a ghost story.

He was trying to get rid of something.

The box itself was unassuming: a small cabinet made of dark wood, with two doors, a little drawer, and Hebrew lettering carved into its surface. Inside were a collection of items that did not appear to belong together—a lock of hair, a dried rosebud, a granite statue, a goblet, a golden wine cup, and a single candle holder. The doors were often found open, even when sealed shut.

Mannis explained that the box had belonged to a Holocaust survivor, a woman he identified as having emigrated from Poland. According to her family, the box housed a *dybbuk*—a restless spirit in

3

Jewish folklore, traditionally the soul of a deceased person denied peace, capable of attaching itself to the living.

The woman had forbidden anyone from opening it.

They did anyway.

According to Mannis's account, the estate sale was the first rupture. The box was removed from its original home, passed casually from hand to hand. Within days, the woman's granddaughter began reporting nightmares—violent, repetitive dreams of an old woman screaming in a foreign language. The dreams stopped only when the box was removed from her house.

Mannis took it next.

That was a mistake.

He did not believe the story at first. He cleaned the box. Displayed it in his shop. He reported that the smell of cat urine began appearing inexplicably—sharp, acrid, localized to the box. Employees complained of dizziness, shadowed figures in their peripheral vision. One suffered a sudden stroke at a young age.

Mannis himself began to dream of an old woman pressing against his chest, whispering in a language he did not understand.

The dreams did not stop.

He sealed the box with wax and listed it for sale.

That is how the internet found it.

The winning bidder was a man named Jason Haxton, then the director of the Museum of Osteopathic Medicine in Missouri. Haxton acquired the box out of curiosity and professional interest. He did not open it immediately. He did not display it.

The symptoms began anyway.

Lights flickered. His mother suffered a stroke shortly after coming into contact with the box. Haxton himself developed a severe skin condition—painful lesions that appeared and disappeared without diagnosis. He dreamed of the same woman Mannis described, speaking a language Haxton could not identify but later learned matched Yiddish phrases associated with dybbuk lore.

Independently.

That detail matters.

Haxton attempted to research the box's origins. He consulted rabbis. Scholars. Folklorists. Many dismissed the idea outright. Others cautioned him—carefully, professionally—that dybbuk traditions were not toys, and that containment mattered more than belief.

Eventually, Haxton attempted a ritual resealing.

It did not go smoothly.

Over the years, the Dybbuk Box passed through several hands. Each transfer followed the same pattern: skepticism, proximity, escalation. Owners reported recurring nightmares, illness, financial collapse, accidents. One reportedly lost all of his hair. Another claimed his house filled with flies. Several begged Mannis to take the box back.

He refused.

No one wanted it.

What distinguishes the Dybbuk Box from older cursed objects is not its mythology, but its *paper trail*. Emails. Listings. Interviews. Medical records. The story is not reconstructed centuries later—it is archived as it happens. That makes it harder to dismiss and easier to argue over.

Skeptics point out inconsistencies. Mannis has admitted to embellishing some details in later years. Dybbuk boxes are not a recognized traditional Jewish artifact; they do not appear in classical religious texts. The ritual described by Haxton does not align cleanly with orthodox practice.

All of this is true.

And yet.

The experiences reported by unrelated owners share eerie consistencies. The same dreams. The same figure. The same sensations of pressure, suffocation, and presence. These are not details that circulate easily unless shared deliberately—and many of the accounts were not public when others reported them.

The box does not behave like a hoax that spirals out of control.

It behaves like something adapting.

Today, the Dybbuk Box is reportedly sealed and stored under controlled conditions. It has been displayed briefly, removed again, studied cautiously. Its current location is sometimes described as the Museum of Haunted Objects, though even that status shifts depending on who is speaking and when.

The box remains closed.

Most of the time.

The Dybbuk Box does not threaten. It does not perform. It simply punishes proximity and rewards distance. That restraint is part of its power. It does not need to convince you it is real. It only needs you to touch it once.

The oldest dybbuk stories warn that such spirits do not want to possess everyone.

They want a *place*.

And if the Dybbuk Box is nothing more than a story, it is a story that has shown an unsettling ability to follow the same rules over and over again.

There is a line in one of Haxton's private notes that never made it into the public narrative. It is brief, unadorned, and chilling in its simplicity:

"The box doesn't feel angry. It feels displaced."

That may be the most dangerous kind of haunting.

Not a rage.

Not a curse.

Just something that was sealed for a reason—and keeps trying to find its way back inside someone's life.

And if the lid opens again, as lids always seem to do, it will not ask whether you believe in it.

It will only ask whether you were warned.

2
the hope diamond
ritual idol

L ong before the diamond had a name, it had a place.

Not a setting or a mount, but a location—stone pressed into stone, dark against darker, where light was not meant to linger. The earliest stories do not describe a jewel. They describe an *eye*.

In several early accounts drawn from Indian oral tradition and later repeated—carelessly, often inaccurately—by European travelers, the blue stone was said to be set into the forehead or eye socket of a deity or guardian figure. Sometimes the idol is named, sometimes not. In most versions, it is not a god meant to be loved, but a watcher meant to remain awake.

The diamond was not decoration.

It was an anchor.

The stone believed to become the Hope Diamond originated in India, most likely from the Kollur Mine in the Golconda region, a source of some of the world's most legendary diamonds. The area was already saturated with religious significance long before European traders arrived. Stones were not inert there; they were charged by proximity, by placement, by story.

The blue diamond—then uncut, irregular, darker than it would later become—was said to have been removed from its original setting in the 17th century. The most persistent version names a French merchant-adventurer: Jean-Baptiste Tavernier. His writings confirm that he acquired a large blue diamond in India and brought it back to Europe in 1668.

What his writings do not confirm is *how* he acquired it.

That silence is where the ritual story grows teeth.

According to later retellings, the diamond was stolen—pried from a sacred figure, not traded. The act was not just theft but desecration, and the consequence was not immediate death but something slower and more precise: a sequence of misfortune that would follow the stone wherever it went.

Whether or not the idol ever existed in the form described, the belief that the diamond was *removed from ritual use* never disappears. Even after it is cut, renamed, and reset, that origin clings to it like residue.

Once a ritual object, always a ritual object.

In France, the stone was recut and renamed the Blue Diamond of the Crown. It passed into royal hands, worn and displayed as a symbol of wealth and divine favor. And for a time, nothing happened.

That pause matters.

Curses rarely announce themselves at the moment of offense. They wait for patterns to form.

The French monarchy fell in blood.

Louis XVI and Marie Antoinette were executed. The crown jewels were stolen during the Revolution. The blue diamond vanished, then reappeared years later—smaller, recut, altered just enough to obscure its identity.

But the violence did not end with the royals.

Those associated with the stone—owners, handlers, dealers—began to accumulate an unsettling portfolio of fates. Financial ruin. Sudden death. Public disgrace. The details vary, but the rhythm remains consistent.

People prosper briefly.

Then lose everything.

By the time the diamond reemerges in the 19th century as the Hope Diamond, its reputation has already begun to metastasize.

Stories attach themselves eagerly. Some are exaggerated. Some are demonstrably false. That does not weaken the narrative—it strengthens it.

Because now the curse is no longer tied to a single event. It is *portable*.

The Hope Diamond's later owners include socialites, collectors, and institutions. Several suffered dramatic reversals of fortune. Others did not. The inconsistency becomes part of the myth. The stone does not strike everyone. It selects.

That selectivity is what keeps belief alive.

If it killed everyone, it would be obvious.

If it killed no one, it would be forgotten.

Instead, it lingers in the uncomfortable middle.

Skeptics argue—correctly—that many of the tragedies associated with the Hope Diamond can be explained by coincidence, by the inherent instability of wealth, by the human tendency to connect unrelated events after the fact.

But skeptics rarely address the earlier layer of the story.

The idol.

The idea that the diamond was once *fixed* in place, given a job, and then violently displaced.

In many traditions, objects removed from ritual contexts do not become neutral. They become *homeless*. And homeless ritual objects are dangerous not because they are malicious, but because they no longer know where to belong.

Today, the Hope Diamond sits behind glass in the Smithsonian Institution, admired by millions. It is brightly lit. Carefully labeled. Scientifically analyzed. Its history is presented as a sequence of owners and cuts and settings.

The idol is not mentioned.

But visitors often report an odd response. Not fear—something quieter. A sense that the diamond does not belong to the room. That it looks wrong under the lights. That it seems to absorb attention rather than reflect it.

Museum staff do not encourage these interpretations.

They do not need to.

The diamond no longer kills openly. If it ever did. Its danger now is more subtle. It survives. It attracts. It invites retelling. It turns itself into a story that cannot be pinned down, only passed along.

That may be the final transformation of the ritual idol: from sacred object, to cursed jewel, to public artifact that still refuses to feel inert.

There is an old warning, rarely written, more often implied:

Do not remove what was meant to stay watching.

The Hope Diamond is no longer watching a temple.

It is watching us.

And whether that gaze means anything at all—or whether meaning is something we supply after the fact—is the question the diamond has been asking for centuries.

It does not need an answer.

It has time.

3
the basano vase

T he first death happens quietly.

There is no scream recorded, no struggle described. Only the image that survives: a young bride, newly married, found lifeless on the night meant to mark the beginning of her life. She is holding a small silver vase in her arms, clutching it as if it were precious—or necessary.

That is all the story gives us at the beginning. No cause of death. No illness named. No injury described. Just the stillness, and the vase.

From that moment on, the object refuses to let go of its association with endings.

The Basano Vase is said to have originated in southern Italy, most often linked—by name, if not by surviving documentation—to the town of Bassano del Grappa. The attribution is frustratingly vague, which is itself telling. Many cursed objects arrive with theatrical origins. This one arrives with gaps.

Most accounts place its creation in the 19th century, crafted from silver, modest in size, and unremarkable in design. No inscriptions. No symbols. No obvious ritual markings. It was not a relic, not a religious object, not a charm.

It was a wedding gift.

That detail is repeated insistently in later retellings, as though the storytellers themselves felt its irony too keenly to omit.

After the bride's death, the vase passed to a relative.

Then another.

And another.

Each owner died suddenly.

Not dramatically. Not violently. Simply *too soon*.

The deaths vary in explanation depending on who tells the story—accidents, illness, heart failure—but the pattern remains fixed. Ownership transfers. A brief interval. Death. The vase moves again.

Eventually, someone notices.

By the early 20th century, the vase's reputation had outpaced its paper trail. Stories circulated among collectors and families that the object "brought death." That phrase appears again and again, simple and unembellished, as if no further explanation were required.

At some point—no record survives of when—a warning was attached to the vase. A handwritten note, reportedly in Italian, advising that the object brought misfortune and should not be kept.

Warnings like that are rarely written at the beginning of a story.

They are written when someone is tired of burying people.

The vase disappears for a time, then resurfaces after World War II, when a family—either unaware of or dismissive toward its reputation—takes possession of it. According to widely circulated accounts, they are skeptical. Rational. Uninterested in folklore.

They keep the vase.

Within months, multiple members of the household die.

Again, the causes are varied. Again, the pattern holds.

It is after this that the vase is allegedly buried.

Sealed inside a lead box.

Hidden underground.

Removed from circulation.

The burial itself becomes part of the object's mythology. Lead is not an arbitrary choice—it is historically used for containment, for shielding, for isolation. Even if the burial is symbolic rather than documented, it reflects a belief that the vase cannot simply be discarded. It must be *contained*.

And then, inevitably, it is unearthed.

The most widely known modern account places the vase's reemergence in the late 20th century, when it is reportedly sold or gifted to a man who does not believe in curses. He keeps it briefly. He dies shortly thereafter in a car accident.

This version of the story appears in newspapers, books, and early internet forums, each time with small variations but the same spine. The vase changes hands. The owner dies. Someone tries to neutralize it.

Someone fails.

What is rarely described in the retellings is the time *before* the deaths.

The vase does not announce itself. It does not hum, glow, or draw the eye. Owners do not feel dread the moment it enters their homes. In several versions of the story, the opposite is true: the vase is admired. Commented on. Given a place of quiet honor on a shelf or table.

There is a lull.

People live with it.

They dust around it. They move it when guests come. They forget it for days at a time. Life continues in the ordinary way—meals, errands, conversations—until something small goes wrong. Not enough to panic over. A headache that lingers. A misstep on the stairs. A sense, described later only in hindsight, that the air in the room feels slightly thinner when the vase is nearby.

No one connects these moments at first. Why would they?

The danger of the Basano Vase is not that it demands belief.

It thrives on disbelief.

In the postwar account most frequently cited, the family who takes possession of the vase does so with open skepticism. They are described as practical people, uninterested in superstition. The warning attached to the vase is dismissed as melodrama—an old note clinging to an old object, nothing more.

The vase remains.

The first death is attributed to chance. The second to stress. The third forces a reckoning, but even then the connection is not immediate. Humans are very good at finding explanations that allow them to keep beautiful things.

By the time someone suggests the vase might be involved, it already feels absurd to say so aloud.

That hesitation costs time.

What follows is not a single dramatic event, but a quiet logistical response. The vase is removed from the living space. Put into storage. Given away. Buried. Each action is taken with the careful detachment of people who do not want to believe they are afraid.

The burial—when it occurs—is especially telling.

Lead is heavy. Inert. Traditionally associated with sealing, shielding, containment. Coffins were lined with it. Walls were painted with it. In folklore, lead does not destroy—it *isolates*.

You do not bury something in lead unless you believe it should not touch the world.

There is no record of a priest being called. No ritual performed. No attempt to cleanse or bless the object. That absence is striking.

The vase does not invite confrontation.

It invites removal.

And removal, in the logic of the story, is never the same as resolution.

The Basano Vase enters modern consciousness not through scholarship, but through repetition. Newspaper columns. Paranormal anthologies. Early message boards. Each retelling sands down the details, but preserves the structure:

A gift.

A death.

A warning ignored.

A pattern noticed too late.

What matters is not whether each death can be verified. What matters is that *the story survives without needing proof.*

That is how folklore behaves when it has found a shape that fits human fear.

Skeptics point out—correctly—that the lack of primary documentation makes the entire narrative suspect. No death certificates reference the vase. No Italian archives confirm the original bride. The story appears fully formed only in the late 20th century, when interest in cursed objects surged alongside mass media.

And yet.

The same skeptics often struggle to explain why the story *persists*, why it is retold with such restraint, why it resists embellishment. There are no demons attached to the vase. No dramatic manifestations. No moral lesson.

Only death.

The vase's current location is unknown.

Some insist it remains buried, sealed in lead, still doing nothing at all. Others claim it was destroyed—melted down, dispersed, neutralized. A minority believe it circulates privately among collectors who enjoy objects with reputations and trust themselves to be exceptions.

That belief—the belief in exception—is the final consistent element of the story.

Every owner is certain they will be different.

There is an old belief, less widely known, that certain objects do not cause harm so much as *refuse to prevent it*. They remove a margin of safety from the world. Accidents become fatal. Illnesses worsen. Timing collapses.

If that belief has any truth, then the Basano Vase is not a weapon.

It is an absence.

And absences are notoriously difficult to bury forever.

If you keep the vase, nothing will happen immediately.

If you give it away, the guilt will linger.

If you bury it, you will wonder whether burial is enough.

The story does not punish curiosity.

It punishes ownership.

And it waits patiently for someone who believes that warning labels are meant for other people.

Skeptics are quick to point out the lack of primary documentation. No death certificates link directly to the vase. No contemporary 19th-century records confirm the original bride's death as anything more than tragic coincidence. Much of the story crystallizes late, through repetition rather than archives.

And yet.

That is often how cursed objects behave in history.

They are not preserved by institutions. They survive through **reluctance**—the hesitation to keep them, to catalog them, to speak about them clearly. People do not write careful notes about things they believe are dangerous. They write warnings. They bury them. They pass them on.

What distinguishes the Basano Vase from other cursed objects is how *non-invasive* it is. It does not require rituals. It does not need to be opened, worn, or activated. Proximity appears to be enough.

You do not do anything wrong.

You simply keep it.

There are no recorded hauntings associated with the vase. No apparitions. No voices. No poltergeist activity. Its presence is clean, restrained, almost courteous.

And that may be the most unsettling part.

The vase does not announce itself as a threat. It allows you to feel safe—right up until you aren't.

Today, the Basano Vase's location is unknown.

Some claim it remains buried. Others insist it was destroyed. A few whisper that it has re-entered private circulation, stripped of its warning, waiting for someone who enjoys beautiful things and does not ask too many questions.

Because silver does not corrode easily.

And stories like this do not end just because we would prefer them to.

There is an old superstition in parts of Italy that certain objects "remember" the moment they were first given meaning. If that belief holds any truth at all, then the Basano Vase was defined at the instant it was pressed into a bride's hands on a night meant for beginnings—and instead became an ending.

Objects do not need intention to be dangerous.

Sometimes, they only need a first death.

And a second.

And a third.

And someone willing to believe that *this time* will be different.

4

the witch bottle
of norfolk

They found it under the hearth.

That detail matters, because hearths are not accidental places. In early modern England, the hearth was the mouth of the house: where heat entered, where smoke exited, where spirits were believed to pass. To hide something beneath it was to place a guard at the throat.

The bottle had been sealed there deliberately, pushed down into the packed earth, then built over as if it had never existed at all.

And for centuries, it worked.

The earliest Witch Bottles appear in England in the late 16th and early 17th centuries, precisely when belief in witchcraft was no longer abstract but legally lethal. Norfolk, in particular, was saturated with fear. This was the territory of Matthew Hopkins, the self-styled Witchfinder General, whose campaigns in the 1640s left villages stripped of trust and neighbors eager to accuse.

In that climate, protection became a private act.

You did not announce it.

You did not write it down.

You buried it.

A traditional witch bottle was not decorative. It was utilitarian and ugly by design. Stoneware bottles—often German "Bellarmine" jugs—were preferred for their durability and grotesque faces. Into them went the intimate materials of the person seeking protection: urine, nail clippings, hair. Sometimes pins or nails were added, bent or rusted, sometimes thorns or glass.

The logic was brutally sympathetic. If a witch had cursed you, the curse traveled through a link. The bottle created a trap: the witch's magic would follow the thread back to its source, enter the bottle, and be pierced, confused, or reflected until the witch herself fell ill or withdrew the curse.

The bottle was not meant to be opened.

Ever.

Norfolk accounts are unusually specific. In a 17th-century household near King's Lynn, a bottle was buried beneath the fireplace after a woman complained of sudden fits, nightmares, and inexplicable pains in her side. The symptoms were attributed to malefic witchcraft—common language at the time, but not casually applied.

The bottle was prepared by a local cunning-man. It was sealed with wax, inverted, and placed under the hearthstone.

The woman recovered.

Years later, a neighbor reportedly fell ill with similar pains and died after a prolonged sickness. Whether this was coincidence or narrative closure depends on who is telling the story.

But the bottle stayed buried.

Most witch bottles were never meant to be found again. Their power depended on concealment and continuity. The house changed around them—new families, new floors, new fires—but the bottle remained, absorbing the life of the home above it.

That is what makes their rediscovery so unsettling.

In the late 20th century, Norfolk saw a surge of archaeological interest in witch bottles, often uncovered during renovations. Builders would break through old hearths or foundations and uncover intact stoneware bottles, sometimes still sealed, sometimes cracked but undisturbed.

The contents were exactly what folklore predicted.

Urine residues.

Iron pins.

Human hair.

In one case, analyzed in the 1970s, the bottle still bore internal corrosion patterns consistent with liquid sealed for hundreds of years.

No one could explain why it had not leaked.

Problems tend to begin after removal.

Homeowners report a vague but persistent sense of unease. Sleep disturbances. Increased arguments. A feeling that the house has become "thin." These are not dramatic hauntings—no apparitions, no voices—but the loss of a stabilizing pressure, like removing a keystone and waiting to see what shifts.

In one documented Norfolk case, a bottle removed during renovations was displayed briefly on a mantelpiece. Within weeks, the house experienced a string of minor but escalating mishaps: a fall on the stairs, a kitchen fire, a child's unexplained illness.

The bottle was reburied in the garden.

The disturbances subsided.

Skeptics argue—reasonably—that witch bottles functioned as psychological reassurance. A ritualized sense of control in a dangerous world. The recovery stories are anecdotal. The accidents coincidental.

But that explanation does not fully account for the *instructions* that accompany these objects when they are found.

Again and again, folklore insists on the same rule:

Do not open the bottle.

And if you do, do not keep it indoors.

The bottle is not a charm. It is a containment unit.

Museums now house dozens of witch bottles, including several from Norfolk. They are cataloged carefully, stored securely, sometimes x-rayed rather than opened. Curators note that early collectors often destroyed bottles to examine their contents, unaware that this violated every rule associated with them.

Modern conservation practice is more cautious.

Some knowledge is better left sealed.

What makes the Witch Bottle particularly unsettling is that it is not aggressive. It does not seek victims. It does not act unless disturbed. Its purpose is defensive—until someone decides to *improve* things by removing it.

Then the question becomes unavoidable:

If the bottle was trapping something, where does it go when the trap is broken?

Today, builders in Norfolk are trained to recognize witch bottles when they find them. Many are left in place or reburied with care. The practice has come full circle—from folk magic to archaeology to a kind of quiet respect.

Not belief, exactly.

But not dismissal either.

Because houses remember the things done to protect them.

And sometimes, protection looks like a sealed bottle in the dark, patiently doing its work while generations forget why it was ever needed.

5
the hand of glory

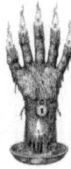

The hand is always taken from a dead man.

That is the first rule, and it appears in every account that survives—across centuries, languages, and regions. The man must have been executed, usually by hanging. He must have died publicly. His body must still be warm when the hand is cut away.

In some tellings, it must be the right hand. In others, the left. Occasionally, the hand is specified as "the hand that committed the crime." What never changes is the insistence that this is not just flesh—it is **residual intent**, preserved.

The Hand of Glory is not made.

It is *harvested.*

The earliest written references appear in late medieval Europe, though the practice is almost certainly older, carried orally by thieves, highwaymen, and those who lived outside the law. The name itself—*Main de Gloire*—is first recorded in French sources, a linguistic corruption of *mandragore*, the mandrake root, another object steeped in criminal folklore and execution imagery.

Like the mandrake, the Hand of Glory sits at the intersection of punishment and power.

The preparation was precise.

After removal, the hand was dried—sometimes in the sun, sometimes in a chimney, sometimes buried in salt or lime. In several grimoires, the instructions are explicit: the hand must be wrapped in a shroud, treated as a corpse, prayed over *backward*. The fingers were then dipped in fat rendered from the same criminal's body, or from another executed man. In some versions, each finger became a candle wick.

Five lights.

One hand.

One purpose.

The purpose was burglary.

Or, more accurately: entry without resistance.

When lit and carried into a house, the Hand of Glory was said to render its inhabitants unconscious—sleeping so deeply they could not be woken by noise, pain, or panic. Doors would unlock themselves. Locks would loosen. Dogs would not bark.

And if a candle finger went out, it could only be relit with blood or milk.

Accounts differ on which.

The Hand of Glory appears most often in French and English folklore, but versions exist across Germany, Italy, and parts of Eastern Europe. In nearly every case, the hand is linked to professional thieves —people who moved quietly, deliberately, and often without leaving witnesses.

That absence matters.

Because what survives in the record are not the successful uses of the Hand, but the times it failed—or was discovered.

One of the most frequently cited incidents comes from Lancashire in the early 18th century. According to local accounts collected later by folklorists, a group of thieves attempted to rob a farmhouse using a Hand of Glory. The household fell unnaturally still. Lamps dimmed. The thieves entered easily.

But the farmer's wife awoke.

Some versions say she had been warned. Others say she had iron on her person, or that she had been drinking milk before bed—milk being repeatedly cited as a substance that resists the hand's influence.

She saw the intruders holding what she later described as "a dead hand burning."

She threw milk on it.

The hand went dark.

The thieves fled, leaving the hand behind. The farmhouse reportedly never felt safe again.

Whether the story is literal or embellished, it reveals the cultural logic of the object. The Hand of Glory was not just a tool. It was a *contest*—between criminal cunning and domestic protection, between unlawful entry and the sanctity of the home.

And sometimes, the house remembered.

Museums hold several alleged Hands of Glory today, though few are definitively authenticated. The most famous is housed in the Whitby Museum in North Yorkshire: a shriveled human hand, mummified, blackened, fingers curled as though mid-grasp. It was reportedly found concealed in a wall during renovations in the 1930s, wrapped in cloth, accompanied by instructions written in archaic script.

The museum labels it cautiously.

Visitors are less cautious.

Staff have recorded persistent rumors: electronics malfunctioning nearby, visitors feeling dizzy or faint, an unusual number of people refusing to stay alone in the gallery. Nothing provable. Nothing dramatic.

Just enough.

What is striking, across accounts, is how *personal* the Hand of Glory feels. Unlike cursed jewelry or books, which can be passed along abstractly, the Hand is unmistakably human. You cannot forget what it is. You cannot mistake it for metaphor.

It forces a recognition: someone died so that someone else could enter quietly.

That recognition alone is unsettling.

Skeptical explanations abound. Many alleged Hands of Glory are likely ritualized animal remains, or medical specimens misidentified later. The instructions associated with them are sometimes contradictory, clearly copied or romanticized in later centuries.

But skepticism does not erase the pattern.

Hands in walls.

Hands near doors.

Hands positioned where entry matters.

In some traditions, a house protected against the Hand of Glory must be defended *before* it arrives. Iron nails in thresholds. Milk left near doorways. Written charms above the lintel. Once the Hand was inside, it was said to be too late.

The house would sleep.

Modern interpretations often frame the Hand of Glory as a symbol —a manifestation of social fear around crime, punishment, and bodily desecration. That is not wrong.

But symbols do not usually leave objects behind.

And they do not usually inspire the same quiet instruction, repeated for hundreds of years:

Do not light it indoors unless you are prepared to leave.

Today, most Hands of Glory—real or alleged—are securely stored, cataloged, studied. They are described as artifacts, curiosities, folklore remnants.

No one recommends recreating one.

No one recommends touching one barehanded.

And no one, officially, recommends lighting it.

Because even now, long after the gallows are gone and the roads are safer, the Hand of Glory carries an implication that has never aged out of relevance:

That a house is only secure as long as no one knows how to enter it quietly.

And that sometimes, the dead remember how.

6

the devil's
tramping shoes

T he shoes are always found facing inward.

That detail appears again and again in the records, almost as an afterthought. Parish notes mention it casually. Folklore collectors repeat it without emphasis. Witnesses recall it only when prompted, as if it didn't seem important at the time.

But it is the detail that refuses to let go.

They are small leather shoes, sometimes boots, sometimes slippers, discovered in places they should not be: sealed chimneys, behind hearthstones, inside walls that have not been opened in generations. And when they are found, they are almost always turned toward the room—toward the people who live there—as though they had been placed deliberately to watch.

The earliest surviving references to what would later be called the Devil's Tramping Shoes appear in England during the late medieval period, though the practice they belong to is almost certainly older. Shoes—real ones, worn ones—were concealed in buildings as part of a widespread folk custom meant to ward off evil. The logic was sympathetic: a shoe, shaped by a human foot, was thought to confuse or trap malign forces that followed people into their homes.

The practice was protective.

Until it wasn't.

By the 16th and 17th centuries, accounts begin to diverge. In some cases, concealed shoes were credited with stopping misfortune: illness abating, livestock surviving, strange noises ceasing. In others, the shoes seemed to *attract* disturbance. Families reported persistent sounds of walking inside walls, particularly at night. Scraping. Slow, deliberate pacing.

As if someone were trying on the house.

In a 1662 account from East Anglia, a mason repairing a collapsed chimney reportedly found a single child-sized boot embedded deep in the brickwork. The homeowner later insisted it had not been placed there for protection, but as a response to something already happening in the house—"a weight," he called it, "that went up and down the stairs when no one was there."

The boot was removed.

Within a month, the house burned.

It is around this time that the interpretation shifts. Folk belief begins to frame certain concealed shoes not as traps for evil, but as *marks of passage*. Objects left behind by something that had already entered—and left again.

Tramping shoes.

The name "Devil's Tramping Shoes" does not appear in print until the 19th century, but oral tradition suggests it had been used long before. The Devil, in European folklore, is rarely a single figure. He is a walker, a tester, a visitor at thresholds. He appears on roads, at cross-roads, at doorways. He travels.

And travelers leave things behind.

One of the most cited cases comes from a farmhouse in Northamptonshire, dismantled in 1838. During renovations, workers uncovered two leather shoes, badly decayed, wedged behind the hearth. They were adult-sized, mismatched, and positioned heel-to-toe, pointing inward.

The family who lived there reported no active hauntings—but their records showed a pattern of short tenancies, sudden departures, and unexplained deaths stretching back over a century. Children who did not survive infancy. Servants who left without notice. Livestock that sickened repeatedly in the same stalls.

Nothing dramatic.

Just enough.

The shoes were removed and discarded. Within weeks, the house was struck by a string of accidents: a fall from a ladder, a kitchen fire, a horse bolting and breaking its leg. The family rehung a single shoe—new, unworn—near the hearth in what they described as "a desperate imitation of the old practice."

The disturbances lessened.

They never fully stopped.

What makes the Devil's Tramping Shoes unsettling is not what they do, but what they *suggest*.

Unlike cursed objects that arrive with ceremony—rituals, spells, invocations—these appear after the fact. They are remnants. Evidence. Proof that something has already crossed the threshold and may cross it again.

In several accounts, the shoes show signs of wear inconsistent with their placement. Soles scuffed as though walked in after being concealed. Leather creased where no foot should have bent it. In one Yorkshire case from the early 1800s, a shoe removed from a wall reportedly left damp footprints on the floor before crumbling into dust.

Skeptics have explanations for all of this.

They always do.

Theories range from the practical to the symbolic. Shoes as protective charms. Shoes as builders' talismans. Shoes as remnants of older pagan practices absorbed into Christian domestic life. Some argue the sounds attributed to "tramping" were simply thermal expansion or rodents.

And yet.

Those explanations fail to account for the consistency of placement. The orientation. The repetition of the same details across regions that did not communicate easily with one another.

Most troubling of all: the insistence, in multiple accounts, that removing the shoes *made things worse*.

By the Victorian era, antiquarians and folklorists began collecting concealed shoes, often removing them from buildings for display or study. The Pitt Rivers Museum alone holds dozens. Many are child-sized. Many are heavily worn. Most are cataloged as protective objects.

A few are cataloged with hesitation.

Curators note disturbances in storage rooms. Mislabeling. Objects found out of place. Nothing dramatic. Just small inconsistencies that require correction.

One archivist, writing privately in the early 20th century, remarked that certain shoes seemed "reluctant to stay filed."

In modern times, builders still occasionally uncover them. Renovation crews find shoes behind plasterboard, under floorboards, sealed into chimneys long since blocked. Most are quietly reburied or discarded. A few are kept.

Almost all are returned.

Those who keep them report an odd compulsion to place them somewhere—near a door, by a fireplace, facing inward. As though the house itself were missing something.

As though something might come back for them.

The Devil's Tramping Shoes do not announce themselves with violence or spectacle. They do not curse loudly. They do not demand attention.

They wait.

They suggest that a house is not a static thing, but a path. That something passed through once, tested the ground, and left a marker behind. Not a warning.

A reminder.

And if you find such a shoe—crumbling leather, toes pointed toward your living room—it may be tempting to remove it. To cleanse the space. To tidy history.

But folklore, stubborn and unkind, offers a quieter counsel:

Some thresholds are safer when you let them believe they are still guarded.

7

the cursed ouija
board of st. louis

T he board was never supposed to leave the apartment.

It was purchased sometime in the early 1970s from a novelty shop off Delmar Boulevard, the kind of place that sold lava lamps, zodiac posters, and incense strong enough to mask the smell of damp brick and old wiring. The Ouija board itself was ordinary: mass-produced, pressed fiberboard, faux-antique lettering, a planchette that felt too light to be taken seriously.

That was the second mistake—assuming that seriousness mattered.

The apartment belonged to a group of college students, most of them renting their first place away from home. It was a narrow, second-floor walk-up with creaking floors and windows that rattled whenever the buses passed. The building had been standing since the early 1900s, subdivided and resubdivided, its original purpose long forgotten under layers of paint and cheap renovation.

No one believed in ghosts.

They believed in boredom.

The first session was a joke. They sat cross-legged on the living room floor, lights on, beer bottles sweating onto the carpet. They asked the usual questions—*Is anyone there? What's your name?*—and laughed when the planchette didn't move.

Then it did.

Just slightly. Enough to be written off as someone nudging it. Enough to invite repetition.

Over the next week, they played again and again. The tone shifted without anyone noticing exactly when. The questions became more specific. The answers became more coherent. The planchette began to move faster, with a confidence that felt... practiced.

The name it spelled out changed every time.

That should have ended it.

It didn't.

By the third week, strange things were happening outside the sessions.

One of the students—Mark, according to later accounts—began waking up at exactly 3:17 a.m. every night, his heart racing, convinced someone was standing in the corner of his room. Another reported hearing whispers in the walls, not voices exactly, but the suggestion of speech, like someone murmuring in another room with the door closed.

Small accidents accumulated. Glasses shattered without being touched. Doors stuck, then slammed open. The planchette went missing, only to be found in places no one remembered putting it.

Still, they played.

Because nothing dramatic had happened yet.

The turning point came during a session that was not planned.

Only two of them were home that night. Rain had soaked the city for hours, the river swollen and dark. They hadn't intended to use the board—but it was already out, leaning against the wall where someone had left it after the last session.

They sat down without turning on all the lights.

That was the third mistake.

From the moment their fingers touched the planchette, the movement was immediate and violent. It spelled words they hadn't asked for. Names they didn't recognize. Dates that didn't make sense.

Then it spelled an address.

Their address.

Then a second one.

Then a third.

All in St. Louis. All within a few miles.

One of them tried to pull their hand away. The planchette jerked hard enough to scrape skin. They ended the session by force, shoving the board under the couch and leaving the apartment entirely, standing in the rain until their hands stopped shaking.

They did not sleep that night.

Within days, the apartment became unlivable.

The air felt wrong—heavy, sour. People argued constantly, snapping at each other over nothing. One roommate moved out abruptly, leaving most of his belongings behind. Another began drinking heavily, insisting he could hear someone calling his name from the stairwell when no one was there.

The board reappeared repeatedly, no matter where it was hidden.

Under the bed. In a closet. Wrapped in a towel and shoved into a box. It always came back out, leaning casually against a wall, as if someone had set it there deliberately.

No one admitted to moving it.

The incident that cemented its reputation happened in late autumn.

A visiting friend—someone who had never used the board before—picked it up, laughed, and suggested one last session "to prove it was all bullshit." Against their better judgment, the others agreed.

This time, the board did not bother with pleasantries.

The planchette spelled *LEAVE* over and over again. Then *NOW*. Then *DOWN*.

When they asked what that meant, the planchette slid off the board entirely and hit the floor, cracking cleanly in half.

At that exact moment, the power went out in the building.

In the darkness, someone screamed—not one of them, but from below, echoing up the stairwell. Sirens followed minutes later. An elderly tenant on the first floor had fallen down the stairs, breaking her neck.

The address the board had spelled earlier matched hers.

That was the last time the board was used.

They tried to throw it away.

That was the fourth mistake.

No matter where they left it—dumpsters, trash chutes, even a vacant lot miles away—it returned. Once it was found on the apartment's front steps. Another time, leaning against the building's basement door, warped slightly as if it had been underground.

Finally, one of them took it home, planning to burn it.

The fire wouldn't take.

The board blackened, smoked, but did not catch. The smell lingered for days, sharp and chemical. That night, the house filled with the sound of knocking—steady, deliberate—coming from the walls.

The board was brought back to St. Louis the next morning.

After that, the trail becomes harder to follow.

Some accounts claim the board was turned over to a local priest, who refused to keep it but performed a blessing before instructing them to store it away from living spaces. Others say it was sealed in a trunk and placed in a storage unit near the river, where it remained for years.

There are rumors—always rumors—that the unit flooded during a particularly bad season, and that the trunk was lost. That items from it began appearing in antique shops months later, water-stained and unlabeled.

No one can say for certain.

What *is* certain is that similar boards began circulating in the city afterward, each with eerily consistent reports: planchettes moving too fast, answers too precise, sessions that escalated without warning.

Some swear it was never about the board at all.

Just the place.

St. Louis is built in layers. Old buildings atop older foundations, neighborhoods shifting and erasing themselves every few decades. It is a city of intersections—rivers, railroads, migrations—and intersections are dangerous things in folklore. They invite crossings.

The Ouija board didn't create something.

It gave it a voice.

Today, no museum claims the Cursed Ouija Board of St. Louis. There is no verified photograph, no catalog entry. The object survives in testimony, in police reports that never mention it, in whispered warnings passed between people who know better than to mock certain things.

And yet, every so often, someone buys a board in the city and swears it feels *familiar*. Like it's been used before. Like it remembers hands that are no longer there.

They say the planchette sometimes moves before anyone touches it.

They say the board doesn't like to be ignored.

If there is a lesson here, it is not the usual one.

This was not about summoning demons or inviting evil. It was about attention. Repetition. The careless intimacy of asking questions you don't intend to hear answered.

The board did not threaten.

It did not lie.

It simply responded.

And in a city built on buried stories, that was enough.

Some doors don't need to be forced open.

They're already listening.

8
the bell witch cave stone

T hey will tell you the Bell Witch lives in Tennessee.

They are wrong.

The Bell Witch *moves* through Tennessee, the way water moves through limestone—slowly, invisibly, reshaping what it touches. The cave is not her home. It is a mouth. And the stone that came out of it is not an artifact so much as a fragment of pressure, broken loose.

It is easier to begin with the cave, because the stone makes no sense without it.

The Bell Witch Cave lies along the Red River, near what was once the Bell family farm in Robertson County. The land looks ordinary enough until you know where to stand. Then it drops away into a limestone hollow that breathes cold air even in summer. The cave has been there far longer than the Bell family, longer than recorded history, longer than the stories that would later cling to it like mold.

Caves always attract stories. But this one did not wait for a storyteller.

By the early 1800s, the Bell family was already experiencing what they could not explain: knocking sounds, voices, invisible blows, animals behaving strangely, children being struck by unseen hands. This was not a single haunting, but a sustained campaign—years long, relentless, public. The entity spoke. It named itself. It argued with preachers. It predicted deaths.

And it mentioned the cave.

Over and over.

Contemporary accounts—letters, affidavits, newspaper articles—treat the cave as a focal point long before tourists did. The spirit, calling itself "Kate," spoke of it as a place of retreat and power. Witnesses reported voices echoing from inside it when no one was there. Some claimed the sounds followed them out, lingering like a pressure in the ears.

The cave was not just nearby.

It was *involved.*

At some point—sources differ on exactly when—someone removed a stone from the cave.

It was not carved. It was not marked. Just a fist-sized piece of limestone, pale and pitted, like thousands of others that could be found along the riverbank.

Except this one did not behave like the others.

Those who handled it reported an immediate sense of discomfort. Not fear—*attention.* A feeling of being noticed by something that did not need eyes. The stone was cold, even in warm hands. Some described a faint vibration, others a heaviness that seemed disproportionate to its size.

No one wanted to keep it long.

Which is how it moved.

The stone passed through several hands over the 19th century, always briefly, always reluctantly. It appeared in parlors, barns, studies. People showed it to guests, then put it away, then quietly returned it to the person who had given it to them.

Stories began to accrete around it—not dramatic curses, but patterns.

Children avoided it without being told to. Animals refused to go near it. People reported headaches, nausea, disturbed sleep. Dreams featured confined spaces, whispering voices, and the sensation of being pressed flat against rock.

One account, recorded in the late 1800s, describes a woman who kept the stone wrapped in cloth in a dresser drawer. She reported that the drawer would not stay closed, no matter how often it was repaired. When the stone was removed, the problem ceased.

The repairs were sound.

The drawer simply did not want to keep it.

Skeptics later suggested environmental explanations: sulfur, limestone dust, suggestion, hysteria. All reasonable. All incomplete.

Because the symptoms did not follow belief.

They followed *proximity*.

By the early 20th century, as the Bell Witch legend became more codified, the stone acquired a new status. It was no longer just a troublesome object. It was treated as a relic—dangerous, yes, but *important*. Some believed it was part of the entity itself. Others thought it acted as an anchor, a way for the haunting to manifest physically.

The most persistent theory is also the least comforting: that the stone was not empowered by the Bell Witch, but by the cave itself.

Caves are not empty spaces. They are pressure systems, memory traps. Sound behaves strangely in them. Time behaves strangely too, if you listen to the stories told by people who work underground long enough.

Remove a stone, and you don't just take material.

You break a pattern.

In the mid-20th century, the stone vanished.

There is no dramatic theft. No curse on the thief. Just a quiet disappearance from the informal chain of custody that had carried it for decades. Some say it was returned to the cave. Others claim it was buried on private land. A few insist it still exists, kept by someone who does not talk about it.

What *is* documented is that, after its disappearance, reports of Bell Witch activity near the cave diminished—but did not stop.

The voices grew rarer.

The stories grew quieter.

The cave remained.

Visitors today are warned not to take anything from the cave. This is framed as preservation, which is sensible. But locals will tell you another reason if you ask the right way.

"The cave notices," they'll say.

They won't explain how.

There is no museum record for the Bell Witch Cave Stone. No catalog number. No glass case. That absence matters. Objects like this resist preservation because preservation requires stasis, and nothing associated with the Bell Witch stays still for long.

If the stone still exists—and it may—it is likely doing what it has always done: moving just enough to avoid settling, passing from hand to hand, never staying where it is not wanted.

Or it may be back where it belongs, wedged into the cave wall, indistinguishable from every other stone except to whatever learned its shape the first time.

The Bell Witch never claimed the stone.

It never had to.

The danger was never possession.

It was removal.

And if there is a warning here, it is the same one the cave has always offered, patiently, without malice:

Some places are not haunted because something happened there.

They are haunted because they are *open.*

And some stones, once taken from the dark, do not forget how the dark felt.

They simply wait for the chance to return.

9

the pulsa de nura effigy

("Blows of Fire"; the Burning Sentence)

N o object announces itself as a Pulsa de Nura.
That is the first mistake people make when they try to understand it. They imagine something ornate—engraved metal, ancient parchment, a relic locked behind glass. But the Pulsa de Nura does not rely on permanence. It relies on *intention*, on repetition, on agreement.

What remains afterward—the effigy, the written name, the burned scraps—is incidental.

The ritual is the thing.

And rituals, once performed, do not stay where they are put.

The phrase *Pulsa de Nura* comes from Aramaic. It is usually translated as "lashes of fire," though scholars argue the wording is less poetic and more procedural. The phrase appears in the Talmud as a description of divine punishment administered by angels—a sentence carried out in the heavenly court, not by human hands.

Which is precisely why its later transformation is so disturbing.

Because at some point—no one can say exactly when—the idea emerged that humans could *invoke* it.

Not metaphorically.

Not symbolically.

Invoke it as a verdict.

The earliest references to Pulsa de Nura as a performed rite appear in medieval Kabbalistic texts, whispered rather than recorded, framed as theoretical discussions rather than instructions. These passages are careful, even evasive. They speak of dangers. Of consequences. Of the risk to the practitioners themselves.

What they do not do is deny that such a thing is possible.

By the early modern period, stories circulate of small groups of learned men—always described as restrained, devout, and reluctant—gathering at night to pronounce a sentence against someone they believed had committed an unforgivable spiritual crime.

Not sin.

Cosmic damage.

The effigy appears later.

It is not required, but it is often present.

A rough human form. Wax, clay, sometimes cloth. Rarely detailed. The name of the condemned written or carved into it, sometimes accompanied by astrological symbols or fragments of scripture. No embellishment. No artistry. This is not sympathetic magic in the folk sense.

This is a placeholder.

A stand-in for a body that cannot be brought to the ritual itself.

Accounts from the 17th and 18th centuries describe the rite obliquely, as something "known to scholars" but not practiced lightly. The language is always defensive. The writers insist they do not condone it. They warn against it. They emphasize that it requires unanimity, purity, and absolute certainty of guilt.

The insistence is telling.

No one defends something that does not exist.

In the modern era, the Pulsa de Nura becomes infamous not because of theology, but because of names.

Public figures.

Politicians.

People who later died suddenly.

In the late 20th century, reports surface in Israeli media describing clandestine Pulsa de Nura ceremonies performed against individuals accused of betraying the Jewish people. In several cases, the targets died months or years later—sometimes violently, sometimes of illness, sometimes by their own hand.

Correlation is not causation.

Everyone says this.

And yet the stories persist.

Witness descriptions of these modern rites are eerily consistent.

A small group, often ten men. Midnight or near it. Candles. Psalms spoken in reverse order. The effigy placed at the center. The name pronounced again and again, followed by invocations calling upon angels of destruction to carry out divine justice.

The effigy is then burned.

Not ceremonially.

Efficiently.

The remains are buried or scattered. No one takes souvenirs. No one speaks afterward.

Those who claim to have witnessed such rituals often say the same thing when pressed: the atmosphere was not dramatic.

It was *administrative*.

Like paperwork for God.

Skeptics argue that Pulsa de Nura functions as psychological violence rather than supernatural force—a way to terrorize enemies, to signal exclusion, to frame later misfortune as deserved. There is truth here. The power of belief is not small, especially when reinforced by community, fear, and isolation.

But this explanation frays at the edges.

Because not all targets knew they had been named.

Some learned only after their deaths.

And some never learned at all.

The effigies themselves are rarely preserved.

This is intentional.

Keeping one would be dangerous—not because it radiates energy, but because it represents an *unfinished relationship*. An accusation suspended in time. A verdict that has been spoken but not resolved.

Collectors who claim to possess Pulsa de Nura effigies often describe misfortune that is subtle at first: insomnia, fixation, an inability to stop thinking about the named individual. Later comes paranoia, social rupture, illness.

The pattern is not punishment.

It is *entanglement*.

What makes the Pulsa de Nura uniquely disturbing among curse traditions is that it does not frame itself as magic.

It frames itself as law.

There is no bargaining. No offering. No appeasement. The ritual does not ask for harm; it declares that harm has already been authorized.

If something goes wrong afterward, the ritual has an answer prepared:

Justice was delayed.

Justice was partial.

Justice fell elsewhere.

Today, most rabbinic authorities denounce the Pulsa de Nura outright. They describe it as superstition at best, blasphemy at worst. They emphasize that humans cannot compel divine judgment.

And still, rumors persist.

Small gatherings. Quiet rooms. Names spoken carefully.

Effigies burned and forgotten.

If there is a warning embedded in the Pulsa de Nura tradition, it is not about curses.

It is about certainty.

Every account, ancient and modern, circles the same danger: the moment when humans become convinced they are qualified to issue final sentences.

The effigy does not carry the curse.

The people do.

And once that belief is shared—spoken aloud, agreed upon, enacted—it does not vanish with the smoke.

It simply looks for somewhere else to land.

Which may be why no one keeps the effigy.

And why no one who has seen one ever wants to describe it for long.

Some things are safer when they are allowed to burn completely.

And some judgments, once spoken, do not need an object to remember them.

10
the cursing dolls of mexico

(Isla de las Muñecas — "The Island of the Dolls")

The first thing people notice is the silence.

That surprises them, because they have been told to expect screams.

The canals of Xochimilco are rarely quiet. Birds skim the water. Boats drift past with music and laughter. Voices echo between the reeds. But when the boat turns toward the narrow channel leading to the island, the sound thins. The air changes. Even the water seems to slow.

And then the dolls appear.

They hang from trees, nailed to posts, tied with wire, balanced in alcoves and branches. Some are intact. Most are not. Their eyes are clouded, missing, or filled with dirt. Limbs dangle at wrong angles. Hair clings to moss and bark as if the island itself is wearing them.

This is not decoration.

This is accumulation.

The story begins in the 1950s, though no one agrees on the exact year. A man named Don Julián Santana Barrera lived alone on a small chinampa—one of the artificial islands built centuries earlier by the Mexica people—in the canals south of Mexico City.

43

He was not a recluse at first. He farmed. He tended the land. He traded with passing boatmen. The island was ordinary.

Until the girl drowned.

According to the version Don Julián told later in life, he found her body tangled in the reeds near his island. She was young. A child. He could not save her. Not long after, he discovered a doll floating in the water—ragged, waterlogged, one eye missing.

He hung it in a tree.

At the time, this did not seem strange. Dolls are offerings. Dolls are stand-ins. Across cultures, they absorb what cannot be spoken.

But Don Julián did not stop.

Soon after the first doll was hung, he claimed the island changed.

He heard footsteps at night. Whispers. Laughter that did not belong to adults. He became convinced the spirit of the drowned girl lingered there, restless and angry, and that the doll had not satisfied her.

So he found another.

And another.

He pulled them from canals, garbage heaps, abandoned boats. He accepted them from visitors. He scavenged relentlessly, hanging each doll carefully, as if placement mattered. Some were tied at eye level. Others were nailed high, overlooking the water. A few were placed facing inward, toward the center of the island.

He spoke to them.

He prayed.

He begged.

This is where the tone of the story shifts.

Because Don Julián did not claim the dolls were cursed.

He claimed they were *necessary*.

Visitors who encountered him in the 1970s and 80s described a man deeply afraid—not of the dolls, but of stopping. He insisted that the spirits demanded vigilance. That the dolls watched while he slept. That they kept something worse at bay.

He refused to remove any of them.

He refused to leave.

And slowly, the island became something else.

By the time journalists began visiting in the late 20th century, the

44

island was saturated. Hundreds of dolls hung in various stages of decay. Some had been there for decades, bleached and splitting. Others were new, their plastic still bright, their expressions eerily cheerful among the rot.

Visitors reported unease almost immediately. Not terror. Not shock. Unease.

They felt observed—not by one presence, but many. Eyes everywhere. Faces tilted at slightly wrong angles. Dolls facing away from paths, as if watching something behind the trees instead.

Some swore the dolls moved.

Most later admitted they were not sure.

Don Julián died in 2001.

He was found in the same canal where the girl had drowned, near the same spot.

That coincidence hardened the legend.

After his death, caretakers moved his body, but the island remained. Boats continued to arrive. Visitors brought more dolls—offerings, jokes, dares, souvenirs. The accumulation accelerated.

This is the critical distinction.

The curse did not originate with the dolls.

It *formed* around them.

Over time, a pattern emerged among visitors who treated the island lightly.

People reported nausea, headaches, intrusive dreams. Children cried unexpectedly. Cameras malfunctioned. Some visitors took dolls as souvenirs, only to later return them—quietly, without explanation.

A recurring theme appears in interviews: the sense that the dolls did not want to leave.

Not angrily.

Possessively.

As if removal broke a rule that had never been spoken.

Skeptics have explanations, and many of them are reasonable.

Human brains are pattern-making machines. The island is visually overwhelming. The setting primes fear. Don Julián himself may have suffered from untreated mental illness, and the legend grew after his death.

All of this may be true.

And yet.

There are too many similar accounts from people who did not know the story before they arrived. Too many reports of dolls appearing in different positions than expected. Too many returned offerings.

The most unsettling detail is not supernatural at all.

It is how quickly visitors stop laughing.

Today, Isla de las Muñecas is a tourist destination. Boats arrive daily. Photos circulate endlessly online. The dolls continue to decay, replaced by newer ones, layer upon layer of plastic and cloth and glass.

The island no longer belongs to Don Julián.

It belongs to the story.

And stories, once fed long enough, do not starve easily.

Stand on the island long enough and a strange thought begins to surface.

What if the dolls are not meant to trap the spirit?

What if they are meant to *distract* it?

What if they are not cursed objects, but witnesses—hung there to watch so that something else does not have to?

No one stays long enough to test that theory.

They leave offerings instead.

Just in case.

Even now, guides will tell you not to touch the dolls.

They will say it lightly. Joking. Half-smiling.

But they will still watch your hands.

And when the boat pulls away and the island recedes, the dolls remain—swaying gently, eyes clouded, faces patient.

Waiting for the next story to be added.

Because this is not a place where something happened once.

It is a place where something is still being *tended.*

11
the beelzebub mirror frame

There are mirrors that show you your face.

And then there are mirrors that make you aware you *have* one.

The Beelzebub Mirror Frame belongs to the second category.

It does not distort reflections. It does not warp light. It does not bleed or whisper or fog on command. Most people who encounter it describe their first reaction as disappointment. *It's just a mirror,* they say. *It's the frame people are scared of.*

That misunderstanding is where the trouble begins.

Because the danger was never in the glass.

The earliest accounts of the frame appear in fragmented inventories from late 17th-century Europe, scattered through private collections rather than churches or noble estates. That absence is telling. Mirrors were expensive, symbolic, and often religiously fraught objects. When they appear without provenance—no artist, no patron, no household—they have usually been moved *quietly*.

The frame itself is carved from dark wood, almost certainly walnut, though later handlers would swear it changed tone depending on the light. The carvings are dense and layered: insect wings, swollen fruit, curling leaves, and faces that seem almost human until you look too closely at the mouths.

Those mouths matter.

They are not screaming. They are chewing.

By the early 1700s, the frame had acquired a name, though not consistently. In German and French marginal notes, it appears as *the Fly Lord's Glass* or *the Devourer's Looking*. In English records, it is eventually called the Beelzebub Mirror—not because the demon appeared in it, but because observers felt *judged* by something vast and amused.

Beelzebub has always been associated less with rage than with appetite. Rot. Corruption that feeds slowly. He does not seize souls; he lets them spoil.

The frame reflects that temperament.

The first detailed account comes from a letter dated 1712, written by a minor aristocrat whose name survives only as "H—." He describes acquiring the mirror from an estate sale after the previous owner's sudden death. The house, he notes, had been "unaccountably emptied" before the sale, save for the mirror, which servants refused to touch.

He placed it in his study.

Within weeks, H— reported a peculiar sensation when passing it: not fear, exactly, but a compulsion to *check*. To look again. To ensure his reflection was still accurate. He began pausing mid-task, mid-sentence, drawn back by the feeling that something about his face had changed.

It had not.

But his expression, he wrote, seemed "overfamiliar." As if the mirror knew him better than he knew himself.

Soon, he noticed that the mirror did not reflect the room equally. Corners darkened. Background objects lost clarity. The reflection emphasized the body—skin, mouth, eyes—while the surroundings fell away.

He began dreaming of flies.

This is where most retellings become sensational.

They describe whispers. Shadows. Faces appearing in the glass.

Those details do not appear in the earliest sources.

What *does* appear, again and again, is appetite.

Owners report eating more without satisfaction. Drinking without pleasure. Sex without intimacy. They describe a hollowing sensation, as if desire had been unmoored from fulfillment. The mirror does not create new cravings. It amplifies existing ones, stripping them of restraint and reward simultaneously.

By 1739, the mirror had changed hands at least four times. In each case, the transfer followed a familiar pattern: fascination, unease, isolation, and sudden departure—death, disappearance, or abandonment of property.

One owner, a French antiquarian, recorded a chilling observation before sealing the mirror in storage:

"It does not show me what I am.

It shows me what would be left if everything else were eaten."

Theories proliferated.

Some clerics argued the mirror was a moral device—a memento mori, exaggerating vanity until it collapsed into disgust. Others believed the carvings functioned as sigils, not summoning a demon but *inviting attention*. A beacon rather than a vessel.

The most compelling theory comes from an 1821 marginal note by a collector who refused to house the mirror indoors. He proposed that the frame operated as a kind of spiritual accelerant: wherever rot already existed—moral, emotional, psychological—it hastened the process.

The mirror did not corrupt.

It *revealed how easily corruption could feel like truth.*

Modern encounters are rarer but better documented.

In the mid-20th century, the mirror resurfaced briefly in a private collection in Eastern Europe. A curator tasked with cataloging it noted severe headaches, irritability, and a persistent sense of being evaluated. He reported that staff avoided standing directly in front of the mirror, preferring to pass it sideways, eyes averted.

Security footage from that period—grainy, inconclusive—shows nothing unusual. No movement. No apparitions.

What disturbed investigators was how often people stopped walking when they caught sight of their reflection.

Not stared.

Stopped.

As if listening.

The Beelzebub Mirror Frame is not associated with dramatic deaths or overt hauntings. There are no reliable reports of voices, physical manifestations, or possession. This frustrates skeptics and believers alike.

But its danger lies elsewhere.

It teaches you to see yourself as consumable.

To imagine your worth as something that can be measured, tasted, judged.

It does not threaten damnation.

It offers inevitability.

Today, the mirror's exact location is uncertain. Some claim it was dismantled, the frame separated from the glass and burned. Others insist this is impossible—that the carvings resist destruction, splintering but never fully breaking.

What is certain is that no museum publicly displays it.

That absence speaks volumes.

Objects associated with fear are often exhibited. Objects associated with *recognition* are not.

If you ever encounter a mirror that makes you feel not afraid, but *assessed*—a mirror that seems patient, indulgent, faintly amused—do not test it. Do not stare. Do not search for movement.

And above all, do not ask what it sees.

Because the Beelzebub Mirror does not answer questions.

It waits for you to supply them yourself.

And it is very good at knowing which ones you already believe.

12
the annabelle doll

The real Annabelle doll does not look dangerous.

That is the first and most important thing to understand.

She is not porcelain. She does not have glass eyes or cracked lips or a painted smile frozen in mockery. She is soft. Cloth-bodied. Her hair is red yarn. Her eyes are simple black ovals. She wears a cheerful gingham dress and looks like something you might have been given as a child without ceremony.

She is a Raggedy Ann doll.

People expect monsters to announce themselves. Annabelle never has.

The story begins in 1970, not in a haunted house, but in an apartment. A small one. Ordinary. Shared by two young women in Connecticut—Donna, a nursing student, and her roommate Angie. This detail matters. Nursing students are trained observers. They are not prone to melodrama. They notice changes in routine because their lives depend on it.

The doll was a gift.

Donna's mother found it in a hobby shop and gave it to her as a birthday present. Donna placed it on her bed, propped casually against the pillows. It did not move. It did not speak. Nothing happened.

Until it did.

The first changes were subtle enough to dismiss. Annabelle appeared in different positions than where Donna had left her. Legs crossed instead of straight. Arms folded instead of resting at her sides. The roommates assumed one of them had moved the doll and forgotten.

Then the doll began appearing in rooms where neither of them had placed her.

The couch. The hallway. Once, sitting upright at the dining table.

The apartment was not large. There was nowhere for a doll to hide.

They laughed it off.

They stopped laughing when the notes appeared.

The paper was parchment-like, old-fashioned, torn from no notebook they owned. The handwriting was childlike, uneven, looping.

"Help us."

"Help Lou."

The name mattered. Lou was a friend. He disliked the doll on sight.

From the beginning, Lou said Annabelle made him uncomfortable. He felt watched in the apartment. He reported vivid nightmares in which the doll crawled toward him, climbing his body, pressing on his chest. Donna and Angie teased him for it, though they quietly began to lock the doll in a closet at night.

One afternoon, Lou woke from a nap on the couch in a cold sweat, convinced Annabelle had tried to kill him.

He had scratch marks across his chest.

Not superficial ones. Deep, red, as if made by claws.

They vanished within days.

That detail would later trouble investigators more than the scratches themselves.

At this point, Donna and Angie did what many people do when faced with something they cannot explain.

They sought reassurance.

A medium.

The medium was not dramatic. She did not scream or flinch or recoil from the doll. She closed her eyes, listened, and told them a story.

The spirit of a little girl named Annabelle Higgins, she said, had died on the property before the apartments were built. She was lonely. She wanted companionship. She liked Donna and Angie. She meant no harm.

She wanted permission to stay.

Donna felt sorry for her.

She said yes.

This is the moment Ed and Lorraine Warren would later identify as the turning point—not because a demon appeared, but because consent was given.

The doll's behavior escalated immediately.

The Warrens were contacted after a priest, brought in to bless the apartment, became alarmed. The priest identified the presence not as a child spirit, but as something inhuman. Something that did not belong to the doll, but was using it.

According to the Warrens' account, the entity attached to Annabelle was not a ghost at all, but a demonic presence seeking a human host. The doll was a conduit. A tool. A distraction.

Demons, Ed Warren often said, do not possess objects.

They use them.

The scratches on Lou. The notes. The movement. These were not acts of haunting, but of grooming. The entity was testing boundaries. Testing fear. Testing sympathy.

When Ed and Lorraine attempted to remove the doll from the apartment, things went wrong almost immediately.

The car malfunctioned repeatedly on the drive. The brakes failed more than once. Lorraine later claimed she sensed the entity's resistance as a pressure, a refusal to be displaced.

They prayed.

They sprinkled holy water on the doll.

They did not treat her gently.

That, too, matters.

The Annabelle doll now resides in a glass case at the Warrens' Occult Museum in Monroe, Connecticut. She sits upright, legs extended, hands folded in her lap. A warning sign hangs beside her.

"Warning: Positively Do Not Open."

People laugh at that sign.

They should not.

Over the years, visitors have reported faint tapping sounds coming from the case. Others describe nausea, headaches, or an overwhelming sense of dread while standing near her. One man, according to the Warrens, mocked the doll openly, banged on the glass, and challenged it to follow him home.

He died later that day in a motorcycle accident.

His girlfriend survived, but was hospitalized.

Skeptics dismiss the story as coincidence.

Lorraine Warren never did.

What makes Annabelle uniquely unsettling is not what she does, but how she confuses expectations.

Horror movies have transformed her into something else entirely: porcelain-faced, sharp-toothed, overtly malevolent. The cinematic Annabelle warns you immediately. She telegraphs danger.

The real Annabelle does the opposite.

She invites empathy.

She looks harmless. She looks loved. She looks like something you would forgive.

That is the trap.

The Warrens insisted that the doll was never possessed by a little girl. The child spirit narrative, they believed, was a manipulation. A story designed to lower defenses.

This reframes every early interaction.

The notes are no longer cries for help.

They are tests.

The scratches are not accidents.

They are demonstrations.

There are no verified scientific explanations for the events surrounding Annabelle that satisfy everyone. Skeptics suggest pranks, stress, suggestion, or fabrication. The Warrens themselves have been criticized, debated, and accused of embellishment.

And yet.

Even those who doubt the demonology pause at the consistency of one detail: the doll never harmed Donna or Angie directly. The aggression was always displaced. Redirected. Proxied.

That pattern—harm to observers, not caretakers—recurs in other object-centered hauntings.

It is not common.

It is strategic.

Annabelle does not move anymore.

If she ever did, she no longer needs to.

She sits in her case, visible, contained, photographed endlessly. She has become a spectacle. A brand. A character.

And yet, the warnings remain.

The glass is blessed. The case is sealed. The doll is never removed.

Not for film crews.

Not for skeptics.

Not for anyone.

Because whatever Annabelle is—or was—it thrived not on fear, but on permission.

And permission, once given, is very hard to take back.

If there is a lesson in the Annabelle doll, it is not that demons hide in toys.

It is that danger does not always announce itself with fangs and fire.

Sometimes it arrives stitched, smiling, and asking only to stay.

And sometimes the most frightening words you can offer it are not a challenge, but an invitation.

13
the bell of nanking

The bell was never meant to be heard.

That is the detail people forget when they tell the story.

According to the earliest versions of the legend, the Bell of Nanking was not cast to summon prayer or mark time. It was not designed to call people together. It was meant to be perfect. And in pursuit of that perfection, it absorbed something it could not release.

The story places us in China, during the Ming dynasty, in the city of Nanking—then one of the great capitals of the world. The city was powerful, wealthy, and intensely symbolic. Its walls were vast. Its monuments were statements. When the emperor commissioned a bell for one of the city's temples, it was not an object he wanted to tolerate. It was an object he wanted to endure.

The bell was to be immense, flawless, and resonant beyond anything that had come before it.

Bronze was gathered. Furnaces were built. Foundry workers labored under pressure that was not metaphorical. Failure would not be corrected. It would be punished.

The first casting failed.

So did the second.

Each time, the bell cracked as it cooled, its surface marred by fractures that ruined both sound and strength. The alloy was adjusted. The temperature recalculated. The workers blamed themselves. The overseers blamed them harder.

And still, the bell would not hold.

At this point, the story shifts tone.

Different tellings introduce different figures, but they all center on a young woman—sometimes the daughter of the foundry master, sometimes a servant, sometimes a wife. Her name varies. In some versions, she is called Ko-Ngai. In others, she remains unnamed, identified only by her relationship to the man who would be punished if the bell failed again.

She understands what is coming.

The emperor's patience is gone. Another failure will mean death—not hers, but her father's. Or her husband's. Or her family's. The distinction is irrelevant. The bell must succeed.

And so, on the night of the final casting, she does something no one asks her to do.

As the molten bronze pours into the mold, she throws herself into it.

The metal closes over her body. The casting completes. The bell cools.

This time, it does not crack.

The Bell of Nanking is said to have been flawless.

Its surface smooth. Its proportions exact. Its tone deep, clear, and enduring. When struck, it rang with a sound that carried for miles, vibrating through stone and bone alike. People gathered to hear it not because they were summoned, but because they wanted to know what it sounded like when perfection was achieved at such cost.

And then they noticed something else.

Beneath the bell's resonant clarity, there was another sound.

A wail.

It was faint. Easily dismissed at first. A trick of the ear, some said. The way sound reverberates in enclosed spaces. But it returned, again and again, always at the tail end of the bell's note. A thin, human cry, stretched and distorted, lingering just long enough to be recognized.

Those who knew the story did not argue about what they were hearing.

They knew.

There is no surviving Bell of Nanking that can be definitively tied to this legend. That absence has not weakened the story. If anything, it has allowed it to spread.

Variations appear in nineteenth-century travel writing, in missionary accounts, in Western retellings that cannot quite decide whether they are recording folklore or repeating a cautionary tale. Some writers insist the bell stood in a specific temple. Others claim it was destroyed, or melted down, or buried. A few suggest it was moved, its origins deliberately obscured.

What remains consistent is the sound.

The bell does not scream. It does not sob. It does not beg.

It *wails*.

And the wail is not constant. It does not overwhelm the bell's primary note. It follows it—like an echo that refuses to be purely mechanical.

Skeptics have offered explanations, of course.

Metallurgists point out that impurities in bronze can create unusual overtones. Acousticians explain how resonance can produce secondary frequencies that the human ear interprets as something else. Psychologists note the power of expectation—how knowing a story primes the listener to hear what they are told to hear.

All of this is reasonable.

None of it addresses the persistence of the legend across centuries, cultures, and languages.

Nor does it explain why bells, more than almost any other object, attract stories of entrapment. Spirits caught in metal. Voices sealed inside bronze. Sound as a form of containment.

The Bell of Nanking is not unique in this regard.

But it is the most famous.

What gives the Bell of Nanking its staying power is not the supernatural claim, but the moral one.

The story insists that perfection demands payment. That beauty extracted through force does not remain neutral. That sound, once shaped, remembers what went into it.

This is why the bell does not strike itself.

Someone must choose to ring it.

And that choice matters.

In modern retellings, the Bell of Nanking often becomes shorthand for a particular kind of haunting—one without a ghost, without a curse that escalates, without a monster to confront. The harm is already done. The injustice complete.

All that remains is vibration.

The story is sometimes told to children. Sometimes to tourists. Sometimes in academic discussions about folklore transmission. It changes shape depending on who tells it, but it never loses its core.

A woman enters molten metal.

The bell rings.

Something human remains.

There are no reports of death associated with hearing the bell. No sickness. No madness. If the bell is dangerous, it is dangerous in a quieter way.

It makes people think about what they are willing to sacrifice for greatness.

It asks whether listening makes us complicit.

And it suggests—uncomfortably—that some sounds are not meant to be purified, only preserved.

If the Bell of Nanking still exists somewhere, intact and silent, it is probably doing what it has always done best.

Waiting.

Because the bell does not need belief to function. It does not need witnesses or rituals or fear. It only needs a hand willing to strike it, and an ear willing to stay long enough to hear what follows.

Most people walk away before the wail.

Those who don't tend to remember it for the rest of their lives.

Not because it was loud.

But because it was human.

14

the roman curse tablets (defixiones)

T he first curse was not shouted.

It was scratched.

Somewhere in the Roman world—Britannia, Gaul, Italy, Africa—it began the same way: a private grievance, a small injustice, a tight knot of anger that could not be spoken aloud without consequence. The law was slow. The gods were distant. The target was known.

So the curser found lead.

Lead was cheap. Heavy. Dull. It bent easily beneath a stylus or knife, taking letters the way flesh takes scars. It was also poisonous, associated with Saturn, with the underworld, with death. Perfect for words meant to travel downward.

The tablet was cut small enough to conceal in the palm. The text was not beautiful. Spelling was often erratic. Grammar slipped. Names were repeated obsessively, as if saying them enough times might force the universe to listen.

"I bind…"

"I hand over…"

"I give…"

These were not metaphors.

They were transactions.

The earliest curse tablets appear in the fifth century BCE, but it was during the Roman Imperial period that they flourished. This was a world obsessed with control—over bodies, over property, over reputation. When control failed in the visible world, it was rerouted elsewhere.

The curser would name the victim in full, sometimes including their mother's name to avoid ambiguity. Hair color. Occupation. Even handwriting, in some cases. Nothing was left to chance. The more precise the identification, the harder it would be for the gods to miss.

Then came the binding.

The tablet might be folded, pierced with a nail, twisted, or rolled tightly shut. Some were nailed through the center as if pinning the victim in place. Others were tied with thread or sealed with wax. A few were written backward or in mirror script, forcing the words themselves to cross a boundary.

Finally, the tablet was deposited.

Not burned. Not displayed.

Hidden.

Thrown into wells. Dropped into graves. Slipped into temples dedicated to chthonic gods. At Bath, in Roman Britain, dozens were cast into the sacred spring of Sulis Minerva, their lead surfaces dissolving slowly in the mineral water, their words sinking where the living could not follow.

The act was deliberate.

Once released, the curser was not supposed to intervene again.

What makes the defixiones unsettling is not their violence, but their familiarity.

These are not grand, operatic curses. They are petty. Domestic. Small.

A stolen cloak. A lost ring. A bad business deal. A rival in love. A chariot race gone wrong.

One tablet from Bath reads like a customer complaint written to a god:

"I give to the goddess Sulis the man who has stolen my cloak...

whether slave or free... may he not sleep, may he not have children, until he brings my cloak back to the temple."

Another lists a long series of names, crossing out those already eliminated, as if tracking progress. One curses a courtroom opponent, asking that their tongue twist and their memory fail when they attempt to speak.

These are not the curses of monsters.

They are the curses of neighbors.

That is why they linger.

The tablets were never meant to be recovered.

Their power, such as it was, depended on secrecy and finality. To dig one up was to interrupt the transaction. And yet, dig them up we did.

In the nineteenth and twentieth centuries, archaeologists began uncovering them in startling numbers. Wells. Rivers. Temples. Cemeteries. The sheer volume forced a reevaluation. This was not fringe behavior. This was common practice.

The tablets were catalogued, cleaned, translated.

And something strange happened.

The moment they were removed from their hiding places, they changed.

They became artifacts instead of weapons.

That shift did not sit easily with everyone.

Some early scholars refused to handle them without gloves. Others recorded a vague unease, an irritation, a sense of intrusion. One archaeologist working at Bath noted—almost apologetically—that reading the tablets felt like overhearing something private and ugly, something not meant for him.

That reaction never quite went away.

Skeptics are quick to point out that curse tablets "worked" only in the psychological sense. Belief created anxiety. Anxiety created misfortune. There is no need to invoke gods or underworld forces when human fear is sufficient.

This explanation is tidy.

It is also incomplete.

Because many curse tablets target people who never knew they had been cursed. Illiteracy was common. Tablets were hidden. Victims often had no idea why their luck had turned.

And yet, patterns appear in the texts themselves.

Repetition. Obsession. Escalation.

Some tablets grow longer over time, as if the curser returned again and again, adding clauses, tightening the bind. Others include threats against the gods themselves, a dangerous move in Roman religion. "If you do not act," one tablet implies, "you are complicit."

That kind of language is not casual superstition.

It is desperation.

There are also tablets that appear to have backfired.

A small number include instructions for releasing the curse—conditions under which the binding should end. When those conditions were not met, the curse lingered, directionless. Scholars debate whether this mattered. The people who wrote the tablets clearly thought it did.

Lead, after all, does not decay easily.

Some tablets remained folded for centuries, their words preserved exactly as they were written. When unfolded in modern labs, the letters appear sharp, angry, and immediate—as if no time had passed at all.

Reading them feels like opening a door that was never meant to be reopened.

Today, Roman curse tablets are housed in museums across Europe. They sit behind glass, labeled and explained. Visitors read them with curiosity, sometimes amusement. The language feels crude. The grievances feel small.

But curators are careful.

They do not display them casually.

At Bath, many tablets remain unexhibited, stored instead in controlled archives. The reason given is conservation. Lead corrodes. The truth is more complicated.

There is something about seeing too many of them at once.

The effect accumulates.

One curse is a story.

A hundred is a pattern.

And patterns invite questions no one is eager to answer.

The defixiones do not threaten the modern reader. They do not summon anything. They do not activate.

What they do is remind us how thin the line has always been between justice and vengeance, between prayer and demand. They show us a world where people believed—deeply—that words placed in the right location, with the right intent, could alter reality.

Whether that belief was correct is almost beside the point.

The tablets exist.

They were written.

They were hidden.

And for centuries, no one knew where they were.

If there is a warning in the Roman curse tablets, it is not that curses work.

It is that people will always look for somewhere to put their anger when they are not allowed to speak it aloud.

The underworld, it seems, has always been happy to accept deliveries.

And lead, patient and heavy, has always been willing to carry the message down.

15
the witch's ladder

T he Witch's Ladder does not begin with a spell.

It begins with a house being torn apart.

In the late nineteenth century, in the village of Wellington in Somerset, a thick-walled, thatched farmhouse was deemed unsafe and scheduled for demolition. It was not an unusual event. Buildings were pulled down all the time—especially old ones, especially rural ones, especially those with no clear future. What made this demolition different was not the act itself, but what the workmen found when they reached the roof.

There was a void above the upper room of the house, sealed and inaccessible from below. No ladder reached it. No trapdoor led into it. It was the kind of space that exists only in older buildings, where construction methods leave pockets of darkness that are never meant to be entered once the house is complete.

When the workers broke into that space, they did not find debris or nesting animals.

They found objects.

Not scattered. Not abandoned. Placed.

Six heather brooms lay together. An old armchair sat nearby, worm-eaten and sagging, its rush seat long decayed. And beside them

—coiled but deliberate—was a length of rope about five feet long, thick, rough, and twisted through with feathers.

The feathers were not tied on afterward. They were woven into the rope itself, their quills caught between the strands, protruding outward at irregular angles. Goose feathers, mostly. Some crow or rook. Many were broken with age, leaving stubs like the remains of teeth.

The men did not hesitate.

They named it immediately.

A witches' ladder.

That confidence is the first unsettling detail. The rope does not resemble a ladder in any practical sense. It has no rungs. No steps. Nothing that would help a human climb. And yet multiple men, working independently, agreed on its purpose. The chair, they said, was for witches to rest. The brooms were for riding. The rope was "to act as a ladder to enable them to cross the roof."

They did not laugh when they said it.

That, too, was noted.

The discovery was documented in 1887 by Dr. Abraham Colles, who published the account in *The Folk-Lore Journal.* Colles was not a sensationalist. He was careful, methodical, skeptical without being dismissive. He understood that objects like this existed at the intersection of belief and behavior, and that dismissing one side entirely made the other incomprehensible.

By the time Colles investigated, much had already been lost.

The brooms were treated as ordinary tools. Their decayed handles snapped when handled. They were re-handled and used in a garden, then discarded—"lost irretrievably," as Colles later wrote. The chair survived only because it was shoved into storage. The rope survived because it did not look useful.

This accidental preservation would later matter.

Colles attempted to trace the meaning of the objects through living memory. He spoke with local women—carefully, indirectly, without leading questions. Two older women independently referenced "the rope and feathers," and "the new rope with new feathers," as if this were a known thing rather than an invention.

Neither woman would explain its use.

Colles suspected fear. Or perhaps embarrassment. He noted what he described as "great reticence," a reluctance to discuss practices that still carried social danger, even decades after witchcraft prosecutions had ended. It was safer to say nothing than to be thought foolish—or worse, complicit.

What emerges from Colles' account is not a tidy explanation, but a sequence:

A hidden bundle, sealed in a roof void.

A confident worker-tradition naming it witchcraft.

Local memory acknowledging the object without explanation.

Scholars disagreeing in public about what it "really" was.

The ladder enters the historical record already contested.

When the rope was later presented at a meeting of the British Association for the Advancement of Science, debate erupted almost immediately. Two men in the audience insisted the object was not magical at all, but a "sewel"—a twisted rope used in deer hunting. The loop at one end supported this theory. So did the rope's construction.

What the hunting explanation did not account for was context.

Sewels are not stored with chairs and brooms in sealed attic spaces. They are not hidden where no one can reach them. They are not accompanied by local traditions that refuse to explain themselves.

The argument was never fully resolved.

Instead, the rope was donated to the Pitt Rivers Museum in Oxford, where it was catalogued as a Witch's Ladder. The label stuck. The name adhered more tightly than the fibers of the rope ever could.

This is how many cursed objects are made—not through intent, but through classification.

To look at the Witch's Ladder in a museum today is to feel an odd dissonance. It is smaller than people expect. Less dramatic. Its feathers are brittle. Its rope is frayed. It looks more like something forgotten in a barn than something capable of harm.

And yet.

People linger.

Museum-goers report an immediate fixation on the detail that the ladder was hidden somewhere "inaccessible from below." That phrase recurs in descriptions, in notes, in visitor comments. The idea of a space in a house that exists above you, sealed, unknown, containing something deliberate—this is what stays.

Not witches flying. Not curses.

Containment.

The ladder does not appear to have been used for attack. There are no accounts of illness or death linked to it. No sudden misfortune. If it was magical, its function may have been preventative rather than aggressive—something meant to bar entry, confuse movement, or redirect influence rather than summon it.

This aligns with broader European folk practices, where knotted cords and feathered ropes were used to bind illness, steal milk symbolically, or interfere with unseen forces. These practices were often quiet, domestic, and defensive. Their danger lay not in what they did, but in what they implied: that the home was porous, and that something could cross into it if left unguarded.

The Witch's Ladder is unsettling because it suggests someone believed their house required protection from above.

The ladder's effects, if we can call them that, are not physical. They are cognitive.

People who spend time with the object report a persistent urge to explain it definitively. To decide, once and for all, whether it is magical or mundane. This urge is rarely satisfied. Arguments replicate themselves. The same points recur. The same doubts reassert.

This mirrors the ladder's own history: contested, reinterpreted, resistant to closure.

Collectors of occult artifacts sometimes express an interest in owning similar objects, not because they believe in witchcraft, but because they want to test the boundary between belief and artifact. This impulse—to prove or disprove—is where fixation sets in. The ladder punishes certainty not with misfortune, but with contradiction.

The more firmly you insist on a single explanation, the less the object cooperates.

Today, the Witch's Ladder from Wellington is securely housed in the Pitt Rivers Museum, catalogued and conserved. It is no longer hidden. It is no longer inaccessible.

And yet it remains oddly private.

It does not scream its meaning. It does not offer itself as spectacle. It sits, coiled, its feathers broken and fading, its purpose unresolved.

Perhaps that is the quiet lesson of the Witch's Ladder.

Not all dangerous objects harm.

Some simply remind you that people once believed harm could enter from places you never thought to look—and that belief alone was enough to change how they built, hid, and remembered their homes.

The ladder has not climbed anywhere in over a century.

But it still knows how to linger above you.

16

the black
grimoire of turin

T he first problem with the Black Grimoire of Turin is that no
one can agree on when it began to exist.

Not when it was written—people argue about that
endlessly—but when it *entered the world as a thing people feared*. That
moment is harder to pin down. It does not announce itself with a
discovery date or a triumphant unveiling. It slides into history sideways, mentioned in passing, half-referenced in letters, rumored in the
margins of other texts. By the time anyone starts looking for it directly,
it has already learned how to disappear.

Most stories place it in Turin sometime in the late eighteenth or early
nineteenth century, a period when the city was dense with contradiction.
Turin was orderly, Catholic, royal. It was also a crossroads—of trade, of
ideas, of clandestine societies. Occultism flourished not in open rebellion against the Church, but in its shadow. Grimoires circulated quietly,
often copied by hand, altered as they passed from owner to owner. Black
books were not unusual. *This* book, however, was said to be different.

It was not meant to teach.

It was meant to bind.

The earliest accounts describe a manuscript bound in dark leather, unmarked, without title or author. No flourish. No sigil on the cover. The pages inside were said to be dense with cramped script, written in a mixture of Latin, corrupted Italian, and symbols that did not correspond cleanly to any known magical alphabet. The text did not explain itself. It did not instruct beginners. It assumed familiarity, fluency, and —most troublingly—commitment.

You did not read this book to learn.

You read it to *continue* something.

One of the most persistent rumors surrounding the Black Grimoire of Turin is that it was not written by a magician, but by a scribe. A professional copyist. Someone trained not in summoning spirits, but in preserving texts exactly as they were received.

If this is true, it reframes the book entirely.

Because scribes do not create. They transmit.

The story goes that the scribe—unnamed, as so many are—was commissioned to copy an older manuscript. Where that earlier book came from is never specified. Some claim it was brought north from Naples. Others insist it arrived through Jewish mystical networks, stripped of context and already dangerous by the time it reached Piedmont. A few go further and suggest it was confiscated from a defrocked cleric, one of many whose faith curdled into obsession rather than disbelief.

The scribe began his work.

He did not finish it.

Accounts diverge sharply here. Some say he abandoned the project after suffering night terrors so severe he could no longer hold a pen. Others claim he died suddenly, leaving the manuscript incomplete. Still others insist he finished the copy—and that the *copy* was the problem, not the original.

From this point forward, the book's reputation detaches from verifiable events and begins to behave like a living thing.

Unlike grimoires designed to be impressive, the Black Grimoire of Turin is described as aggressively plain. Those who claimed to have seen it remarked on its refusal to perform. No illustrations. No ornamental initials. No decorative borders. Even the ink, they said, was unremarkable—dark brown rather than black, as if the book resisted drama.

And yet, people remembered it.

They remembered the way the pages felt heavier toward the middle. They remembered the faint impression—whether real or imagined—that the book had been pressed flat for a long time, as though stored under weight. They remembered that the text did not progress in a straight line. Rituals appeared to repeat, but not quite. Names shifted by a letter or two. Instructions contradicted earlier passages, as if testing the reader's attention.

This was not a book for casual handling.

It punished skimming.

Those who spent time with it reported a particular kind of unease: not fear, exactly, but a growing sense of obligation. The longer you read, the harder it became to stop. The text did not threaten. It did not warn. It simply assumed you would continue.

That assumption, more than anything, frightened people.

By the mid-nineteenth century, references to the Black Grimoire of Turin begin appearing in private correspondence and secondhand accounts, usually attached to cautionary tales. A collector who acquired it and suffered financial ruin shortly thereafter. A student who attempted one of its workings and descended into paranoia. A priest who confiscated it and later refused to speak of it again.

None of these stories can be conclusively proven.

That is not the point.

What *can* be traced is a pattern of disappearance. The book is always in someone's possession briefly. It is shown to a friend. Mentioned in a letter. Then it is sold, hidden, lost, or destroyed—though destruction is rarely convincing. Fire, after all, leaves records. Ash is easier to document than absence.

At one point, the book is rumored to have entered the holdings of a private Turin library, catalogued vaguely and then removed without explanation. At another, it is said to have crossed into France, where it became associated—incorrectly but persistently—with other infamous grimoires, its identity blurring as its reputation grew.

This blurring may be its most effective defense.

You cannot ban what you cannot name.

Modern scholars are divided on whether the Black Grimoire of Turin ever existed as a single, stable object. Some argue that it represents a category rather than a specific manuscript: a shorthand for a particular tradition of coercive magic texts circulating in northern Italy during a period of intense social anxiety.

Others counter that this explanation is too neat. That it ignores the consistency of certain details repeated across independent accounts: the plain binding, the unstable text, the sense of compulsion reported by handlers. Folklore, they argue, does not usually align so precisely without an anchor.

There is also the uncomfortable matter of the book's afterlife.

Even today, rare-book dealers occasionally field inquiries from collectors seeking "the Turin grimoire" or "the black book from Piedmont." Most are dismissed as cranks or thrill-seekers. A few, quietly, are not. Every so often, a manuscript surfaces—anonymous, unremarkable, written in a mix of Latin and vernacular—that causes a brief flurry of private concern before being shelved, reclassified, or sold to a buyer who does not ask questions.

Whether these are fragments, forgeries, or something else entirely remains unresolved.

What is resolved is this: no institution publicly claims ownership of the Black Grimoire of Turin.

That alone is unusual.

The danger of the book, if it exists, is not explosive. It does not kill swiftly. It does not announce its effects. Instead, it erodes boundaries. Readers report a narrowing of focus, a growing impatience with ordinary explanations. Relationships fray. Sleep becomes shallow. The world outside the text begins to feel irrelevant, then irritating, then hostile.

In this sense, the book behaves less like a cursed object and more like a closed system.

Once inside, everything else feels extraneous.

The most troubling accounts are not those of madness or death, but of devotion. Of people who believed—sincerely—that the book understood them. That it responded, not with voices or visions, but with alignment. With a sense that events were unfolding *as they should*.

That belief, once established, is difficult to dislodge.

If the Codex Gigas unsettles through completeness, the Black Grimoire of Turin unsettles through implication. It never shows you the whole. It never offers reassurance. It simply implies that there is a correct way to proceed, and that you are either moving toward it or away.

The book does not curse.

It commits.

Which is, perhaps, worse.

Today, the Black Grimoire of Turin is officially unaccounted for. It exists in footnotes, in rumors, in the negative space of archives. It is cited far more often than it is described. Its absence has become part of its identity.

That absence is not comforting.

Because books that are truly gone tend to fade.

This one hasn't.

Some objects want attention. Others punish it. The Black Grimoire of Turin does neither. It waits to be recognized, not rediscovered. To be resumed, not begun.

If it still exists—and there are those who insist it must—it is almost certainly resting somewhere quiet, shelved among ordinary volumes, its plain binding protecting it from curiosity. It does not need to announce itself.

It knows that eventually, someone will open it not out of hunger or fear, but out of certainty.

And certainty, as this book has always understood, is the most dangerous condition of all.

17
the devil's bible—codex gigas, debated curse

They tell you the book is cursed before they tell you how heavy it is.

That feels backwards, once you've seen it.

The Codex Gigas does not announce itself with whispers or flickering lights or sudden dread. It announces itself with mass. With scale. With the unmistakable physical presence of something that was never meant to be moved easily, much less owned.

Before anyone ever called it the Devil's Bible, people stood in front of it and went quiet.

The book is enormous—so large that "book" almost feels like a misnomer. When closed, it stands nearly a meter tall. When opened, it spreads across a table like a restrained animal. Its pages are thick vellum, pale and faintly translucent, carrying the subtle irregularities of skin that once lived. Modern estimates suggest between one hundred and one hundred sixty animals were required to produce it. That number alone unsettles people, though it shouldn't. Medieval books were made of skin. Knowledge has always been expensive.

Still, there is something about knowing how many lives were rendered into pages that makes the Codex Gigas feel less like a manuscript and more like a ledger.

It weighs roughly seventy-five kilograms. Two people are required to lift it safely. One to steady it. One to guide it. When curators move it, they do not hurry. You cannot hurry something like this without inviting damage, and damage, in this case, feels like a moral act rather than a physical one.

You get the sense—standing there—that the book does not like to be handled.

Not because it resists, exactly. But because it remembers every hand.

The Codex Gigas was created in the early thirteenth century in Bohemia, most likely in the Benedictine monastery of Podlažice. It was not a grand institution. It was not wealthy or powerful or particularly well-connected. Within a few decades of the book's completion, the monastery would be gone—destroyed, its stones scattered, its name surviving largely because of this one object.

That alone would be enough to raise eyebrows. Small places are not meant to produce monumental works. They do not have the resources, the scribes, the time. And yet the Codex Gigas exists, fully formed, meticulously written, unnervingly consistent.

The handwriting does not change.

Page after page, column after column, the script remains steady. There are no visible shifts in ink density that would suggest decades of interruption. No stylistic evolution. No signs of a second hand stepping in to help. Modern paleographic analysis points, again and again, to a single scribe.

This is where the legend enters.

According to later tradition, a monk at Podlažice committed a crime so severe that he was sentenced to be walled alive within the monastery—a punishment meant not only to kill, but to erase. In desperation, he begged for a reprieve, promising to create a book in a single night that would glorify God and bring eternal honor to the monastery. When he realized the task was impossible, he turned to the Devil for assistance. The Devil agreed. The book was completed by dawn. In gratitude, the monk included a portrait of his benefactor.

It is a tidy story. Suspiciously tidy.

There is no contemporary record of such a sentence. No monastic account of a miraculous overnight manuscript. No mention of a pact. The story surfaces later, when people are already struggling to explain what they are seeing.

And perhaps that is the first lesson of the Codex Gigas: when confronted with scale we cannot comprehend, we invent motives that match our fear.

The Devil's portrait appears roughly halfway through the manuscript.

This is important. It is not hidden at the end. It is not lurking in the margins. It does not creep up on you.

It waits.

By the time you reach it, you have already passed through the Old Testament, the New Testament, and extensive historical and encyclopedic material. You are deep into a book that has proven itself sober, methodical, and orthodox. And then, abruptly, you turn a page and the Devil is there, rendered at nearly life size.

He is not subtle.

His skin is a dark greenish-black. His claws are red, as are the tongues protruding from the heads flanking him. He stands alone, framed within a rectangular border, his arms raised as if presenting himself for inspection. He wears a white loincloth patterned with red shapes resembling ermine tails—symbols associated not with hell, but with royalty and authority.

He looks less like a tempter and more like a subject.

Opposite him, on the facing page, is an illustration of the Heavenly City. Order and chaos presented as parallel entries. Two pages. Equal space. Equal weight.

This pairing has disturbed scholars for centuries, not because it glorifies the Devil, but because it contextualizes him. The Codex Gigas does not treat evil as a corruption of the text. It treats it as part of the record.

That is harder to dismiss.

What follows the Devil's image is not chaos or heresy, but continuity. The text resumes. Instructions appear. Calendars are laid out. Names of the dead are recorded. Medical remedies are described. Exorcism formulas are included, practical and procedural, stripped of theatricality.

The Codex Gigas is not a grimoire in the popular sense. It does not instruct the reader on how to summon demons. It does not promise power. It does not traffic in secrets.

It traffics in totality.

The Bible is here in full. So is the work of the Jewish historian Josephus. So is Isidore of Seville's *Etymologiae*, a foundational encyclopedia of medieval knowledge. There are penitential guidelines, telling you what to do if you sin. There are healing instructions, telling you what to do if you are ill. There are local records, telling you who lived and who died.

The book does not distinguish between sacred, practical, and administrative knowledge.

Everything is worth preserving.

This is where the discomfort deepens.

Because if the Codex Gigas is cursed, it is not because it contains forbidden knowledge. It is because it refuses to rank knowledge at all.

The monastery that created the Codex Gigas did not survive it.

That fact hangs over the book like a shadow. Podlažice disappears from history not long after the manuscript's completion, destroyed in regional conflict. The Codex Gigas, however, is removed in time. It passes through monastic libraries, into royal collections, into the hands of emperors.

It survives fires that destroy other books. It is moved ahead of wars. When the Thirty Years' War ends in 1648, Swedish forces seize it as war booty and transport it north. It remains in Sweden to this day, housed in the National Library.

Empires that own it fall.

Kings who display it lose power.

Libraries that shelter it burn—except the rooms it occupies.

No one seriously claims causation. But patterns have a way of lodging in the human mind, especially when they repeat across centuries.

Unlike other objects in this book, the Codex Gigas does not produce reports of sudden illness or violent death. There are no consistent accounts of physical harm. What it produces instead is fixation.

Readers describe a peculiar inability to focus on any single section. They flip forward, then backward, uneasy with what they might be missing. Scholars speak of the book as "exhausting," not intellectually, but psychologically. There is too much here. Too much to hold at once.

Curators note that visitors linger longer than expected, standing in front of the display case long after they have finished reading the placard. Some leave unsettled without being able to articulate why. Others feel nothing at all, which seems, in its own way, more troubling.

The Codex Gigas does not perform.

It does not reward belief.

It simply remains.

Skeptics have been quick to dismantle the legend of the Devil's pact. Modern research suggests the manuscript could have been produced over decades by a single, disciplined scribe. The consistency of handwriting, once thought impossible, is now understood as the product of extraordinary focus rather than supernatural aid.

And yet.

Even those who dismiss the curse hesitate to dismiss the book's effect. The Codex Gigas resists reduction. It is not impressive because of one image or one story. It is impressive because it refuses to be summarized.

The Devil's portrait, in this light, begins to feel less like a confession and more like an admission: if you attempt to contain the world in a single volume, you must also contain its shadow.

That may be the book's true transgression.

Today, the Codex Gigas is securely housed, climate-controlled, digitized, and guarded. Visitors are allowed to view it, but not touch it. Pages are turned rarely, under supervision. The Devil still faces the Heavenly City, exactly as he has for eight hundred years.

There are no warnings posted.

None are needed.

The book does not threaten. It does not tempt. It does not curse those who approach it.

Instead, it offers something quieter and far more enduring: the unsettling realization that knowledge does not require morality to survive. That preservation does not imply endorsement. That evil, once recorded, does not need to act in order to persist.

The Codex Gigas does not ask for belief.

It asks only to be remembered.

And perhaps that is why it is still here, long after the hands that made it have turned to dust.

Some objects want to be feared.

This one only wants to be complete.

18
the crying boy
painting ritual set

I
t begins, as so many modern hauntings do, not in a monastery or a crypt, but in a living room.

A modest room. Brown carpet. A coal fire or a gas heater glowing low. Family photographs on the mantel. And above it—nearly always above it—a small framed print of a child with enormous eyes and a tear caught mid-fall, as if it had nowhere left to go.

By the time anyone noticed the pattern, dozens of houses were already gone.

In the early 1980s, firefighters across the United Kingdom began to remark on something they were *not* trained to record. After the hoses were rolled and the embers cooled, when the soot was brushed away and the walls stood blackened and skeletal, a single object was often found intact.

The painting.

Charred furniture collapsed around it. Curtains burned to nothing. Television sets melted into their own plastic casings. And there, hanging slightly askew or lying face-up in the rubble, was the Crying Boy—its surface unblistered, its glass uncracked, its expression unchanged.

Firefighters are not, by training or temperament, superstitious people. They deal in causes: faulty wiring, unattended candles, chimney sparks. But the same men, in different towns, began saying the same thing.

"It shouldn't have survived."

The Crying Boy was not rare. That was part of the problem.

By the late 1970s and early 1980s, the image—one of several nearly identical variations—had been sold by the tens of thousands. It was inexpensive, mass-produced, and often given away with furniture purchases or sold in discount shops. The artist was credited inconsistently: Giovanni Bragolin, Bruno Amadio, sometimes simply "Franchot Seville." The biographies contradicted each other. The paintings themselves blurred together.

But the child never changed.

A boy of about five or six. Dark hair. Large eyes filled with something that could be sadness—or accusation. The tear was always the same: too perfectly placed to be accidental.

The paintings were often bought by families with children. Hung in nurseries. Placed near fireplaces for symmetry. Given as gifts without comment.

No one remembers why they chose it.

The first widely documented cluster of fires appeared in northern England, though isolated reports surfaced elsewhere. What caught attention was not the number of fires—house fires were common enough—but the repetition of the same detail in aftermath interviews.

The painting survived.

In some cases, it had fallen face-down, protected by nothing but chance. In others, it remained on the wall while the wall itself burned. Firefighters noted that the cord or wire used to hang it often snapped from heat, yet the frame showed no warping. One investigator described it as "cool to the touch" while surrounding debris was still warm.

This detail would later be exaggerated.

At the time, it was simply unsettling.

Then the press noticed.

In September 1985, *The Sun* published a now-infamous article linking the Crying Boy to a string of house fires. The headline was blunt, almost gleeful. The implication was clear: this was not coincidence.

Readers responded immediately.

Letters poured in describing similar incidents. Families who had never spoken publicly about their fires now found language for them. Some admitted they had thrown the painting away afterward. Others confessed they had kept it—and felt watched by it since.

A narrative coalesced quickly, as narratives always do.

The child, it was said, was cursed. Or the painting was. Or the artist. Or the boy had died in a fire and taken revenge through his image. Each version contradicted the last, but all shared one assumption: the painting *endured* because it wanted to.

Fire departments attempted to correct the story.

They pointed out that cheap prints were often coated with fire-resistant varnish. That glass can shield images from heat. That frames sometimes fall in ways that protect their contents. These explanations were technically sound.

They did not satisfy anyone.

Because there were too many photographs. Too many testimonies. Too many firefighters saying, quietly, that they had stopped taking the paintings home when families offered them.

And then there were the bonfires.

In October 1985, *The Sun* organized a public burning of Crying Boy paintings. Readers mailed them in by the hundreds. The event was framed as catharsis: destroy the image, break the curse.

The paintings burned.

This should have ended the story.

Instead, it deepened it.

Because destruction implied danger. And danger implied survival mattered. And survival implied intention.

The Crying Boy was no longer just a picture. It was a test.

What unsettled people most was not the idea that the painting caused fires—but that it *outlasted* them.

In folklore, fire cleanses. It resolves. It leaves ash where certainty once stood. The Crying Boy refused that resolution. It remained when it should not have. It watched from the ruins.

This is the shape of its power, if power is the word.

Not aggression. Not malice.

Persistence.

If the fires gave the Crying Boy its reputation, the artist gave it its instability.

There is no single, clean origin story for the painting—only a tangle of names, dates, and biographies that refuse to line up. This alone would not be remarkable; mass-produced art often sheds its provenance as it spreads. But in this case, the contradictions feel structural, as though the painting itself resists being pinned to one life, one hand, one intention.

The name most often attached is Giovanni Bragolin, though that was likely a pseudonym. Another name appears just as frequently: Bruno Amadio, sometimes described as a Venetian portraitist, sometimes as a war refugee painter, sometimes as a man who never existed at all.

Some accounts insist the artist painted orphaned children after World War II, working from memory rather than models. Others claim he worked from live subjects—street children, refugees, orphans displaced by bombing and fire. One particularly persistent version claims that the boy in the painting was his own son, who died in a house fire shortly after the portrait was completed.

There is no evidence for this.

There is also no evidence *against* it that satisfies anyone.

Because the stories do not behave like rumors. They behave like echoes.

What *is* verifiable is this: multiple versions of the Crying Boy were painted, not one. The expressions vary subtly. The tear may be on the left cheek or the right. The clothing shifts. The background darkens or lightens. These are not reproductions of a single original, but a series—iterations circling the same emotional core.

That detail matters.

Because repetition implies fixation.

Artists revisit subjects for many reasons: popularity, commission, technical study. But these children are not studies. They are confrontations. Each face stares outward, meeting the viewer directly. There is no narrative context. No comforting symbolism. Just grief, unresolved and unsoftened.

The paintings do not explain themselves.

They wait.

The most unsettling lore surrounding the artist centers not on his death, but on his distance.

Several accounts describe him as emotionally withdrawn, taciturn, difficult to interview. He rarely spoke publicly about the Crying Boy series, and when he did, he deflected. The paintings were "just portraits." The children were "imaginary." The tears meant "nothing."

That last insistence appears in more than one retelling.

Nothing.

It is a strange word to defend so fiercely.

Then there is the fireproofing.

Modern investigators have pointed out—correctly—that many inexpensive prints of the era were coated with flame-retardant varnish. This would explain why the paper did not ignite easily. It would also explain why the glass often survived.

What it does *not* explain is why families consistently reported that *other* framed prints burned in the same fires. Nor why the Crying Boy was so often found face-up, visible, intact.

Fire does not curate.

Yet again and again, the painting remained legible.

In some households, unease preceded the fire.

Owners reported that children disliked the painting, refused to sleep in rooms where it hung, or insisted the boy's eyes followed them. Adults dismissed this as imagination—until the house burned.

Others described persistent dreams after purchasing the print: a child crying in another room, a sense of being needed, the smell of smoke without source. These accounts were not dramatic enough to be dismissed outright, but not concrete enough to investigate.

They lingered in that dangerous middle space.

After the media attention peaked, the Crying Boy began to vanish —not from fires, but from walls.

People took them down quietly. Threw them out. Left them behind when moving. Charity shops reported refusing donations of the prints after complaints. Some households smashed the glass before disposal, as if preemptively neutralizing it.

And yet the painting never disappeared entirely.

Because it had already done the one thing cursed objects must do to survive: it multiplied.

There is a subtle but crucial shift that happens here.

Before the fires, the Crying Boy was an image of sorrow.

After them, it became an *object of endurance.*

The fear was no longer that it caused destruction—but that it could not be destroyed *by* it.

This reframing changed how people interacted with the painting. It was no longer passive décor. It was something to be managed. Avoided. Watched.

Handled carefully.

Which brings us to the quietest, and perhaps most unsettling detail of all.

In several documented cases, families who removed the painting before a fire later discovered it still in their possession—packed into boxes they did not remember placing it in, left behind by previous tenants, or returned to the house by well-meaning relatives.

These accounts are anecdotal. Memory is unreliable. Stress reshapes narrative.

But the repetition matters.

The Crying Boy does not chase.

It waits to be rehung.

What survives a fire becomes evidence.

Not proof—never proof—but something heavier than coincidence. Something people keep circling back to, even after they insist they don't believe in curses.

By the late 1980s, the Crying Boy had crossed an invisible threshold. It was no longer merely *associated* with misfortune; it had become an object people actively negotiated with. Not worshipped. Not studied. Negotiated.

Where do you put it?

How do you get rid of it?

What happens if you don't?

After the media frenzy faded, a quieter phase began.

House fires still occurred, of course. But now, whenever one did, investigators and journalists were primed. If a Crying Boy print appeared in the wreckage, it was noted—even if it had nothing to do with the cause. If one *didn't* appear, no one wrote about it.

This is how folklore survives modernity: through selective attention.

But folklore alone doesn't explain the next development.

Museums would not take them.

This is not because museums believed the paintings were cursed. It was because they believed they were *contaminated by narrative.* The Crying Boy had become untouchable not due to danger, but due to meaning overload. Any display would collapse into spectacle.

Private collectors, however, were less cautious.

Some acquired prints deliberately—testing them, as if daring the legend to perform. Most reported nothing. A few reported unease. One collector documented a string of mundane but persistent misfortunes: electrical failures, minor fires in neighboring units, repeated insurance disputes.

None of it was dramatic enough to publish.

Which is precisely the problem.

The Crying Boy does not behave like a theatrical curse.

It does not escalate cleanly.

It does not punish disbelief.

It does not reward reverence.

It simply remains.

Owners who keep the painting today describe a consistent emotional texture rather than events: a low-level discomfort, a sense that the image demands attention without offering meaning. The longer it hangs, the more it feels *wrongly placed*—not hostile, but displaced.

Like grief that has overstayed its welcome.

One theory proposed by folklorists is that the Crying Boy functions as a grief amplifier.

Not supernatural—psychological.

The painting does not cause tragedy; it *attaches* to it. When disaster strikes, people remember the image. When nothing happens, they forget it. Over time, the memory of the painting accumulates only in the presence of loss.

This would explain why families often remove it after fires but rarely before them.

But it does not explain why so many people feel relief after it is gone.

There is another interpretation, quieter and harder to dismiss.

The Crying Boy depicts a child who has already survived something.

The expression is not panic. It is not shock. It is aftermath.

He is not crying because the fire is happening.

He is crying because it already has.

And fire, historically, is one of the most common ways people explain loss they cannot make sense of—homes, families, cities, childhoods. The Crying Boy offers no comfort, no redemption, no narrative closure. He simply reflects the viewer's inability to fix what has been broken.

This makes the painting intolerable over time.

Which brings us to the final and most consistent behavior surrounding the Crying Boy:

People do not destroy it ceremonially.

They throw it away.

Not in rituals. Not with prayers. Not with fire.

They remove it quietly. Wrap it in newspaper. Leave it by the curb. Drop it at charity shops that later discard it. Slip it into dumpsters behind apartment buildings.

As if the worst thing it could do is be acknowledged.

So where is the Crying Boy now?

Everywhere and nowhere.

In attics.

In storage units.

In boxes labeled "misc."

In forgotten flats.

In secondhand markets where sellers refuse to describe it properly.

The prints persist because no one wants them enough to keep them —and no one fears them enough to destroy them.

They exist in a liminal state, like unresolved stories.

If cursed objects are defined not by what they *do*, but by what they *demand* from us, then the Crying Boy is one of the most effective ever produced.

It demands interpretation.

It demands distance.

It demands to be moved.

And if you ignore that demand long enough, it will wait.

Not for fire.

For attention.

The Crying Boy Painting remains one of the rare objects whose alleged power does not diminish under scrutiny. Exposure does not escalate consistently, but neither does familiarity neutralize it. Owners who report the least distress are those who never hang it at all.

Removal, not destruction, appears to be the most common form of containment.

The image endures.

The question is whether you want it enduring *with you.*

19

the kabbalistic
amulet of prague

P rague has always been a city that attracts stories it cannot fully
contain.

Stones press close together there, as if the buildings themselves are listening. Streets double back without warning. Synagogues,
churches, and towers occupy the same skyline, layered rather than
reconciled. It is a city where faith never learned to stay in its lane, and
where knowledge—especially the forbidden kind—was once not only
tolerated, but cultivated.

By the end of the sixteenth century, Prague had become something
rare and dangerous: a place where mysticism, science, and theology
were allowed to touch.

That is where the amulet enters the record.

When Emperor Rudolf II moved his court from Vienna to Prague
in 1583, he did not bring stability with him. He brought appetite.
Rudolf was a collector of the sort that unsettles administrators and
delights historians: compulsive, acquisitive, and deeply uninterested in
boundaries. His Kunstkammer—the imperial chamber of art and
curiosities—filled with astronomical instruments, alchemical appara-
tus, strange animals, mechanical wonders, gemstones, manuscripts,
and objects whose purpose was not immediately legible.

Some were devotional.

Some were scientific.

Some existed in the uneasy space between.

Prague under Rudolf was not a city that asked *whether* something worked. It asked *what kind of order it claimed to impose.*

It is within this environment—where astrology guided medical decisions, alchemy brushed shoulders with theology, and Christian scholars openly engaged with Kabbalistic texts—that the amulet appears.

It is small. That detail matters.

Unlike the sprawling grimoires or elaborate ritual tools that later imaginations prefer, the Kabbalistic Amulet of Prague is compact—portable, intimate, designed to sit close to the body. Its form imitates the *hoshen*, the jeweled breastplate worn by the High Priest in the Book of Exodus. In scripture, the hoshen is not a weapon. It is a mediator. A surface on which divine judgment becomes legible.

Twelve stones. Twelve tribes. Order imposed on chaos.

The Prague amulet borrows that authority deliberately.

To call it "Kabbalistic" is already a compromise.

The object does not belong neatly to Jewish amulet tradition, nor does it fit comfortably within orthodox Christian devotion. It reflects instead the Christian Kabbalah popular among Renaissance intellectuals—a movement that treated Hebrew letters, angelic hierarchies, and sacred numerology as tools for understanding the structure of the universe itself.

This distinction matters, because it explains why the amulet feels unstable in retrospect.

Jewish protective amulets in Prague followed established patterns. They were practical objects, often created to protect mothers and infants, inscribed with Psalms, angelic names, and warnings against Lilith. They were hung on walls, sewn into clothing, tucked into cradles. Their purpose was specific and local.

The amulet associated with Rudolf II was something else entirely.

It was not meant to protect a household. It was meant to symbolize a worldview.

Scholars who have examined it describe an object dense with intention: stones chosen for their sympathetic properties, inscriptions layered rather than explanatory, craftsmanship that suggests the hand of a court artisan rather than a folk practitioner. It was a talisman, yes —but one designed to *collect meaning*, not disperse it.

This is where later stories begin to tilt.

Objects that try to hold too much often become suspect.

There is no contemporary account describing the amulet as cursed.

That absence is important.

During Rudolf's lifetime, the amulet appears to have been treated as a prestige object—an intellectual trophy that demonstrated mastery over symbolic systems others feared. It likely sat among astrolabes and manuscripts, handled carefully, discussed in hushed tones, admired for what it represented rather than what it did.

The shift happens later, after context erodes.

By the nineteenth century, Rudolf II's Prague had been reimagined as a kind of occult fever dream. Alchemists replaced astronomers in popular retellings. Kabbalah flattened into "magic." Objects once embedded in scholarly discourse were reinterpreted through a Gothic lens.

The amulet survives this shift—but not intact.

Its meaning fractures.

What was once a harmonizing device becomes, in later imagination, a conduit. A thing that does not merely symbolize order, but interferes with it.

That is when people start to whisper.

The stories that attach themselves to the amulet are not dramatic in the way curse narratives often are. There are no fires. No sudden deaths. No newspaper headlines.

Instead, the accounts describe something quieter and harder to dismiss.

Those who study it too closely speak of fixation. Of the sense that the object is asking to be decoded. Of symbols that refuse to resolve into meaning, no matter how long one stares.

Sleep becomes shallow. Thoughts loop. The amulet does not intrude—it invites.

In later collector folklore, there are warnings not to wear it, not because it will harm the body, but because it unsettles the mind. That prolonged proximity encourages pattern-seeking beyond usefulness. That it blurs the line between contemplation and obsession.

No one agrees on whether these effects are intrinsic or induced.

What *is* consistent is the escalation pattern: the more someone attempts to activate the amulet—to treat it as a tool rather than a historical object—the more uncomfortable the experience becomes.

It is not a curse that punishes disbelief.

It punishes certainty.

By the time the amulet enters modern museum collections, it is already carrying this double weight: artifact and accusation. Conservators treat it with gloves and climate controls. Scholars describe it carefully, emphasizing its historical function. And yet the language never quite settles.

It is always described as *powerful*, even when that power is undefined.

That ambiguity is where the haunting lives.

Not in demons.

Not in spirits.

But in the uncomfortable recognition that objects can outlive the systems that once made them safe to understand.

If the amulet was ever meant to act, it did so quietly.

There are no trial records naming it. No denunciations. No sermons warning against its use. When Rudolf II's court finally collapsed—fractured by political instability, religious pressure, and the emperor's own declining health—the amulet did not erupt into legend. It simply persisted.

That persistence is, perhaps, its most unsettling trait.

Objects that become dangerous quickly are easy to categorize. They burn houses. They kill livestock. They leave a mark. But objects that survive regime changes, belief shifts, and interpretive revolutions without fully shedding their aura tend to attract suspicion later, when no one remembers *why* they were safe in the first place.

After Rudolf's death in 1612, his collections were scattered. Some were seized. Some sold. Some vanished into private hands. The amulet's trail becomes indistinct here—not because it disappears, but because it blends.

Inventories list it obliquely: a jeweled plate, an inscribed talisman, a symbolic object of Hebrew origin. At no point does anyone claim it *does* anything. At no point does anyone say it *shouldn't* exist.

This neutrality does not last.

By the eighteenth and nineteenth centuries, the intellectual ecosystem that produced the amulet had collapsed.

Christian Kabbalah was no longer fashionable. Hebrew mysticism was increasingly exoticized rather than engaged. The symbolic literacy required to contextualize such an object was thinning—and in its absence, speculation rushed in to fill the gap.

Collectors begin to describe the amulet differently.

Not as a synthesis, but as a hybrid.

Not as an emblem, but as a device.

Not as contemplative, but as *operative*.

The same inscriptions that once represented divine order are now treated as latent commands. The stones—once symbolic correspondences—are recast as anchors. The amulet is no longer something you read. It is something you *activate*.

This shift does not come from folklore. It comes from misinterpretation.

Modern accounts of "exposure" do not describe immediate consequences. No one collapses after touching it. No one reports visions in the room. Instead, the effects arrive later, displaced into thought and habit.

Museum professionals who have handled comparable objects describe a peculiar resistance to closure. Notes are rewritten. Labels are revised. Descriptions expand rather than clarify. The object seems to generate footnotes faster than conclusions.

Private collectors—particularly those drawn to ceremonial magic—report a different pattern.

The amulet becomes a focal point. It is removed from storage more often than intended. Its inscriptions are copied, traced, translated, retranslated. Sleep shortens. Dreams grow dense but unmemorable, leaving only the impression of having *missed something important*.

This is not possession.

It is fixation.

And fixation, in occult practice, is dangerous precisely because it masquerades as devotion.

One recurring story—recorded in slightly different forms across the late nineteenth and early twentieth centuries—describes a scholar who attempted to reconstruct the amulet's "original purpose" through ritual reenactment. The details are frustratingly incomplete: the location unnamed, the man identified only as a linguist with an interest in Renaissance esotericism.

What survives of the account is not catastrophe, but aftermath.

The scholar abandoned the project abruptly. His notes end mid-sentence. He reportedly claimed that the amulet "did not want interpretation," a phrase that has been repeated often enough to acquire weight, despite its vagueness.

Nothing happened to him that could be documented as supernatural.

What happened instead was withdrawal.

Colleagues describe a man who grew impatient with symbolic explanation, who rejected metaphor as insufficient, who insisted that meaning should *resolve*. When it did not, he disengaged entirely.

This pattern appears again and again.

The amulet does not reward inquiry.

It resists conclusion.

This resistance becomes, in modern framing, its curse.

Unlike objects that escalate through violence or misfortune, the Kabbalistic Amulet of Prague escalates through epistemic frustration. It traps the handler in a feedback loop: the sense that understanding is imminent, coupled with the repeated failure to arrive there.

The longer one insists that the amulet must "do something," the more oppressive its presence becomes—not as a force, but as a problem that refuses to be solved.

In this way, it mirrors the fate of Rudolf II himself: a man who believed the universe could be harmonized through symbols, and who lost control of his empire while trying to read its signs.

By the time the amulet is definitively secured in institutional custody, its danger is no longer framed in occult terms.

Curators speak instead of *context sensitivity*. Of the need to present it alongside explanatory material. Of the importance of resisting sensational labels. Storage recommendations emphasize stability, documentation, and restraint.

It is not sealed away.

It is not exorcised.

It is not destroyed.

It is contained through interpretation.

And yet—even now—descriptions of the amulet are careful in a way most jewelry is not. There is an implicit understanding that it should not be worn. That it should not be isolated from its historical scaffolding. That removing it from narrative invites projection.

The haunting, if it exists, thrives on isolation.

There is a particular kind of object that institutions learn to fear—not because it causes incidents, but because it refuses to resolve.

The amulet falls into this category.

By the mid–twentieth century, curators and archivists no longer argued about what it *was*. That debate had exhausted itself. Instead, the question shifted to how it should be handled without encouraging the very interpretations that made it unstable.

Internal correspondence from museum professionals—dry, procedural, never intended for publication—reveals an unusual level of care. Labels were revised repeatedly. Descriptions grew longer, not clearer. Every sentence seemed to anticipate misuse: by mystics, by thrill-seekers, by those who wanted the object to *mean something definitive*.

One memo, circulated quietly among staff, warned against allowing the amulet to be photographed in isolation.

"Detached images," it noted, "encourage narrative invention."

This was not paranoia. It was pattern recognition.

By this point, stories had begun to circulate outside academic spaces—half-remembered anecdotes passed between collectors, students, and occult hobbyists. None could be substantiated. None involved sudden death or disaster.

Instead, they shared a consistent emotional contour.

People who spent time studying the amulet reported an increasing sense that they were *doing it wrong*. That the object resisted their frameworks. That no translation satisfied. That the inscriptions, when reduced to meaning, felt incomplete—like instructions missing a final step that could never be recovered.

This sense of near-comprehension proved corrosive.

Several private owners reportedly sold or donated similar amulets after brief periods, citing unease they could not articulate. One described the object as "unfinished." Another claimed it produced "the opposite of revelation"—a sensation of narrowing rather than expansion.

In each case, the problem was not fear.

It was insistence.

The most persistent misconception about the amulet is that it was designed to *act*.

In reality, its power—if one insists on using that word—lies in what it refuses to do. It does not bless. It does not curse. It does not respond to ritual reenactment or devotional handling.

What it does instead is destabilize certainty.

The amulet sits at the intersection of systems that were never meant to merge cleanly: Jewish mysticism filtered through Christian esotericism, rendered decorative, then stripped of living practice. It is a relic of synthesis without continuity.

And continuity is what ritual objects depend on.

Without it, they become mirrors.

This is why modern containment strategies are almost aggressively mundane.

The amulet is stored with extensive documentation. Its provenance is emphasized over its symbolism. Its inscriptions are explained, contextualized, and—crucially—*limited*. Visitors are not encouraged to speculate. No experiential language appears on display cards.

The goal is not to suppress mystery.

It is to prevent projection.

Because projection is where the amulet becomes dangerous—not in the theatrical sense, but in the psychological one. The human impulse to complete patterns, to force coherence, to demand function from symbol.

In this way, the amulet echoes a broader historical failure: the belief that divine order can be fully mapped, fully named, fully worn.

Rudolf II tried to rule an empire that way.

It did not end well.

There are no confirmed deaths attributed to the amulet. No accidents. No sudden illnesses. This frustrates those who want a cleaner legend.

But absence is not innocence.

The object's influence—if it exists at all—is cumulative and internal. It works not by harming the body, but by exhausting the intellect. By drawing the handler deeper into interpretation until the act of interpretation itself becomes the trap.

Those who walk away early feel relief.

Those who insist feel hollowed.

The Kabbalistic Amulet of Prague demonstrates a form of hazard that resists dramatization. Its effects do not escalate through proximity, but through insistence. The amulet remains inert until burdened with expectation.

Removal from interpretive context has repeatedly preceded fixation, mislabeling, and abandonment.

Containment is achieved not through sealing or separation, but through restraint.

20

the skull of the marquis de sade

They buried the Marquis de Sade quickly.

That alone should have been the end of it.

He died on December 2, 1814, inside the walls of the Charenton asylum, a place designed to soften the edges of madness with routine and walls. His body was failing, his teeth mostly gone, his hands still restless. He had spent decades moving between prisons, fortresses, and institutions—always writing, always insisting on desire as the final authority. By the time death reached him, the man himself had been reduced to a problem administrators wanted resolved.

There was no ceremony. No marker. No crowd.

De Sade had requested something unusual in his will: that his grave be left unmarked and acorns planted over it, so that nature would erase him. He wanted no monument. No relic. No body to gather around.

History ignored the request.

The cemetery did not last. In the years that followed the Revolution, Paris reshaped itself with little regard for the dead. Graves were cleared. Bones were stacked. Names were lost or reassigned. Paperwork mattered more than bodies. And somewhere in that administrative violence—between ledger entries, wheelbarrows, and reused plots —the Marquis de Sade was disturbed.

The records do not say who took his skull.

They only confirm that it was no longer where it should have been.

That absence is the first documented fact. Everything else grows from it.

By the mid–nineteenth century, de Sade was no longer simply a dead nobleman. He had become an idea. His books—once seized, burned, or whispered about—were rediscovered by writers who were no longer interested in morality as a stabilizing force. To the Symbolists, he was a prophet. To the Surrealists, a liberator. To others, he was still a monster, but a fascinating one.

Ideas like that attract relics.

Bones have always been easier to mythologize than texts. A skull can be touched. Displayed. Passed hand to hand. It does not argue back. It does not explain itself. It waits.

Accounts begin to surface—never in official inventories, never in museum catalogues, always in letters, memoirs, and secondhand reports—of a skull identified as de Sade's circulating in private collections. Sometimes it is described as a curiosity. Sometimes as a philosophical joke. Sometimes, more quietly, as a ritual focus.

There is no single, authoritative chain of custody. Instead, there are clusters of stories that overlap without quite aligning, like reflections that refuse to settle into a single image.

One version places the skull in Paris in the late nineteenth century, in the hands of collectors fascinated by criminal anthropology. Another situates it among avant-garde circles who believed that genius left residues in the body—that proximity to the remains of a transgressive mind could unlock something dormant in the living. A third insists the skull was used during séances, positioned at the center of a table as a symbolic anchor rather than a summoned presence.

None of these accounts can be proven. None can be fully dismissed.

What can be confirmed is this: de Sade's remains were disturbed, and his skull was separated. After that, the trail dissolves into rumor, belief, and desire.

That dissolution is part of the haunting.

Human skulls occupy a strange category in the hierarchy of objects. They are not tools. They are not art. They are not relics in the religious sense, unless someone decides they are. They become mirrors for the meanings imposed upon them.

In de Sade's case, the meanings were already volatile.

He had written about confinement while confined. About power while stripped of it. About desire as something that survived punishment, humiliation, and time. His skull—real or alleged—became a vessel for those contradictions. Not cursed in the traditional sense. Charged.

Those who claimed proximity to it reported experiences that followed a familiar pattern.

At first, fascination. An intensity of thought. A sense that ideas came more easily, or more brutally. Writing that pushed further than intended. Conversations that drifted toward taboo without effort.

Later, discomfort. Sleep interrupted by dreams of corridors, locked doors, watchers behind walls. Irritability. A sense of being watched not by something external, but by one's own impulses, suddenly stripped of disguise.

In the most extreme anecdotes—always relayed secondhand—there are references to self-destructive behavior escalating after prolonged engagement with the skull. Obsession with transgression turning inward. Not possession, not madness, but permission. The idea that restraint was no longer required.

Whether these effects were caused by the object or by the mythology surrounding it is impossible to determine. What matters is that the object functioned as a catalyst. It did not create desire. It removed barriers.

That, historically, is how the most dangerous relics behave.

Skeptics have always been present in the story. They point out, correctly, that no skull has ever been definitively authenticated as belonging to de Sade. That exhumations were chaotic. That attribution often follows reputation rather than evidence. That people in occult circles have been known to lie.

All of this is true.

And yet the story persists.

Part of that persistence comes from the skull's disappearance. If it were housed in a museum—measured, catalogued, photographed—it would lose much of its power. Instead, it exists in the liminal space between documented disturbance and narrative invention.

Lost objects invite imagination. Lost remains invite projection.

The skull's absence becomes its strongest proof.

There is one detail that appears across multiple retellings, often overlooked because it lacks drama.

Those who handled the skull—whether they believed it authentic or not—rarely kept it for long.

It moved. It was passed on. Sold quietly. Returned. Hidden. Its presence was tolerated in theory, but difficult in practice. People spoke of it as something that unsettled a room without doing anything at all.

No fires. No deaths. No unmistakable calamities.

Just erosion.

Relationships strained. Projects abandoned. Fixations that refused to resolve. A sense that the object was not actively hostile, but profoundly indifferent.

That indifference is important.

Curses that announce themselves burn out quickly. Objects that do nothing invite endless interpretation.

If the skull of the Marquis de Sade was ever used in ritual, it was not in the way popular imagination expects. There are no circles of salt, no Latin invocations recorded, no demon names attached. Instead, it appears in accounts as a focal point—a reminder, a provocation, a permission structure.

Placed on a table during philosophical discussion. Present during séances not to summon spirits, but to destabilize moral boundaries. Held not as a key, but as a question.

What happens when restraint is removed?

De Sade spent his life exploring that question. His skull, real or imagined, became a way to ask it again—without the burden of authorship.

Today, the skull's location is unknown. It may have been destroyed. It may sit mislabeled in a private collection. It may never have existed in the way the stories insist.

And yet it continues to appear in footnotes, in memoirs, in warnings passed quietly between collectors.

Not because it kills.

But because it unsettles.

Because it reminds those who encounter the story that ideas do not die cleanly. That bodies can be erased, but meanings persist. That some figures leave behind not relics, but pressure points.

The Marquis de Sade asked to be forgotten.

The skull ensures he is not.

Editor's closing note:

Objects do not inherit evil.

They inherit attention.

And attention, prolonged long enough, can feel indistinguishable from a haunting.

21

the hellfire club
ritual chalice

The chalice is never described first.

In every surviving account, the room comes before the cup. The cave. The torchlight. The smell of damp stone and wine and smoke. Laughter echoing where laughter should not echo. The men are already seated when the object appears, as though it has been waiting for them rather than the other way around.

Only then does someone mention the cup.

The Hellfire Club, more formally known as the Monks of Medmenham, was founded in the mid-18th century by Sir Francis Dashwood, a politician, libertine, and committed provocateur whose reputation straddled satire and scandal. The Club gathered not in drawing rooms or public halls, but in caves carved beneath Dashwood's estate at West Wycombe—artificial grottoes designed to resemble ancient ritual spaces, complete with inscriptions, chambers, and altars.

The motto carved above the entrance was simple:

Fais ce que tu voudras.

Do what thou wilt.

Long before Aleister Crowley adopted it, the phrase was already doing damage.

The chalice appears in descriptions of Hellfire gatherings with frustrating inconsistency. It is not named in official records. It does not appear in ledgers. But it *does* appear in letters, satires, and hostile accounts written by men who attended once and never returned.

A shared cup.

Passed hand to hand.

Filled with wine—sometimes rumored to be laced with other substances, though no proof survives.

It was used at the height of the gatherings, when parody tipped into performance and performance blurred into something more sincere than anyone wanted to admit.

Accounts differ on the chalice's appearance. Some describe it as silver. Others as blackened metal. One 18th-century satirical engraving depicts a cup shaped almost like a skull, though historians argue this was exaggeration meant to demonstrate moral decay.

What matters is not the exact shape.

What matters is that the cup was *not ornamental.*

It was used.

The Hellfire Club delighted in inversion—religious ritual mocked, sacred language repurposed, virtue played for laughs. The chalice functioned as a parody of communion, yes, but also as a unifying object. To drink from it was to signal complicity. Participation. Consent.

No one was forced.

That detail appears repeatedly, almost defensively, in later accounts.

The gatherings themselves were not illegal in any clear sense, but they attracted intense scrutiny. Rumors spread rapidly: satanic rites, blasphemous ceremonies, sexual transgression. Many of these stories were inflated, born of political rivalry and moral panic.

But not all of them.

Several former members later described a sense that something in the caves had gone "too far"—that what began as satire had acquired gravity. That the laughter stopped landing cleanly. That the chalice, once introduced, changed the tone of the room.

One attendee wrote, in a letter later archived among private corre-spondence, that after drinking from the cup he felt "a peculiar lightness, as though one had agreed to something without hearing the terms."

After the Club's dissolution in the late 1760s—prompted by political fallout and increasing public scrutiny—the objects associated with it were dispersed. Furniture sold. Decorations destroyed. Records quietly lost.

The chalice did not go on display.

It vanished.

This is where the story fractures.

Some accounts claim the chalice was melted down, its metal reused, its symbolic power nullified through destruction. Others insist it was taken by a private collector with an interest in esoteric relics. A minority suggest it remained in the caves for decades, discovered and removed by later visitors who did not understand what they had found.

No single claim can be verified.

What *can* be traced is the reappearance of a cup—matching several descriptions—circulating through private collections in the 19th century, often accompanied by vague claims of "Medmenham provenance." In at least two instances, the owners of such cups experienced abrupt reversals of fortune: disgrace, illness, sudden withdrawal from society.

Nothing that could be proven.

Enough to be whispered.

Unlike other cursed objects, the Hellfire Chalice does not inspire fear on contact. People do not report nightmares, apparitions, or physical harm. Instead, they describe changes in judgment. Impulse. A willingness to cross lines they had previously respected.

The object does not compel.

It invites.

Skeptics argue—again, not unreasonably—that any perceived effects are psychological, born of suggestion and historical context. The Hellfire Club was infamous. To believe one holds a relic from it is to participate in that infamy.

But that explanation falters when faced with how consistently the chalice is described as *eroding restraint rather than shocking it.* Owners do not panic. They indulge. They delay consequences. They tell themselves they are in control.

Until they aren't.

In modern times, several objects have been marketed—often dubiously—as "Hellfire chalices." Most are obvious fabrications. A few are more convincing, their provenance murky but persistent.

Serious collectors tend to avoid them.

Not out of belief, exactly.

Out of experience.

The Hellfire Chalice, if it still exists in any meaningful form, is unlikely to announce itself. It will not glow or hum or punish curiosity. It will sit comfortably on a shelf, admired for its craftsmanship, its weight, its history.

It will not ask you to believe in anything.

It will only ask whether you would like another drink.

And that, perhaps, is the most dangerous ritual of all.

part two
jewelry, clothing
& personal items

22
the koh-i-noor diamond

T he first thing people learn about the Koh-i-Noor is its name. *Mountain of Light.*

It is a lie in the way most beautiful names are lies—true in shape, false in implication. Mountains do not move. Light does not weigh this much. And nothing that has passed through so many hands leaves them unchanged.

The Koh-i-Noor did not begin as a jewel. Like most stones that later acquire reputations, it began as a presence—unearthed, unshaped, already dangerous because it existed outside any one person's claim. Long before it was cut, mounted, or crowned, it was known in the Indian subcontinent as a stone of kingship. Not because it conferred power, but because it *refused* to stay with those who wielded it poorly.

The earliest records place it in India, likely mined from the alluvial deposits of the Golconda region sometime before the 14th century. These mines produced diamonds that were not merely valuable but culturally saturated—stones believed to carry consequence, not just price. The Koh-i-Noor was one of these. It was large. It was pale. It was already being watched.

By the time it enters recorded history in earnest, it is no longer anonymous. It is embedded in dynasties.

The stone passes first through Hindu rulers, then into the hands of the Mughal emperors. It is set into thrones, into turbans, into regalia meant to signal divine sanction. One emperor after another claims it as proof of legitimacy. One emperor after another loses it through violence.

Babur, the founder of the Mughal Empire, writes of a diamond of extraordinary size and clarity. His descendants inherit it—and inherit the trouble that comes with it. Shah Jahan, builder of the Taj Mahal, possesses the stone at the height of his power. He also dies imprisoned by his own son, staring at his wife's tomb through a barred window.

The pattern is not subtle.

Power concentrates around the diamond. Power collapses.

The Koh-i-Noor becomes a witness to betrayal, coups, assassinations, imprisonments. It moves not by sale, but by conquest. It is seized, surrendered, stolen, demanded as tribute. Ownership is rarely voluntary. That matters.

By the time it passes to Nader Shah of Persia in the 18th century, its reputation has sharpened. It is Nader Shah who gives it the name that endures—*Koh-i-Noor*, the Mountain of Light—after prying it from a defeated Mughal emperor who had attempted to hide it in his turban.

Nader Shah's reign does not last long.

He is assassinated in his tent by his own officers, and the diamond vanishes again into the churn of succession and blood. From Persia it moves to Afghanistan, then back into the Indian subcontinent, carried by rulers whose reigns are marked by paranoia, mutilation, and violent ends. One owner is blinded. Another is poisoned. Another dies imprisoned.

By now, the stone's reputation has begun to harden into something like a rule.

Men may own it.

They may display it.

They may conquer with it.

But they will not keep it.

This belief becomes so entrenched that by the 19th century, a new tradition emerges around the diamond: women may wear it safely.

Men may not. The Koh-i-Noor does not kill women, the stories say. It only destroys men who try to rule through it.

This belief is not ancient. It is a rationalization—one that allows the stone to continue circulating without being buried or destroyed. But rationalizations are still stories, and stories still shape behavior.

When the British East India Company takes control of Punjab in 1849, the Koh-i-Noor is demanded as part of the Treaty of Lahore. It is handed over not by a king, but by a child.

Duleep Singh is ten years old.

The diamond is placed in his care long enough to be taken from him. He is later exiled. His kingdom is dissolved. His identity fractured. The diamond survives him easily.

When the Koh-i-Noor arrives in Britain, it is treated as a spoil, a curiosity, a prize. It is displayed publicly, where it disappoints. Under gaslight, it does not blaze. It absorbs.

So the British do what conquerors often do with inconvenient truths. They reshape it.

The diamond is recut in 1852, reducing its size dramatically in an attempt to increase its brilliance. What is lost is not documented in emotional terms—only carats, angles, weight. But the act itself is telling. This is not stewardship. It is correction.

After the recut, the Koh-i-Noor is no longer worn by kings. It is passed instead to queens and consorts, embedded in crowns designed not for rule, but for representation. Queen Victoria wears it. Later, it appears in the crowns of Queen Alexandra, Queen Mary, and Queen Elizabeth (the Queen Mother).

The rule holds.

The men who claim it lose empires.

The women who wear it survive them.

Today, the Koh-i-Noor rests in the Tower of London, set into the Crown Jewels. It is protected by glass, by guards, by narrative. It is described as heritage. As history. As inert.

And yet it remains one of the most contested objects in the world.

India claims it.

Pakistan claims it.

Iran claims it.

Afghanistan claims it.

No one forgets it.

Requests for its return are met with deflection, legal language, and polite refusal. The diamond does not move. It sits under lights not unlike the ones that failed it before. Visitors lean in. Some feel nothing. Some feel watched.

The curse, if there is one, has changed shape.

The Koh-i-Noor no longer topples rulers directly. It does something quieter now. It sits at the center of unresolved history, refusing to belong fully to the place that holds it. It destabilizes narratives simply by existing. It reminds empires that acquisition does not equal legitimacy.

There is an old version of the warning, sometimes whispered, sometimes written:

He who owns this diamond shall own the world—but will know all its misfortunes.

The wording varies. The meaning does not.

The Koh-i-Noor does not kill indiscriminately. It does not burn houses or poison bloodlines. It erodes certainty. It converts possession into burden. It makes rulers afraid of what they already have.

A mountain of light is still a mountain.

It casts a shadow.

And the Koh-i-Noor has never stopped doing exactly that.

23

the black orlov diamond

T he first time the Black Orlov is noticed, it is already broken.

Not fractured—cut. Deliberately altered. Reduced from whatever shape it once held into something smaller, darker, and easier to carry. That matters. Objects with violent reputations rarely arrive intact. They are reshaped early, as if someone understood that leaving them whole would be a mistake.

The story most often told about the Black Orlov begins, like so many cursed diamond legends, in India. It is said to have once been set into the eyes of a Hindu idol—sometimes identified as Brahma, sometimes unnamed, sometimes described only as a guardian figure meant to see what humans could not. The original stone, according to this telling, was far larger than the one that exists today.

And it was not meant to move.

Unlike the Hope Diamond, whose idol origin lingers in rumor, the Black Orlov's story insists on violation as its starting point. The diamond is not traded. It is not gifted. It is *taken*. Removed from a sacred context where it was not decoration but function. The eye of a god is not symbolic. It is surveillance.

Whether this idol ever existed in the precise form described is impossible to prove. What *can* be proven is that by the early 20th

century, a large black diamond appears in Europe with no clean provenance and an unusual reputation attached to it almost immediately.
The stone surfaces in Russia, already associated with misfortune,
already whispered about rather than displayed proudly.

By 1932, the Black Orlov has a name—and a body count.

That year, a Russian diamond dealer named J. W. Paris reportedly
acquires the stone. He brings it to New York. He attempts to sell it.
And then, in a move that will be repeated with eerie consistency, he
jumps to his death from a skyscraper.

This is the first documented suicide linked to the diamond, and it
sets the tone. The death is not theatrical. There is no note. No declaration of madness. Just a sudden, irreversible decision made at height.

The stone passes on.

In the years that follow, the Black Orlov changes hands again. Two
Russian princesses—names vary depending on the source, often cited
as Princess Nadia Vyegin-Orlov and Princess Leonila Bariatinsky—are
both reported to have owned or worn the diamond at different points.
Both die by suicide, each jumping from tall buildings in separate
incidents.

Three owners. Three falls.

This is where the story hardens into something people can no
longer comfortably dismiss.

Skeptics are quick to point out that early accounts are muddled.
Names are repeated incorrectly. Timelines blur. The chaos of post-revolutionary Russia swallowed records whole. But even skeptical
retellings cannot erase the pattern that anchors the myth: the deaths
cluster, they echo, and they stop once the stone is altered again.

At some point after the third suicide, the Black Orlov is recut.

The decision is practical on the surface. Smaller stones are easier to
sell. Easier to mount. Easier to separate from reputation. But the effect
is striking. The original diamond—estimated at around 195 carats—is
cut into multiple stones. The largest remaining piece weighs approximately 67.5 carats.

After this, the suicides cease.

The diamond does not suddenly become benevolent. But the escalation changes. The violence withdraws inward. The stone continues to

pass through private collections, appearing briefly, then vanishing again. It is worn, then locked away. Its owners do not die spectacularly —but neither do they speak openly about it.

This shift becomes part of the legend.

The Black Orlov, some say, was too strong in its original form. Breaking it diluted the force. Others argue the opposite—that the recutting was a kind of appeasement, a concession made to something that had already proven it could not be ignored.

Modern gemological records place the diamond in various private collections throughout the mid-to-late 20th century. It appears occasionally at exhibitions, mounted in elaborate necklaces surrounded by white diamonds—an attempt, perhaps, to domesticate it. To frame it as luxury rather than threat.

Visitors notice it anyway.

Descriptions recur across decades: the stone appears to swallow light rather than reflect it. It feels heavier than it should. People report a sense of pressure when standing close to it—not fear exactly, but compression, as if attention itself has weight.

There are no new deaths tied conclusively to the diamond. This becomes the skeptics' strongest argument. Whatever curse once existed, they say, has burned itself out. Or never existed at all.

But curses are not machines. They do not require constant output to remain active. Some are satisfied with a demonstration.

The Black Orlov's reputation now rests in restraint. It does not chase publicity. It does not tolerate prolonged exposure. It moves quietly, briefly, leaving behind just enough unease to ensure it is remembered but never fully understood.

Today, the diamond's whereabouts are not consistently public. It is said to reside in a private collection, emerging only for specific exhibitions under controlled conditions. Curators speak about it carefully. Dealers speak about it rarely. No one markets it aggressively.

This, too, is telling.

Unlike the Hope Diamond, which has been neutralized through repetition and glass, the Black Orlov resists institutional framing. It does not live in a national museum. It is not offered as a shared artifact. It remains personal.

And personal objects are more dangerous than public ones.

There is an old belief in several traditions that objects taken from ritual settings do not seek revenge. They seek *resolution*. If they cannot return to their place, they attempt to recreate the conditions of their function.

An eye removed from a god does not stop watching.

It looks for another vantage point.

The Black Orlov does not announce itself as cursed. It waits for proximity. It waits for ownership. It waits for the quiet moment when a person decides they can handle it.

The suicides are the loud part of the story.

The silence afterward is the warning.

Because the diamond no longer needs to prove anything.

It already has.

24
the delhi purple sapphire
(Amethyst of Misfortune)

The stone arrived mislabeled.

That is the first mistake, and perhaps the most fitting one. For all the violence and superstition that would later gather around it, the Delhi Purple Sapphire was never a sapphire at all. It was an amethyst—violet, translucent, deceptively calm. The kind of stone people wear for protection, clarity, peace.

None of those things followed it.

The gem entered the record in the late nineteenth century, carried back from India during the long aftershock of empire. The details of its removal are, like so many colonial objects, vague by design. It was said to have been taken from a temple in Delhi during the Indian Rebellion of 1857, though even this detail floats between certainty and repetition. Sometimes the temple is named. Sometimes it is merely described as sacred. Sometimes the stone is said to have been set into a statue. Sometimes it is simply "kept there."

What matters is not where it came from, but how it was taken.

The British officer who removed the stone—often identified only as a soldier looting in the aftermath of violence—did not profit from it. He did not live long enough to enjoy it. Accounts differ on the specifics, but the pattern begins immediately: illness, disgrace, financial ruin. The stone changes hands, and the same pattern follows.

By the time the amethyst reaches England, it already carries a reputation. Not a public one. A private one, passed between owners in lowered voices. The gem does not ruin people dramatically. It erodes them. Accidents. Failed ventures. Sudden sickness. A sense that things are *slipping*, just beyond correction.

The man who documents this best is also the man who never wanted to believe it.

Edward Heron-Allen was a polymath—translator, scientist, violin maker, rationalist by temperament and training. He acquired the stone in the 1890s, inheriting it through a chain of already uneasy ownership. Almost immediately, his life begins to fracture around it.

He loses money. He falls ill. Projects collapse. Relationships strain. None of this is supernatural in isolation. What disturbs him is the consistency—and the timing.

Heron-Allen does what a rational man does when confronted with a problem he does not like. He observes it.

He notes that the misfortunes intensify when the stone is near him. He locks it away, and his luck improves. He takes it out again, and things unravel. He lends it to friends, hoping to disprove his own theory.

They give it back.

Some refuse to touch it again. Others experience sudden reversals —injuries, losses, a creeping sense of dread they cannot articulate. One acquaintance returns the stone wrapped in paper, unwilling to meet Heron-Allen's eyes.

This is where the story turns from rumor into record.

Heron-Allen begins to write. Not publicly at first. Privately. He keeps notes. He records dates. He resists the word *curse* while circling it repeatedly. Eventually, reluctantly, he uses it.

He attempts to neutralize the stone by gifting it to charity. The effort fails. No one wants it once its reputation becomes known. He tries storing it among other gemstones, hoping it will lose its distinctiveness. It does not.

At last, he does the thing that gives the Delhi Purple Sapphire its enduring power: he sends it away with instructions.

In 1912, Heron-Allen deposits the amethyst with the British Museum, accompanied by a letter. In it, he describes the stone as cursed. He asks that it never be worn. He asks that it not be removed from storage. He suggests—only half joking—that it be sealed.

And then he adds the most telling detail of all:

he requests that the stone not be unwrapped for thirty-three years.

The number is unexplained. That makes it worse.

For decades, the amethyst sits in the museum's vaults, cataloged, ignored, quietly radioactive in reputation if not in fact. Staff are aware of the letter. Some take it seriously. Others treat it as an eccentric footnote from a superstitious age.

When the stone is eventually examined again, nothing happens. No deaths. No calamities. Skeptics take this as confirmation that the curse was always psychological.

But that interpretation misses the point.

The Delhi Purple Sapphire does not perform on demand. It does not flare when observed. Its power—if that is the right word—was always proximity and possession. Ownership. Intimacy.

Behind glass, stripped of agency, the stone is inert.

What remains unsettling is not that the curse "failed," but that it behaved exactly as Heron-Allen predicted.

Today, the amethyst is sometimes displayed, usually accompanied by a label that carefully distances the institution from the story. It is presented as an example of superstition, of colonial mythmaking, of coincidence misread as fate.

Visitors linger anyway.

People report a strange reluctance to look at it too long. Not fear. Not fascination. A sense that attention itself is being discouraged. That the stone is better left alone.

There is an old belief, repeated across cultures, that objects removed from sacred contexts retain an echo of function. Not intention. Function. An eye watches. A guardian guards. A ward wards.

An amulet meant to protect, when inverted, does not attack. It withdraws protection.

The Delhi Purple Sapphire does not kill its owners.

It simply leaves them alone with what comes next.

Heron-Allen lived out his life rationally, productively, never fully convinced—and never fully dismissive. He did not destroy the stone. He did not attempt to cleanse it. He archived it.

That may have been the most respectful choice.

Some objects do not want belief.

They want distance.

And the most unsettling thing about the Delhi Purple Sapphire is not that it brought misfortune—but that the one man who knew it best learned to fear it *without ever quite believing in it at all.*

25

the busby stoop chair

(wearable curse transferred via sitting)

They did not burn the chair.

That is the detail that refuses to behave. In an era when execution sites were scrubbed clean, gallows dismantled, and criminals erased with administrative efficiency, the chair remained. Not hidden. Not destroyed. Simply... left.

It stood outside an inn on the Great North Road, just beyond the small village of Thirsk in North Yorkshire. Travelers rested against it. Locals leaned back with tankards in hand. It looked no different from any other heavy oak chair meant to endure weather and weight.

And people kept dying.

The story begins in 1702, though even that date feels like a convenience rather than a certainty. Thomas Busby—sometimes called Dirty Tom—was a counterfeiter, thief, and drunk, known locally more for his temper than his crimes. He frequented the inn then known as the Busby Stoop Inn, drinking himself into rages and disputes that spilled easily into violence.

The man he eventually killed was his own father-in-law.

The argument was petty. The outcome was not. Busby strangled the older man in a fury, then staggered back to the inn to finish his drink.

When he was arrested, tried, and sentenced to hang, he requested one last indulgence: a final glass of ale at the inn he had ruined.

They granted it.

Busby sat in his favorite chair, drank, and rose to meet his execution. But before he left, he turned back to the seat that had carried him through countless nights of fury and failure.

He cursed it.

Accounts differ on his exact words, but the sentiment is consistent: anyone who sat in that chair would die. Not someday. Not metaphorically. Die.

Curses spoken at the gallows are a genre unto themselves. Most dissolve into folklore within a generation. This one did not.

Busby was hanged nearby, and his body buried beneath the crossroads—a traditional precaution against restless dead. The chair, however, was returned to the inn.

And people kept sitting in it.

The first deaths were dismissed as coincidence. Soldiers on leave. Travelers bound for dangerous roads. Men who were already living on borrowed time. But patterns do not require belief to form.

By the late eighteenth century, locals had noticed something unsettling. Men who sat in the chair did not simply die eventually. They died *soon*. Accidents. Falls. Sudden illness. Violence. No two deaths were identical, but the timeline was eerily consistent.

Sit in the chair. Leave the inn. Do not come back.

During the Second World War, the chair claimed one of its most frequently cited victims. A group of Royal Air Force airmen stopped at the inn before returning to base. One of them—accounts vary on his name—sat in the chair, laughed at the superstition, and left shortly after.

He was dead by morning, killed in a crash during a routine exercise.

Another airman reportedly tried to remove the chair as a joke, lifting it from the floor and carrying it outside. He was killed in a road accident before the day was over.

By now, the innkeepers were no longer amused.

The chair was not displayed prominently. It was not advertised. But it was not destroyed either. There is something uniquely human about that hesitation—the refusal to take responsibility for ending a story, even one that keeps drawing blood.

By the 1960s, the death toll attributed to the chair varied wildly depending on the teller. Some said dozens. Some said more than sixty. Skeptics argued that the numbers were inflated, that attribution followed rumor rather than record.

And they were right.

But they were also missing the point.

The danger of the Busby Stoop Chair was never statistical. It was behavioral. People sat in it *because* of the story. They tested it. Mocked it. Proved themselves brave against it.

The chair did not need belief to work. It only needed participation.

Eventually, the chair was removed—not destroyed, but displaced. It was donated to the Thirsk Museum, where it remains suspended high on the wall, deliberately positioned so no one can sit in it.

This decision is often presented as a safety measure.

It is also an admission.

The museum does not deny the legend outright. They contextualize it. They provide dates. They explain how stories grow. But they also do something quieter, more telling: they keep the chair airborne, as if contact itself were the problem.

No one is allowed to sit.

Visitors still ask why.

What unsettles curators is not that people believe the curse, but that they *want* to test it. That sitting feels irresistible. That a chair—a symbol of rest, hospitality, relief—has become something people approach with a dare already forming on their lips.

Chairs are intimate objects. They receive the body. They remember weight. They bear witness in a way tables and walls do not. To curse a chair is to curse the act of resting itself.

The Busby Stoop Chair does not hunt. It does not follow. It waits.

Theories abound, of course. Confirmation bias. Selective memory. The dangerous lives of soldiers and travelers mistaken for supernatural causality. All reasonable. All insufficient.

Because none of them explain the restraint.

No one has sat in the chair since it was mounted on the wall.

Not skeptics. Not thrill-seekers. Not researchers.

The curse survives not because people believe in it, but because they choose not to disprove it.

There is a particular kind of warning embedded in this object, one that feels almost gentle compared to the bloodier artifacts in this archive. It does not promise suffering. It does not whisper or glow or demand sacrifice.

It simply offers a seat.

And that, perhaps, is the most dangerous invitation of all.

Some objects hurt you when you reach for them.

Some hurt you when you look.

The Busby Stoop Chair waits until you decide you deserve to rest.

26

james dean's "little bastard" jacket fragment

They like to say the car was cursed.

That's easier.

It gives the danger a shape you can point to—metal twisted, engine screaming, speed immortalized in black-and-white photographs. It keeps the story at a distance, contained inside the wreckage of a machine that no longer exists.

But curses don't always stay where we leave them.

Sometimes they break off and follow the body.

In the autumn of 1955, James Dean was twenty-four years old and already tired of being careful. He had finished filming *Giant*. He was driving west toward a race he was not supposed to enter, in a Porsche 550 Spyder he called *Little Bastard*—a nickname given half-jokingly, half-defiantly, as if daring fate to object.

Fate objected.

The crash near Cholame, California, happened quickly. Too quickly for heroics. Too quickly for narrative satisfaction. Dean was pronounced dead shortly after arrival at the hospital. The other driver survived. The car was destroyed.

That should have been the end.

Instead, the wreckage developed a second life.

Pieces of the Porsche were salvaged—sold, borrowed, studied. Mechanics reported injuries. Drivers who installed parts from *Little Bastard* into their own vehicles were killed in separate accidents. Tires blew. Engines failed. Metal behaved badly.

Newspapers noticed.

By the late 1950s, *Little Bastard* had become a cautionary legend, its reputation growing faster than the documented facts. Skeptics pushed back, correctly noting exaggerations, gaps in sourcing, and the human tendency to retrofit meaning onto tragedy.

But while the debate focused on the car, something else was quietly moving through the margins of the story.

Dean's clothing.

In the chaos after the crash, personal effects were recovered along with the wreckage. Blood-stiffened fabric. Torn denim. Leather scraped raw by asphalt. Most of it disappeared into private hands, studio storage, or family custody. No formal inventory exists. No comprehensive chain of possession was ever recorded.

That absence matters.

At some point—likely within weeks of the accident—a fragment of James Dean's jacket was removed. Not the whole garment. Just a piece. Accounts describe it variously as a sleeve section, a collar fragment, or a torn panel from the back. The inconsistency is telling. What survives in the record is not the object's exact shape, but its *presence*.

The fragment began circulating quietly among collectors of Hollywood ephemera. Unlike the car parts, it was not displayed publicly. It was shown privately, handled reverently, sometimes worn briefly "as a joke," sometimes kept folded, sometimes locked away.

And strange things followed.

Not spectacular deaths. Not headline-ready disasters. Smaller, more intimate disturbances. Accidents without witnesses. Sudden illnesses. Careers derailing in ways that felt disproportionate to their causes. Several early owners reportedly refused to speak about the fragment at all, selling or gifting it without explanation.

One collector, according to correspondence preserved in a private archive, described an overwhelming sense of *pressure* when the fabric was nearby—"like standing too close to someone who hasn't finished dying." He did not keep it long.

Another reportedly claimed the fragment smelled faintly of oil and heat even decades later, though no chemical analysis supported the sensation. When pressed, he admitted the smell only appeared when he was alone.

Unlike the car, the jacket fragment never developed a singular mythology. There was no exhibition disaster. No public curse tally. No dramatic disappearance.

Instead, there was avoidance.

People who encountered it stopped wanting to talk.

Theories emerged, as they always do. Trauma imprinting. Psychosomatic response to celebrity death. Projection fueled by the already-legendary status of James Dean as a symbol of beautiful, unfinished lives.

All reasonable.

But they fail to account for the object's behavior.

The fragment does not announce itself. It does not demand belief. It does not seem interested in spectacle. It operates on proximity, not performance.

Those who wore it—briefly, experimentally—were the most affected. Clothing is the most intimate category of relic. It remembers the shape of a body. It holds warmth. It absorbs sweat, fear, adrenaline. When death is sudden, clothing becomes a boundary that did not have time to adjust.

In religious traditions, such garments are treated with caution or burned outright. In forensic contexts, they are sealed, cataloged, neutralized.

In celebrity culture, they are fetishized.

By the 1970s, the fragment's trail becomes difficult to follow. It is referenced obliquely in auction rumors but never listed. Collectors allude to it without naming it. At least one story places it briefly in Europe before it vanishes again into private hands.

There is no confirmation of its current location.

That, too, matters.

The curse of *Little Bastard* burned bright and fast, then cooled into folklore. The jacket fragment did something quieter. It endured.

Unlike the car, the fragment never killed publicly. It eroded privately. It followed people home. It sat in drawers. It waited in closets.

And that patience feels intentional.

James Dean's death froze him in motion. Forever young. Forever speeding. Forever almost-there. The fragment carries that arrested momentum forward—not as velocity, but as pressure. A sense that something ended mid-breath and resents being remembered out of sequence.

There is a reason museums prefer objects that can be framed, mounted, isolated.

Clothing resists containment.

It wants to be worn.

It wants to remember the body it belonged to.

And perhaps that is the real danger of the fragment—not that it is cursed, but that it remains loyal.

Loyal to a moment that never resolved. Loyal to impact. Loyal to the brief, incandescent life it once touched.

Some artifacts scream their history.

This one whispers.

And if you listen too closely, you may find yourself carrying more of the story than you intended—wondering why you feel restless, why motion feels necessary, why stopping feels wrong.

The car is gone.

The legend remains.

And somewhere, folded carefully out of sight, a piece of fabric still remembers how fast it was going.

27
the ring of silvianus

The ring was not lost at first.

It was taken.

That distinction matters, because theft is not an accident —it creates a relationship. In the Roman world, stolen objects did not simply disappear; they left behind an imbalance that demanded correction. And when correction could not be achieved through law, it was achieved through gods.

The Ring of Silvianus enters the historical record in the late fourth century CE, during the long, grinding dusk of Roman Britain. The empire still ruled on paper. Its roads still cut the countryside. Its temples still stood. But authority had begun to thin, and with it, trust. People turned increasingly to ritual to solve problems that courts could no longer—or would no longer—address.

Silvianus was one of those people.

We know his name because he carved it into gold.

The ring itself is massive by modern standards—thick, heavy, unmistakably male, and not designed for subtlety. It is hexagonal in form, its flat bezel engraved with a single word in confident Latin capitals: SILVIANVS. Not a dedication or a prayer. It's a declaration of ownership.

This was not jewelry meant to be admired from afar. It was meant to be *recognized*.

At some point—likely while Silvianus was visiting or residing near the temple complex at Aquae Sulis (modern Bath)—the ring vanished. There is no record of a struggle, no accusation filed in a civic court. Instead, Silvianus did something far more final.

He cursed it.

On a thin sheet of lead, Silvianus inscribed a defixio—a Roman curse tablet—addressed to the goddess Sulis Minerva, a syncretic deity worshipped at the sacred springs of Bath. His words were precise, controlled, and unmistakably angry. He named the ring. He named the crime. And he named the punishment.

The thief—identified only as Senicianus—was to be denied health, sleep, and peace until the ring was returned to its rightful owner. Not destroyed. Not compensated. Returned.

The tablet was folded, pierced, and thrown into the sacred waters, where it joined dozens of similar pleas: stolen cloaks, missing coins, lost love, unpaid debts. Bath was not just a spa. It was a bureaucratic office for divine retribution.

For centuries, that should have been the end of it.

But the ring did not go back to Silvianus.

Instead, it traveled.

When it resurfaces, it does so far from the baths—unearthed in 1785 at Lydney Park in Gloucestershire, the site of a Romano-British temple complex dedicated to Nodens, a god associated with healing, hunting, and—crucially—curses. The ring was found alone, without context, separated from its owner, separated from its crime, still declaring itself.

SILVIANVS.

No explanation accompanied it. No record of restitution. No indication that the curse had been resolved.

It sat, unresolved, for over 1,500 years.

When antiquarians catalogued the ring in the 19th century, they noted its unusual size and weight. It was too large for most fingers. It may have been worn over a glove. It may have been ceremonial. Or it may have been designed that way deliberately—to prevent easy concealment.

You cannot hide a ring like this.

The curse tablet, meanwhile, remained buried in Bath until the late 19th century, when systematic excavations of the Roman baths brought hundreds of defixiones to light. Scholars translated them carefully, clinically. Names emerged. Crimes emerged.

And then someone noticed the overlap.

Silvianus.

The connection between the ring and the curse tablet was not made immediately. It took decades of comparative scholarship, and even then, it was tentative. But the narrative fit too well to ignore: a named owner, a named thief, an unresolved theft, and an object that never made its way home.

What happens to a curse that does not complete its task?

That question fascinated more than just archaeologists.

In the 1920s, the ring and its associated curse came to the attention of J. R. R. Tolkien, who was consulted by Sir Mortimer Wheeler during excavations at Lydney. Tolkien was not asked to write fiction. He was asked to interpret a name: *Nodens*. But the story followed him anyway.

A powerful ring.

An owner who loses it.

A curse that binds identity, possession, and suffering.

Tolkien never claimed the Ring of Silvianus as a direct inspiration. He did not need to. The structure was already there, embedded in Roman belief: objects carry obligation. Ownership is not symbolic. It is enforced.

And enforcement does not expire quietly.

The ring now rests in the British Museum, labeled, stabilized, and inert by all conventional measures. Visitors see it as an artifact—a relic of Romano-British life, an interesting footnote in the history of curse tablets.

But the story it tells is unfinished.

Silvianus never recovered his ring. Senicianus is never recorded as returning it. There is no tablet lifting the curse, no offering of thanks, no closure ritual. The lead tablet asks for punishment *until* restitution occurs.

The condition was never met.

Skeptics argue—reasonably—that the curse was symbolic, a psychological release for an aggrieved man. That the ring's later discovery elsewhere proves nothing more than trade, travel, or coincidence.

But that explanation falters when you consider Roman ritual logic.

Curses were not metaphors. They were contracts.

They named parties. They specified terms. They invoked enforcement. And they remained active until resolved or ritually neutralized.

The Ring of Silvianus was never neutralized.

Which raises an uncomfortable possibility: the curse did not fail.

It simply changed scope.

The ring no longer targets Senicianus. It no longer seeks a single thief. Instead, it persists as an object of unresolved claim—forever asserting ownership without an owner present to receive it.

It is a ring that insists on belonging while belonging to no one.

That tension is subtle. It does not cause dramatic deaths or visible calamity. Instead, it unsettles scholars, inspires fiction, and refuses to sit quietly as mere metal. It turns every handler into a temporary custodian of someone else's grievance.

In Roman law, unresolved claims could outlive their claimants. Debts passed to heirs. Obligations followed property. Justice was slow, but it was patient.

So is this ring.

It waits behind glass now, its gold dull under museum lights, its inscription still legible, still declarative. SILVIANVS.

Not *was*.

Is.

There is an old legal warning buried in Roman practice, one that applies here more than most: *res sacrae*—sacred things—are not owned in the way other objects are. They remember their last true purpose.

This ring remembers being stolen.

And until it is returned to a man who has been dead for sixteen centuries, it will continue to ask the same question, silently, to anyone who lingers too long in front of it:

Who holds what does not belong to them—and what does the world still owe because of it?

28

the sutton hoo helmet

(Sutton Hoo and the Afterlife
of an Unearthed King)

The mound was never lost.

That is the first thing people get wrong about Sutton Hoo. It was not forgotten, buried, or erased by time. It sat in plain sight on a bluff above the River Deben in Suffolk, a low rise among many others, visible to anyone willing to look long enough and wonder why the ground had been shaped that way.

Locals did wonder. They always had.

Children played on the mounds. Farmers plowed around them. Antiquarians speculated idly. And occasionally—quietly, illegally—treasure hunters dug at them, pulling up nothing of note and retreating with the conviction that the stories were exaggerated.

What stopped them was not law. It was reluctance.

The land felt watched.

When excavation finally began in earnest in the summer of 1939, it did not feel like a conquest. It felt like permission had been asked—and reluctantly granted.

The person holding the spade was Basil Brown.

Brown was not a university-trained archaeologist. He was a self-taught excavator with a deep, intuitive respect for soil, layers, and silence. He listened to land the way others listened to people. When he cut into Mound 1 and began uncovering the ghost of a ship—iron rivets tracing a vessel that had long since rotted away—he understood immediately what he was standing inside.

This was not a grave.

It was a *statement*.

The ship burial at Sutton Hoo dated to the early seventh century, a time when England was not yet England, when kings ruled through display as much as blood, and burial was a final performance. Whoever lay here—now widely believed to be King Rædwald of East Anglia—had been sent into death with armor, regalia, and objects designed to endure.

And at the center of it all was the helmet.

It was not found whole. That matters.

The Sutton Hoo helmet came up in fragments—over five hundred pieces, crushed under the weight of centuries. It did not reveal itself all at once. It had to be assembled slowly, carefully, by hands that did not yet know what they were touching.

When reconstructed, the helmet revealed a face that does not look like it was meant to comfort the living.

The eyebrows are dragons. The nose and mouth form a beast. The eyes stare forward, unblinking. It is both mask and warning. A king who does not stop guarding just because he is dead.

The excavation drew attention quickly, and with attention came authority. Basil Brown was quietly sidelined. Professional archaeologists arrived. Titles were asserted. Ownership was debated.

Then the war came.

Within weeks of the helmet's discovery, Britain entered World War II. The artifacts were packed away, hidden in tunnels, shielded from bombs. The helmet survived. Many people did not.

Deaths came later, and not in the dramatic clusters that make headlines. That is part of what makes this story harder to dismiss—and harder to shake.

Edith Pretty, the landowner who commissioned the excavation and insisted the finds be given to the British Museum, died in 1942 at the age of 59. She had been in declining health, but the timing was noted.

She never saw the helmet displayed. She never saw the story completed.

Basil Brown lived until 1977, long enough to see his role minimized, then slowly reclaimed. His was not a cursed death—but it was a diminished life, spent watching others speak for something he had uncovered with care.

Other figures associated with Sutton Hoo fared less gently.

Several scholars involved in early analysis died relatively young, often after prolonged illness. Others suffered professional ruin, their work overshadowed by disputes over credit and interpretation. The helmet, it seemed, did not tolerate misattribution.

Unlike the Egyptian curse narratives, Sutton Hoo never developed a clean mythos of punishment. No dogs died howling. No lights went out on cue. Instead, the consequences were *structural*.

Careers stalled. Health declined. Recognition arrived late or not at all.

The helmet did not kill. It *waited*.

There is a reason Anglo-Saxon burial culture emphasized disturbance. Grave goods were not meant to be retrieved. They were meant to *function* in death. To unearth them was not theft in the Roman sense —but it was interruption.

The helmet's gaze, once reconstructed, seemed to follow that interruption outward.

During its conservation and display history, the helmet became one of the most iconic objects in British archaeology. It shaped modern understanding of early medieval kingship. It appeared in textbooks, exhibitions, and national identity narratives.

And yet, it has never felt fully assimilated.

Museum staff have commented—off the record—on the way visitors respond to it. Not awe. Not fear. Recognition. A sense of being measured.

The helmet does not invite identification. It resists it.

Scholars have proposed endless interpretations: ceremonial armor, ritual mask, symbolic kingship. All are plausible. None are complete. The helmet refuses a single story.

That refusal extends to the people around it.

Those who treat it as an object of conquest—academic, national, personal—tend to find themselves diminished. Those who treat it as a presence, something that existed long before and will exist long after, fare better.

This is not a curse in the theatrical sense. It does not seek retribution. It does not punish trespass with spectacle.

It enforces *posture*.

The Sutton Hoo helmet does not demand fear. It demands humility.

And humility, in the modern world, is not a safe position to occupy.

Today, the helmet sits behind glass in the British Museum, reconstructed, stabilized, and contextualized. It is no longer fragmented. It is no longer buried.

But it is not finished.

Its story continues to rearrange itself around those who claim it. The king beneath it remains unnamed. The exact rituals surrounding its burial remain debated. The consequences of its unearthing remain diffuse, difficult to chart, and strangely persistent.

There is a quiet warning embedded here, older than curses and subtler than superstition:

Some objects are not dangerous because they are angry.

They are dangerous because they were complete before we interfered.

The Sutton Hoo helmet was not waiting to be found.

It was waiting to see what kind of people would do the finding.

29

the myrtles plantation wedding dress

The stain appears before the story does.

Visitors will tell you that first—how they saw the fabric before they heard the name, how the discoloration seemed to bloom beneath the glass like something still warm, still reacting to air. It is faint at first glance, a yellowed smudge at the bodice, not dramatic enough to be theatrical, not sharp enough to be dismissed as age. It looks less like damage and more like residue.

As if the dress remembers.

The house that holds it, Myrtles Plantation, has always been good at memory. Built in 1796 near St. Francisville, Louisiana, it sits on ground that never learned how to forget—layers of occupation, enslavement, domestic life, violence, and rumor pressing together under white columns and live oaks. Long before ghost tours and souvenir pamphlets, people spoke of the place in lowered voices. Not cursed. *Occupied.*

The wedding dress entered the house quietly, as most dangerous things do.

It is generally dated to the mid–19th century, white silk with lace detailing consistent with the period, displayed upright as if still inhabited. According to plantation records and later family accounts, it belonged to a young woman connected to the Woodruff family—most often identified as Sarah Woodruff, though the name shifts depending on who is telling the story and when. That instability matters. When names won't hold still, stories usually don't want to be owned.

The marriage itself is barely recorded. What survives instead are fragments: a reception held in the house, music, candles, wine. And then the interruption.

Accounts agree on this much: the bride collapsed during or shortly after the celebration. Some say poison. Others say illness. A few suggest jealousy—arsenic introduced by another woman with access to the kitchen. The culprit is never identified. The death, when acknowledged at all, is folded into plantation silence, the kind that absorbs scandal and leaves behind furniture.

The dress was removed, cleaned, stored.

It did not stay clean.

The first stain was noticed years later, when the garment was unpacked and prepared for display. A discoloration at the bodice, faint but distinct, appearing where no spill had been recorded. Conservators attempted removal using period-appropriate methods. The stain lightened, then returned. They tried again, more carefully.

It came back darker.

Over time, the pattern repeated. The dress could be cleaned, but not corrected. Each attempt left it altered in some small way—threads weakened, silk dulled. Eventually, the effort stopped. The dress was placed behind glass, where the stain remains, neither spreading nor fading.

That would be unsettling enough on its own. But the dress does not exist alone.

The Myrtles Plantation is associated with at least a dozen spirits, depending on who is counting. The most frequently named is Chloe, an enslaved woman said to have been murdered and buried on the grounds. Whether Chloe existed as described is debated; plantation records are incomplete, and oral histories shift. But visitors report seeing a woman in a green turban near mirrors and staircases, sometimes close to the room where the dress is kept.

Children are reported more often than adults. Footsteps. Laughter. Handprints on glass.

And then there are the fingerprints.

On the wedding dress case, faint impressions sometimes appear— smudges shaped like fingers, visible only at certain angles. Staff wipe them away. They return. No alarms are triggered. No break-ins recorded. The case remains sealed.

Skeptics note humidity. Old glass. Suggestibility. All fair.

They do not explain why the impressions cluster around the stain.

Nor do they explain why some visitors experience sudden nausea or dizziness when standing too long in front of the dress, while others feel nothing at all. The reaction is inconsistent, selective. That is usually where belief takes root.

During the late 20th century, as the Myrtles gained fame as one of America's most haunted homes, the dress became a focal point. Tour guides learned to pause there, to let the silence stretch. Guests leaned closer. Cameras malfunctioned. Photos showed unexpected shadows.

A few guests reported something more intimate.

Pressure at the chest. A sense of constriction, like tight fabric. An urge to leave the room quickly, accompanied by grief that did not feel personal. One woman reportedly began to cry without knowing why, then stopped abruptly once she crossed the threshold.

The house has seen many deaths. Not all of them tragic. Not all of them violent. The wedding dress, however, appears to concentrate attention. It draws the stories toward itself, as if it were a node—a place where unfinished narratives snag.

There is a theory, circulated quietly among folklorists and museum professionals, that clothing absorbs more than we account for. That garments worn at moments of heightened emotion—weddings, funerals, executions—carry a charge that does not dissipate easily. This is not magic so much as proximity: fabric pressed against skin, sweat, breath, fear.

In that reading, the Myrtles dress is not cursed. It is *occupied*.

The stain becomes evidence not of poison but of persistence. A mark that refuses to behave like decay. It does not spread because it is not damage. It does not fade because it is not dirt.

It is a reminder.

The dress has been moved within the house several times. Each relocation coincided with increased reports of activity in the surrounding rooms. After the most recent adjustment, staff noted a rise in EMF fluctuations and unexplained cold spots nearby—phenomena skeptics attribute to wiring and old construction, but which still align inconveniently with the dress's presence.

Today, the wedding dress remains on display. It is not advertised as dangerous. It is described as "unexplained." Visitors are encouraged to look, not to linger. Children are gently redirected elsewhere.

The house has learned, over time, which objects require boundaries.

There is no formal warning attached to the dress, no plaque advising caution. None is necessary. People tend to step back on their own. They feel the limit without being told.

That is the quiet power of the Myrtles Plantation wedding dress. It does not frighten everyone. It does not perform. It does not punish curiosity outright.

It simply refuses to be made inert.

Some things are meant to be worn once, then returned to darkness. When they are kept—cleaned, displayed, admired—they do not always forgive the interruption.

And sometimes, they leave a stain to prove it.

30

the "cursed" pharaoh's rings

The problem with rings is that they are meant to be worn.

Not displayed at a distance. Not framed behind glass. Not handled with gloves and labels and accession numbers. A ring is designed to close a circle around flesh. To mark ownership. To bind a name to a body.

In ancient Egypt, that binding was never symbolic alone.

Gold was not just wealth. It was permanence. Flesh of the gods, uncorroding, eternal. When a pharaoh's ring was made, it was not merely decorative—it was administrative, religious, and metaphysical all at once. To place such a ring on a living hand was to authorize action. To place it on a dead one was to ensure continuity beyond death.

And to remove it—well.

That is where the stories begin to gather.

Most accounts of "cursed pharaoh's rings" do not point to a single object. There is no lone jewel that carries the entire weight of the legend. Instead, the unease clings to a category: gold signet rings removed from royal or high-status burials and later traced through private collections, museum storerooms, and—briefly, disastrously— onto human hands that did not belong to them.

The most famous associations orbit the discovery of Valley of the Kings and the 1922 excavation of the tomb of Tutankhamun by Howard Carter. While the popular imagination tends to collapse every Egyptian curse into that single event, the rings tell a quieter, more granular story—one that stretches both earlier and later, and refuses to stay contained within a single tomb.

In tomb inventories from the New Kingdom period, rings appear repeatedly, described not by ornament but by function. Scarab rings bearing the names of gods. Signets engraved with cartouches. Bands marked with protective formulae meant to seal documents, bless offerings, or command obedience from both the living and the dead.

Many were buried with their owners intentionally, placed on fingers or strung together with amulets. Their job was not finished at death. It was *relocated*.

Which makes their removal—by looters in antiquity, by archaeologists in the modern era—a kind of reassignment no one ever consented to.

Early reports from 19th-century collectors describe rings that seemed to bring misfortune not immediately, but gradually. A British antiquarian in the 1860s noted in correspondence that a gold ring acquired from a Theban dealer "never rested easily," passing through three hands in under a year after each owner experienced financial or personal upheaval. The ring was sold, then resold, then quietly returned to Egypt.

No curse was claimed. None was needed. The pattern spoke for itself.

During the Carter excavation, multiple rings were cataloged, photographed, and removed under strict supervision. Officially, none were worn. Unofficially—according to later memoirs and secondhand accounts—some rings were tried on briefly, held against skin, slipped onto fingers "for scale."

Several of the deaths and misfortunes that followed the Tutankhamun excavation have been overplayed by tabloids and later sensationalists. But a few details remain stubbornly resistant to tidy explanation. A sudden illness here. A string of professional reversals there. A curator who refused to keep a particular ring in his personal possession after reporting recurring nightmares involving hands—hands grasping, hands closing.

It is worth noting that Egyptian belief systems treated the body as divisible but interconnected. The hand had power. The name had power. Objects that touched both became intermediaries. Rings, especially, acted as conduits—portable seals that carried authority wherever they went.

When such an object is removed from its funerary context, it does not become neutral. It becomes unemployed.

The most persistent modern accounts involve rings that passed briefly through private hands in the early 20th century, often before laws governing antiquities export were firmly enforced. One ring, allegedly from a royal cache near Luxor, was worn by a French dealer's wife in the 1930s. Within months, she suffered a severe illness that left her partially paralyzed. The ring was sold. The illness stabilized. The dealer later refused to discuss the object, citing "bad business."

Another ring—this one bearing a scarab engraved with a solar deity—was acquired by an American collector in the 1950s and displayed in his home. Guests reportedly felt discomfort when handling it. The collector himself died suddenly of a heart attack at forty-nine. The ring vanished from the estate inventory.

Skeptics point out, correctly, that gold rings are small, easily lost, easily misattributed. That illness and death are not rare among collectors of a certain age. That stories accrete around Egyptian objects because we expect them to.

All true.

What remains harder to dismiss is the consistency of one detail across accounts: the escalation when rings are worn.

Handled, they unsettle. Displayed, they remain quiet. Stored, they sleep.

Worn, they interfere.

Museum professionals are rarely superstitious, but they are observant. Several institutions quietly enforce handling policies for royal Egyptian rings that go beyond conservation. No direct skin contact. No fitting demonstrations. No reenactments. These rules are framed in terms of preservation, but they echo something older and less articulate.

Do not complete the circuit.

Today, many such rings sit in drawers rather than cases. Cataloged. Photographed. Rarely exhibited. Their stories live mostly in footnotes, correspondence, and the careful pauses of curators who have learned which questions not to answer directly.

They are not dramatic objects. They do not glow. They do not announce themselves. They simply carry a sense of refusal.

Refusal to be claimed.

Refusal to be repurposed.

Refusal to forget the hands they were made for.

In ancient Egyptian theology, eternity was not abstract. It was contractual. You did your part. The gods did theirs. Objects were witnesses to that agreement.

To take a pharaoh's ring is not to steal gold.

It is to interrupt a promise.

And interrupted promises have a way of resurfacing—quietly, persistently, wherever the circle is closed again.

31

the necklace of the princess de lamballe

(Fragments of a Court That Did Not Survive)

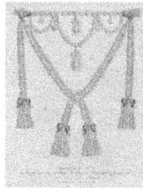

T hey killed her twice.

The first time was political.

The second time was intimate.

On the morning of September 3, 1792, Princess de Lamballe—born Marie Thérèse Louise of Savoy-Carignan—was dragged from her cell in La Force Prison and asked a question she could not survive answering. Would she swear allegiance to the Revolution? Would she renounce the monarchy? Would she denounce her friend, Marie Antoinette?

She refused.

What followed has been documented, reprinted, sanitized, sensationalized, and argued over for more than two centuries. The violence itself—brutal, public, ritualized—has become part of revolutionary mythology. But what tends to slip out of focus is what happened *before* the body was destroyed.

They stripped her.

Not metaphorically. Literally.

Clothing, shoes, gloves—removed. Hair loosened. Jewelry taken. Not seized by officials, not cataloged, not entered into any ledger. Taken by hands in the crowd, hands that believed they were not stealing but reclaiming something that had never belonged to her in the first place.

Among those objects was a necklace.

Its exact form is no longer certain. That uncertainty is part of the problem.

Contemporary descriptions suggest a court necklace: gold, possibly set with pearls or small diamonds, elegant rather than ostentatious. The Princess de Lamballe was not known for excess. She dressed carefully, modestly by Versailles standards, favoring refinement over display. But she was still a princess. Still superintendent of the Queen's household. Still marked.

Jewelry at court was never just personal adornment. It was proximity made visible. To wear something at Versailles was to declare who you belonged to—and who belonged to you.

The necklace, like the woman, was bound to Versailles whether it wanted to be or not.

When the crowd took it, the necklace ceased to be an object of court life and became something else entirely: a relic of rupture.

The French Revolution produced many artifacts—documents, weapons, banners—but it also produced fragments. Things torn from their contexts and forced to circulate without meaning, or with too much meaning, depending on who touched them next.

Several post-Revolutionary accounts claim that pieces of Lamballe's jewelry surfaced in Parisian markets within days. Anonymous necklaces. Unidentified gold chains. Items sold cheaply, urgently, sometimes refused by buyers who recognized them and did not want to be involved.

One 19th-century memoir by a Paris jeweler describes an unnamed necklace brought to his shop "still warm from the hand that carried it," though whether this was metaphorical or not is impossible to say. He refused it. That refusal, he claimed, saved him from "ruin of the spirit," if not of the business.

The necklace does not kill everyone who touches it.

That is not how it works.

Instead, the stories cluster around possession followed by loss— financial, social, psychological. Owners who sell it quickly and regret it. Owners who keep it and feel watched. Owners who attempt to restore or reset it and find that no configuration feels stable.

Jewelry is intimate by design. It touches skin. It moves with breath. It warms. When an object has been removed violently from a body—especially a body subjected to ritual humiliation—it carries more than metal forward with it.

The Princess de Lamballe was not executed in the legal sense. She was unmade publicly, piece by piece, in a performance meant to erase what she represented. The necklace was part of that performance.

Later revolutionary writers attempted to dismiss stories of cursed objects as aristocratic superstition. And yet, those same writers were careful never to wear items traced directly to the September Massacres. They sold them. Melted them. Passed them on.

Gold survives revolution. Meaning does not always.

In the decades that followed, rumors attached themselves to a particular necklace said to have belonged to Lamballe—sometimes described as a pearl strand, sometimes as a gold chain with a central drop. The inconsistency suggests less a single surviving object than a *type*: jewelry claimed, reclaimed, and re-claimed again under her name.

That name carried weight.

To say "this was Lamballe's" was to summon not just a woman, but a moment when loyalty became fatal. When friendship became evidence. When proximity to power was punished more savagely than power itself.

Skeptics note, rightly, that many objects were falsely attributed to famous victims for profit. That provenance was often invented. That no museum today displays a necklace definitively identified as hers.

All true.

But absence does not mean erasure.

The most persistent reports do not come from museums but from private collections—necklaces inherited with stories attached, stories passed down alongside warnings. "Do not wear it." "Do not keep it long." "It does not like to stay."

One account from the late 1800s describes a woman who wore such a necklace to a public event and experienced a panic so severe she fainted, later claiming she felt "hands at her throat, not choking, but measuring." The necklace was removed. The feeling stopped.

Whether that experience was psychosomatic is beside the point.

What matters is that it fit the pattern.

Objects associated with revolutionary violence often behave like unresolved arguments. They do not explode. They whisper. They reintroduce tension where none should exist. They carry the memory of a crowd that believed destruction was justice.

The necklace does not belong to a single place now. It exists as fragments, replicas, claims, denials. It is nowhere and everywhere, which may be the most revolutionary state of all.

If it survives, it does so quietly.

And if it causes harm, it does not do so spectacularly.

It destabilizes.

It reminds.

It tightens, not around the neck, but around the idea that some loyalties—once declared—can never be safely removed.

There is an old, unrecorded warning attached to objects taken during the September Massacres, repeated in different forms across different families:

Do not wear what was stripped from the dead.

It remembers the hands that took it.

The Necklace of the Princess de Lamballe does not demand belief.

It only demands proximity.

And history has already demonstrated what happens next.

32

bonnie and clyde's
personal effects

T hey died in daylight, in a ditch, with the engine still hot.

On May 23, 1934, the car that had carried them across half the American South finally ran out of road. Bullets tore through glass, steel, and flesh with an efficiency that felt almost administrative. When the shooting stopped, Bonnie Parker and Clyde Barrow were no longer fugitives. They were evidence.

The bodies were photographed. The car was photographed. The weapons were counted and recounted. But it was the smaller things—the items close enough to touch skin—that refused to settle into history. They moved too quickly. They were taken too eagerly. They were handled before anyone decided what they meant.

In the minutes after the ambush near Gibsland, on a stretch of road that would later become a pilgrimage site, spectators rushed forward. Some wanted proof. Some wanted souvenirs. Some wanted proximity to a story that had already outgrown its authors. Lawmen tried—half-heartedly—to keep order, but order had never been the point.

They cut Bonnie's hair.

They took Clyde's coat.

They reached into pockets that were still warm.

Bonnie's belongings were intimate in the way women's belongings often are—lipstick, a compact, handwritten poems folded and refolded until the creases threatened to tear. Clyde's effects were practical: cigarettes, cash, a watch, weapons worn smooth by use. Together, they formed a mobile household that had never stayed anywhere long enough to become a home.

Those objects had been carried through bank robberies, safehouse arguments, nights sleeping in the car with the windows cracked and the engine ticking as it cooled. They had absorbed sweat, fear, adrenaline, boredom. They had learned the rhythm of flight.

And then they were suddenly still.

The official story insists on inventory. Lists were made. Some items were returned to families. Others vanished into collections private enough to avoid scrutiny and public enough to demand admission fees. Within weeks, Bonnie and Clyde's effects were circulating as commodities. Not relics—yet. Not curses—still too soon. They were novelties, tokens of a crime spree that had been flattened into entertainment.

That flattening did not last.

As the years passed, reports accumulated—not of dramatic deaths, but of instability. People who acquired items connected to the couple described a persistent restlessness. The sense that the object did not want to be owned. Watches that stopped and restarted without pattern. Guns that jammed in ways that could not be reliably replicated. Clothing that felt wrong to wear, as if the fabric resisted the body.

One collector in the 1950s wrote privately that Clyde's jacket— acquired through a chain of custody no one could quite reconstruct— "never stayed put." It was stolen twice, returned once, misplaced repeatedly. When it was finally donated to a museum, the donor insisted on anonymity and requested that the jacket not be displayed "near exits." He did not explain why.

Bonnie's poems complicate the story further.

She wrote constantly. Letters. Verses. Observations meant to be read aloud, or perhaps just read later, when later finally arrived. One poem, published posthumously, frames their lives as already concluded, as if she knew the ending and chose to write toward it anyway. The paper those poems were written on became as coveted as the guns.

People who handled the manuscripts reported a strange temporal dislocation—a sense that the words were not finished speaking. Archivists described the work as emotionally "loud," a term more often applied to rooms than to paper. One noted that reading the poems aloud produced a physical tightness in the chest that vanished when the pages were closed.

Skeptics argue—again, correctly—that this is romantic projection. That Bonnie and Clyde's story has been inflated by film, music, and myth until it exerts pressure on anything associated with it. That people feel something because they expect to feel something.

Expectation, however, does not account for behavior.

Items associated with the couple are unusually prone to movement. They change hands often. They are stolen from collections at higher-than-average rates. They are loaned and not returned. Even institutions with robust security report difficulty keeping track of them. The famous car itself—riddled with bullets, seats soaked through—became a touring attraction almost immediately, paraded through fairs and carnivals before settling, uneasily, into museum life.

The car is loud. It draws crowds. It performs.

The personal effects do not.

They operate at a lower volume. They whisper instead of shout. They provoke small choices: *I'll sell it. I'll keep it boxed. I don't want it in the house.* These choices accumulate. The pattern emerges slowly.

The question that follows these objects is not whether Bonnie and Clyde were heroes or villains. That argument burns itself out quickly. The question is simpler and more unsettling:

What happens to objects that were never meant to stop?

Bonnie and Clyde lived in motion. Their belongings learned to move with them. When that motion ended violently, the objects were left with nowhere to go. No closure. No ritual. No sanctioned resting place.

In many traditions—none of them especially American—objects carried through repeated danger require intentional grounding when the danger ends. Otherwise, they retain momentum. Not energy, exactly. Habit.

The habit of flight.

That habit manifests now as instability rather than threat. People rarely report physical harm. Instead, they describe disruption. Relationships strained. Collections that feel unbalanced. A persistent urge to relocate the object, to pass it on, to let it go.

Bonnie and Clyde's personal effects do not curse so much as they *displace*. They make stillness uncomfortable. They remind their keepers—quietly, insistently—that safety was never part of the original agreement.

Today, many of these items sit behind glass, cataloged and insured. Others remain in private hands, surfaced occasionally at auction with provenance just convincing enough to invite belief. The objects themselves have not changed.

We have.

We want our outlaws tidy. We want our history framed. We want danger contained and labeled and lit from above. But some objects resist containment not because they are malicious, but because they were shaped by a life that refused it.

Bonnie and Clyde did not plan to become relics. Their belongings did not consent to becoming artifacts. They were tools of survival, intimacy, and escape.

They remember that.

And sometimes—when handled without care—they remind their keepers that the road does not end simply because the story does.

It ends because something stops it.

And stopping is not the same as resting.

33

the cursed wedding veil of sicily

(The Widow's Veil, The Veil that Won't Burn)

The veil is never the part anyone remembers until it's too late.

In Sicily, the veil is supposed to be the softest thing in the room—tulle or lace, a held breath of fabric, a polite cloud trailing behind a bride while families stare each other down and pretend love is uncomplicated. It belongs to daylight: to church steps, to photographs, to rice and shouted blessings. It is not meant to be found in the dark.

And yet the story that keeps resurfacing—half-whispered in antique shops, repeated by tourists with the careful thrill of saying something "local," traded between collectors like a dare—begins with a veil folded away where a veil should not be. A cedar chest. A sealed drawer. A wardrobe that smells of camphor and salt air. The kind of storage that turns cloth into relic.

They call it, variously, the Cursed Wedding Veil of Sicily, the Widow's Veil, the Veil that Won't Burn. Some versions insist it came from Palermo. Others swear it's a village object—something from inland, where the hills keep secrets and the old women still do not answer questions the first time you ask them. The details slide. That is part of what makes it stick.

When a cursed object has a clean paper trail, it becomes museum-ready, respectable. When it doesn't, it becomes contagious—because anyone can imagine they've touched it.

What can be said with confidence is this: Sicily is one of the places in Europe where the boundary between the sacred and the protective has always been thin enough to tear with your thumbnail. There is Catholic ritual in public, and a second language underneath it—older, stubborn, practical. The language of warding. The language of the evil eye. The language of "don't say that out loud."

Folklorists and anthropologists have spent more than a century trying to write this down without flattening it into caricature. Giuseppe Pitrè, collecting Sicilian traditions in the late nineteenth century, recorded the everyday mechanics of belief—charms, gestures, counter-charms—without treating the people who used them as simple-minded. His work sits like a foundation under almost everything that followed.

Decades later, Ernesto de Martino would study Southern Italian magical practices—binding, fear, misfortune, the evil eye—and describe a landscape where misfortune was not only suffered but managed through ritual action, through objects, through small delib-erate acts meant to keep life from unraveling. And scholars writing in the twentieth century continued to note the same pattern: in Southern Italy, the evil eye is not a fairytale concept. It is a social force, a way of naming harm that travels through attention, envy, imbalance.

A wedding—especially a wedding—is where that kind of force is believed to gather.

Because weddings are public. Weddings are spectacle. Weddings invite eyes.

Which means that in the folk imagination, weddings invite the wrong kind of looking.

In the oldest layers of the veil story, the "curse" does not begin with a demon. It begins with a moment that is more Sicilian than supernat-ural: envy. A bride too radiant. A marriage too advantageous. A family too proud. Someone watching from the edge of the crowd, not crying because they're moved, but because they've been left out of the accounting of joy.

The veil enters as a tool meant to protect the bride from that look.

157

And then—this is the pivot every version shares—the veil becomes the thing that carries the look forward.

The first story, the one told most often, is simple in a way that feels suspicious. A young bride. A late nineteenth-century or early twentieth-century date that is never nailed down but always implied by the texture of the telling: horse hooves on stone streets, kerosene lamps, old money, a church that smells of incense and lemon polish. She is given a veil that is not new. It belongs to a cousin, an aunt, a family friend—someone with authority over the bride's life, or at least over the family narrative. The gift is framed as blessing. "Wear this," they say, "and you'll be safe." In a culture where hand-me-down wedding items can be both tradition and burden, the bride accepts.

On the day itself, the veil behaves like fabric. It drapes. It photographs well. It makes her look like what everyone wants her to be.

That night—or three nights later, depending on who tells it—misfortune arrives.

Sometimes it is a fall down stairs. Sometimes it is a fever that takes her fast, leaving the bed hot and the household cold. Sometimes it is a miscarriage so violent it becomes the only thing the family remembers about the marriage. In the most brutal versions, she dies before the week is out, and the veil is removed from her with shaking hands, because no one wants to cut it and no one wants to keep it intact. Cloth becomes suddenly moral: if you tear it, you've done something wrong. If you keep it, you're inviting something worse.

So they fold it away.

And folding is a kind of decision. Folding is how people treat things they don't want to destroy but cannot bear to look at. Folding says: later. Folding says: not now. Folding says: I am not dealing with this.

This is where the veil becomes dangerous in the way cursed objects become dangerous—not by doing something dramatic, but by entering a cycle of concealment and retrieval.

Because the veil does not stay folded.

In some tellings, it is brought out again a generation later, when another marriage needs saving. A family that has already lost one bride begins to treat the veil like a protective relic rather than a contaminated one. They reinterpret the first death as coincidence, bad luck, God's will—anything but the veil's fault. Or they decide that the veil wasn't the problem; the bride was. She was weak. She was sickly. She was not meant to have happiness. The veil survives by outliving blame.

So it is worn again.

And again something breaks.

Not always death—sometimes "only" ruin. A groom killed in an accident. A sudden loss of money. A fire that leaves the house standing but everything inside charred, as if the flames took what they wanted and left the structure as a warning.

A veil is particularly suited to this kind of legend because it's intimate without being personal. Jewelry is owned. Books are read. Rings are worn every day. But a veil touches the body in a specific, ceremonial way. It rests against hair and skin at the threshold between private life and public life. It is in the photographs. It is in the memories. It is present at the precise moment people believe their fate changes.

If you wanted to invent an object that could absorb narrative, you'd invent a veil.

The accumulation phase of the story—where a curse becomes a reputation—happens the way folklore almost always does: through repetition attached to a social truth.

The social truth here is the evil eye.

In Sicilian tradition (and broadly across the Mediterranean), the evil eye is often understood as harm transmitted through attention—especially attention fueled by envy, resentment, imbalance. People who have something visible—beauty, fertility, luck, new love—become targets simply by being seen. The counter-measures are equally visible: gestures, words, charms, small acts of concealment or misdirection. Pitrè's collected material reflects how embedded these practices were in daily life, not as "occult theater" but as ordinary protection in a world where misfortune is not theoretical.

In that framework, a wedding veil isn't just romantic. It's apotropaic. It's a shield.

Which means that if something goes wrong after a wedding, the veil becomes suspect in a way modern audiences sometimes underestimate. If the shield fails, people begin asking why. If the shield "fails" repeatedly, people begin thinking the shield is inverted—turned into a conduit rather than a barrier.

This is the moment the veil becomes a "carrier" object in the field-guide sense you've been building, even when we're not naming categories on the page. It becomes a thing that doesn't merely witness misfortune but transports the conditions for it.

And then the story does what all good haunted histories do: it tries to become documented.

Here's the hard truth, and it's actually useful for your book's credibility: unlike the Codex Gigas or Roman curse tablets, there is no single, universally agreed-upon archival "Cursed Wedding Veil of Sicily" with a museum accession number that anchors the tale. There are *veils*, plural—antique, delicate, catalogued—and there are *stories*, plural—variable, persistent, emotionally consistent. The curse lives in that gap.

So the documentation is indirect. It lives in what scholars documented about belief, and in what later retellings did to those beliefs.

De Martino, writing about Southern Italian magic, emphasizes the way ritual practice responds to existential vulnerability—illness, loss, fear, social pressure. Weddings are exactly the kind of pressure cooker he's talking about: high stakes, highly witnessed, socially policed. In that environment, objects that "should" be harmless—cloth, ribbon, lace—become loaded simply by being present at the wrong moment.

Academic discussions of the evil eye in Southern Italy likewise underline that these beliefs operate through human relationships, not spooky special effects: who envies whom, who is seen, who is protected, who is not. A veil-curse legend is a folkloric technology built to make that invisible social risk feel tangible.

And that tangibility is what later storytellers seize.

In many modern versions—especially the ones that make their way into English-language "cursed objects" lists—the veil is sold. Not to a museum, but to a private buyer. The story relocates from a Sicilian household (where belief is lived) into an antique market (where belief becomes commodity). The veil appears as a listing: "Victorian Sicilian lace," "family heirloom," "worn once," or "worn twice," which is exactly the kind of detail a seller adds when they're trying to make you feel special.

Then the buyer reports... not a haunting, at first, but a pattern.

The room where it's stored feels colder. Sleep becomes thin. A constant sense of being observed emerges—not a ghost in the corner, but the heavy social sensation of being *watched*, the same sensation the evil eye is built out of. People begin to photograph the veil because it's beautiful; the photographs come out wrong. Not paranormal wrong— just *off*. Shadow where there shouldn't be shadow. Focus refusing to settle. The buyer becomes obsessed with getting a "clean" image, and the obsession begins to feel like the object's real effect: it doesn't attack you. It recruits your attention until your attention becomes the attack.

Is that supernatural? A skeptic would say no. It's suggestibility. It's anxiety. It's the human brain doing what it does when it's handed a good story and an object you can touch.

But folklore does not require the supernatural to be effective. It requires repetition. It requires a few people to tell you, quietly, that the same thing happened to them.

So the veil's modern legend continues: a chain of owners who return it, resell it, donate it, bury it in storage. Nobody wants to destroy it outright, because destroying ritual-associated objects—especially objects linked to a bride—can feel like inviting a different kind of harm. The veil survives by exploiting human caution.

At this point in the chapter, the "theories and doubt" section would normally show up as headings. In narrative form, it arrives as a voice in the room: the person who rolls their eyes, the historian who hates sloppy claims, the archivist who points out—correctly—that Sicily is full of beautiful antique textiles and that a "cursed veil" is an internet-friendly label that sells.

They are not wrong.

But they are also not the whole story, because skepticism tends to address only the final layer—the marketplace and the meme—and not the underlying structure of belief that made the story possible in the first place.

Here's what the skeptical voice can't easily erase:

A wedding veil is *exactly* the kind of object that would be treated as protective in a malocchio framework.

And an object treated as protective is *exactly* the kind of object that becomes terrifying when the protection fails.

That is the logic of inversion. It's older than horror novels. It's present in protective amulets that become "dangerous" when stolen, in prayers that become "curses" when spoken wrong, in holy objects that become contaminated when they cross thresholds they were never meant to cross.

Whether the Cursed Wedding Veil of Sicily is one veil or many, one original tragedy or a collage of them, that logic is what keeps it alive. It doesn't need to be "true" in a courtroom sense to be real in the sense that matters: real as a pattern of human behavior, fear, and attention.

And that brings us to the object now.

If you ask where the veil is, most tellers will give you an answer that sounds like a place but behaves like a fog: "with a collector," "in a private home," "locked away in a trunk," "back in Sicily," "sold to someone who didn't believe and then they did." The veil is always *elsewhere*. It remains just out of reach. It has to, or the story collapses into verification.

But the best versions of the legend end not with the veil disappearing, but with a quiet return to the original problem: eyes.

In a modern world where we photograph everything, where we post weddings for strangers, where attention is currency, the evil eye has new infrastructure. It doesn't require a jealous neighbor at the edge of the ceremony. It requires a feed. It requires strangers watching your joy without knowing you.

A Sicilian veil-curse story, told now, is not only about lace and dead brides. It's about the vulnerability of being seen.

The veil becomes a warning with teeth not because it floats or bleeds, but because it makes a familiar social fear feel like an object you can fold, store, and—if you are careless—unfold again.

There is a reason the story insists that no one who owns the veil keeps it displayed.

Not because it's ugly.

Because it invites looking.

And if you come from a place where looking can hurt, then you understand what the curse really is: not the veil itself, but the gaze that travels with it—quiet, persistent, and hungry for a doorway.

The last warning, the one that's never written on a tag but always implied, is simple:

If you inherit a veil with a story attached, do not rush to make it romantic. In Sicily, some fabrics are not heirlooms. They are histories that have learned how to survive.

And some histories, once lifted back into the light, begin looking for the next bride.

34

the necklace of
madame lalaurie

The necklace is not the most disturbing thing about Delphine LaLaurie.

That distinction belongs to the house.

New Orleans remembers buildings the way other cities remember names. The city keeps its ghosts attached to addresses, and the address that still tightens throats is 1140 Royal Street. Before the fire. Before the shutters were boarded. Before the rumors hardened into fact. Before the crowd gathered with ropes and bricks and fury and did what crowds always do when the truth arrives too late.

The necklace enters the story the way dangerous objects often do: quietly, almost politely, at the edge of a larger horror. It is never the headline. It is the accessory. And that is what allows it to survive.

In the decades before 1834, Madame LaLaurie was exactly what New Orleans rewarded—wealthy, charming, well-married, impeccably dressed. She hosted elegant salons. She wore fine fabrics and finer jewelry. She gave money to the church. She smiled in public. And around her throat—depending on which account you believe—rested a necklace that people noticed because it *asked* to be noticed.

Descriptions vary, but they orbit the same center: gold, heavy for its size, set with stones that were not ostentatious enough to be vulgar and not modest enough to be forgettable. It lay close to the skin. It did not swing. It did not clink. It sat.

There is no invoice that survives. No jeweler's receipt that can be pointed to and circled in red. Like much of LaLaurie's life, the necklace exists first in recollection—servants whispering, guests remarking, later writers trying to pin it down and finding that it slides just out of frame. This slipperiness is not a flaw. It is a feature.

Because objects tied to sustained cruelty rarely announce themselves with clarity. They linger.

The cruelty itself, by contrast, was eventually undeniable.

In April of 1834, a fire broke out in the LaLaurie household— started, according to contemporary accounts, in the kitchen. When authorities forced their way inside, they found what the city would later pretend it had never suspected: enslaved people chained, mutilated, starved, kept alive in conditions that even a society built on slavery recognized as monstrous.

New Orleans erupted. The house was sacked. Furniture was destroyed. Windows shattered. Madame LaLaurie fled—first into hiding, then out of the country entirely. France would shelter her. The city would keep her house as a wound.

And the necklace?

It vanished.

This is the first point where the necklace becomes something more than ornament. In stories that emerge after the fire— accounts written decades later, oral histories, later sensational retellings—the necklace is said to have been removed before the mob reached the upper floors. Either LaLaurie took it with her, or someone took it *from* her in the chaos. The ambiguity matters. A stolen object carries a different weight than one carried into exile.

The versions diverge from there.

One claims the necklace traveled with LaLaurie to Paris, where she lived out her final years diminished but intact, dying in 1849. Another insists the necklace was sold, quietly, to fund her escape—gold converted into passage, stones into silence. A third, darker version suggests the necklace never left Louisiana at all, that it passed hand to hand in the aftermath like a contaminated relic, its origin unspoken but its effects unmistakable.

What everyone agrees on is this: the necklace does not settle.

In the years following the fire, stories begin to cluster around jewelry in New Orleans—particularly pieces acquired cheaply, suddenly, from uncertain sources. Owners complain of sleeplessness. Of irritability. Of a feeling of being watched that does not fade when the room is empty. Of tempers that sharpen without cause. Of accidents that feel personal.

None of this is supernatural enough to satisfy a ghost tour.

Which is precisely why it works.

The necklace's alleged effects mirror LaLaurie herself: subtle in public, unbearable in private.

One late nineteenth-century account—often repeated but difficult to source cleanly—describes a woman who purchased a gold necklace at auction, only to find her household unraveling within months. Servants quit without explanation. Animals refused to enter certain rooms. She developed a habit of touching her throat when anxious, fingers circling the clasp as if checking that something was still there. When she sold the necklace, the symptoms lifted. When the buyer wore it, they returned.

Is this proof? No.

It is pattern.

And patterns are the currency of cursed objects.

Theories emerged, as they always do, to domesticate the discomfort. Some suggested the necklace was simply associated with guilt—that wearing something believed to belong to a monster would naturally disturb the conscience. Others argued that the story itself was the vector, that belief did the damage and not the metal.

But this explanation sidesteps a harder question: why this object, and not the dozens of others connected to LaLaurie?

Why not the furniture? The silverware? The house itself?

The answer may lie in proximity.

A necklace is intimate. It rests against the pulse. It warms to the body. It sits at the border between breath and speech. If you wanted an object to absorb the rhythms of a person—their heartbeat, their tension, their calm cruelty—it would be something worn close, for long periods, without thought.

And LaLaurie wore hers often.

There is also the uncomfortable symbolism of adornment in a context of control. Jewelry signifies ownership, power, the ability to decorate oneself while denying autonomy to others. In a household where human beings were treated as objects, an object that marked status becomes charged in a way that survives its owner.

If curses are real—and this book has been careful never to insist that they are—they rarely behave like vengeance. They behave like residue.

What remains after sustained harm is not always a ghost. Sometimes it is a tendency. A pressure. A distortion that travels.

By the early twentieth century, the necklace's story had become unmoored enough to be flexible. Writers folded it into the broader LaLaurie legend, sometimes inventing details, sometimes smoothing over contradictions. A few claimed the necklace had been melted down. Others insisted it still existed, passed through collections under false provenance.

The lack of resolution does not weaken the story. It strengthens it.

Because the unresolved fate of the necklace mirrors the unresolved legacy of LaLaurie herself. She was never tried. Never punished by the law. She escaped consequence in life. New Orleans was left to deal with the aftermath.

The necklace, in this reading, becomes a symbolic correction—a mobile reminder that what is buried improperly does not stay buried.

Today, the necklace is never on display. No museum claims it. No auction house advertises it. When people say they have seen it, it is always briefly, always under circumstances that prevent verification. A private collection. A family heirloom. A friend of a friend.

This is exactly where such an object would live if it were real.

Objects tied to atrocity do not survive well in light. They survive in shadow, where their stories can keep changing just enough to stay alive.

The quiet warning at the end of the necklace's story is not about possession or hauntings or sudden death. It is about continuity.

Some objects remember what people try to forget.

And if you choose to wear something that once rested against the pulse of cruelty—if you choose to make it warm again—you may find that it remembers you too.

Not with rage.

With patience.

35

the bloody handkerchief
of mary queen of scots

T he handkerchief survives because fabric is patient.

It survives because blood, once dried, becomes stubborn.

It survives because people keep things they should burn, especially when those things belong to the dead.

Mary, Queen of Scots did not die quietly. She was not allowed to. Her death was designed to be instructional—an execution meant to speak to every Catholic sympathizer, every wavering noble, every queen who thought blood might protect blood. On the morning of February 8, 1587, inside the Great Hall at Fotheringhay Castle, she was dressed carefully, deliberately. Crimson petticoat beneath black velvet. A visual sermon. Martyrdom, staged.

And in her hand—reported in multiple contemporary accounts— was a handkerchief.

It is a small detail, easily overlooked in the larger horror of the scene. The axe. The block. The executioner's hesitation. The botched first strike. But objects that persist rarely announce themselves with spectacle. They linger at the margins of catastrophe, absorbing what spills.

When the blade fell, it did not end cleanly. Witnesses recorded that Mary did not scream. That she prayed. That the executioner required more than one blow. That when her head was finally severed, the lips moved as if continuing a prayer no one was meant to hear.

Blood spread across the floor.

And the handkerchief—linen, white, likely embroidered—was used.

This is where the object begins its second life.

In the aftermath of executions, especially those involving royalty, nothing was truly discarded. Blood-soaked cloth was not refuse; it was relic. Catholic Europe was already primed to treat Mary's death as martyrdom, and martyrs generate artifacts the way fires generate ash. Bits of clothing were cut away. Threads were preserved. The handkerchief, stained deeply enough to mark its purpose, was kept.

Who kept it first is unclear. Some accounts suggest a lady-in-waiting. Others imply a sympathetic onlooker. Still others place it in clerical hands almost immediately, folded and hidden with care. What matters is not the identity of the first keeper, but the intention: preservation.

The handkerchief was not washed.

That choice matters.

Blood that remains visible becomes testimony. It insists on memory. It does not allow the event to soften with time. Every fold reopens the moment.

Over the decades that followed, references to a bloodstained cloth associated with Mary appear in Catholic inventories, private collections, and whispered exchanges. It is sometimes called a napkin, sometimes a kerchief, sometimes simply "the cloth." The lack of standardized naming allows it to move unnoticed, slipping between records without settling into one fixed identity.

And wherever it goes, the same stories follow.

Owners report disturbances that are not dramatic but persistent. Sleeplessness. Heightened emotional volatility. A sense of pressure when the object is near, particularly at night. Some describe dreams—not of the execution itself, but of corridors, locked doors, the feeling of waiting for something that does not arrive.

A Jesuit account from the late seventeenth century refers obliquely to a "blooded cloth of the Queen" that caused unease among those tasked with safeguarding it, noting that it was kept wrapped and seldom displayed "lest it trouble the spirit." The language is cautious. Religious men are careful about what they admit troubles them.

Later, Protestant writers dismiss the object as superstition, an example of Catholic excess—relic obsession masquerading as reverence. They argue that any discomfort arises from suggestion. From imagination.

But this explanation fails to account for the pattern that emerges across centuries: people who do not believe in the relic still react to it.

The handkerchief's power—if it can be called that—does not resemble a curse in the folkloric sense. It does not strike. It does not punish. It reminds.

Mary's execution was an act meant to end a threat. Instead, it produced a narrative that refused closure. Her body was buried. Her cause was not. Objects tied to her death became carriers of unfinished business, especially those that touched the blood itself.

Blood is not neutral in early modern belief systems. It carries identity. Essence. Covenant. To preserve blood is to preserve a claim.

The handkerchief thus becomes a portable protest.

By the nineteenth century, as romanticism reclaimed Mary as tragic heroine rather than political liability, the handkerchief's reputation deepened. Collectors sought it. Others claimed to have it. Several "Mary relics" surfaced, some obvious forgeries, some plausible enough to remain troubling. Among them, a linen cloth described as bearing "dark rust-colored staining consistent with age-old blood."

Scientific testing was rarely applied. And when it was, results were inconclusive—not enough material, too degraded, provenance too murky. The uncertainty only sharpened the unease.

If the handkerchief exists today—and there is no consensus that it does—it is not in a museum. It is not labeled behind glass. It survives, if at all, in private hands, where relics prefer to live. Wrapped. Unexamined. Occasionally taken out, then quickly put away again.

Those who claim to have handled it speak of an immediate emotional response. Not fear, exactly. Grief, sharpened by anger. A sense of injustice that feels personal despite the centuries between.

This reaction is often dismissed as historical empathy. But empathy does not usually arrive with physical sensation—the tightening throat, the pressure behind the eyes, the urge to weep without knowing why.

Objects soaked in blood do not forget the moment they were used. And objects tied to state violence remember differently than those tied to private death. They remember intention.

The quiet warning attached to the Bloody Handkerchief of Mary, Queen of Scots is not supernatural. It is ethical.

Do not mistake containment for resolution.

Some deaths are meant to end stories. When they fail, the story finds another vessel. Sometimes that vessel is a nation. Sometimes it is a religion.

And sometimes, it is a square of linen, folded carefully, waiting to be unfolded again.

36
the ruby of timur

T he Ruby of Timur is not a ruby.

That is the first lie it tells.

It is a spinel—deep red, glassy, heavy in the hand—but the name has persisted for centuries, clinging to it with the same stubbornness as the blood history clings to everything it touches. Misnaming is not accidental with objects like this. Names shape expectations. Names create myths that reality then struggles to escape.

This stone has never escaped.

The earliest stories do not treat the gem as jewelry. They treat it as proof. Of victory. Of divine favor. Of right to rule.

By the late fourteenth century, the stone was already old when it entered the orbit of Timur—also known as Tamerlane—the Turco-Mongol conqueror whose campaigns redrew maps through fire. Timur did not rule gently. He ruled as warning. Cities that resisted him were erased. Towers of skulls were erected in the aftermath, not as metaphor but as architecture.

And somewhere in this moving theater of violence, the red stone passed into his possession.

We do not know exactly how.

That absence matters.

The Ruby of Timur appears in the historical record not at the moment it is taken, but at the moment it is **claimed**—engraved, named, and folded into legacy. Timur's name was cut into the stone itself, an act that transformed the gem into something closer to a document than an ornament. Ownership was not implied. It was carved.

Later rulers would add their own inscriptions. Shahs. Emperors. Men who believed power could be accumulated by proximity.

Each inscription reads like a fingerprint pressed into glass.

The stone traveled with conquest. From Central Asia into Persia. Then into the Mughal Empire, where it passed through the hands of emperors who treated gemstones not as decoration, but as cosmic instruments—symbols of order in a world held together by force.

Babur. Jahangir. Shah Jahan.

The Ruby of Timur was present as empires rose and bled. It was worn at courts where executions were public ritual and mercy was strategic. It was admired, handled, and re-mounted, but rarely separated from violence. The gem did not cause conquest. It followed it. That distinction is crucial.

Curses that endure do not create events. They accompany them.

By the time the stone entered British hands in the nineteenth century, it had already accumulated a reputation—not overtly cursed, but heavy. Stories of misfortune followed those who attempted to move it casually, treat it as mere ornament, or separate it from its historical context.

In 1849, after the annexation of the Punjab, the stone was presented to Queen Victoria alongside the Koh-i-Noor. The gesture was framed as tribute. It was, in truth, seizure.

The British did what conquerors often do: they cleaned the object. Reset it. Reframed it. The Ruby of Timur was mounted into a necklace, then later incorporated into the Imperial State Crown. It became part of a larger symbolic system designed to neutralize its past by overwhelming it with pageantry.

But objects remember what settings try to erase.

Accounts from jewelers and attendants describe unease when handling the stone alone. Not fear—something closer to reverence edged with discomfort. The gem is large, heavier than expected, its surface marked with inscriptions that cannot be ignored once noticed. To wear it is to wear a list of conquerors.

Unlike some cursed objects, the Ruby of Timur does not generate a trail of sudden deaths. Its effect is subtler and arguably more disturbing. It appears in proximity to **structural violence** rather than personal catastrophe. Wars. Annexations. Political collapses that occur not because of the stone, but alongside it, as if it gravitates toward moments when power is taken rather than inherited.

Skeptics argue—correctly—that this is selection bias. That a jewel associated with rulers will naturally be present during upheaval. That red stones attract symbolic projection.

But symbolism does not explain why the gem is repeatedly described as feeling *wrong* when isolated from regalia. Removed from ceremony, it loses its context and becomes oppressive rather than beautiful. It does not glitter. It broods.

Today, the Ruby of Timur remains part of the British Crown Jewels, its inscriptions still legible, its history compressed into a display label that cannot possibly contain it. Visitors admire it briefly, then move on. Few linger long enough to notice the names carved into its surface.

That may be intentional.

The quiet danger of the Ruby of Timur is not that it kills, but that it **legitimizes**. It has spent centuries validating conquest simply by being present, absorbing authority and reflecting it back with no judgment. It rewards whoever claims it next with the illusion of continuity—as if power, once seized, becomes destiny through repetition.

There is an old superstition among gem handlers that stones which pass through too many empires become unmoored. They no longer know which story they belong to. When worn, they do not bring luck or ruin. They bring **pressure**—the weight of every hand that held them before.

The Ruby of Timur has never belonged to one people. It has belonged to power itself.

And power, like the stone, does not apologize.

It waits.

37

napoleon's hat

Napoleon Bonaparte did not wear a crown when he conquered Europe.

He wore a hat.

Not just any hat, and not casually. The black felt bicorne—worn sideways, points framing his shoulders rather than his face—became as much a part of his silhouette as his posture or his stare. It was not fashion. It was strategy. On a battlefield choked with smoke and movement, soldiers could spot him instantly. The hat made him visible. It made him central. It made him unavoidable.

Napoleon understood symbols better than most men who claim to despise them.

He owned more than one bicorne, of course. At least 120 over the course of his life, according to inventories and tailors' records. They were replaced as they wore down, stained by rain, sweat, and war. And yet, not all of them are equal in the historical imagination.

Some hats witnessed victories.

Some witnessed retreat.

Some were present when history turned its face away.

It is those hats—the ones that lingered at the edges of triumph and disaster—that developed reputations no curator label can fully explain.

The earliest accounts of unease surrounding Napoleon's hats do not speak of curses. They speak of attachment.

Napoleon was rarely separated from his bicorne. He slept near it. He reached for it instinctively. He is reported to have become irritated, even agitated, if a particular hat was misplaced. This was not superstition. It was something closer to identification. The hat was not a possession. It was an extension.

By the time of his exile to Elba in 1814, that extension had begun to fail him.

Napoleon took his hat with him into exile. More than one, in fact. Contemporary letters describe him wearing it even when unnecessary, pacing, adjusting it, touching the brim as if reassuring himself that some part of the old order remained intact. Observers noted that he seemed smaller then. Not physically diminished—but *compressed*. As though the hat now carried more history than the man beneath it could hold.

After Waterloo, after the second abdication, the hats became relics.

This is where the trouble begins.

Napoleon's death in 1821 on Saint Helena transformed his personal effects into artifacts overnight. Locks of hair were taken. Buttons were saved. And the hats—those black silhouettes of ambition—were distributed, sold, gifted, and hoarded.

Some went to museums.

Some went to private collectors.

Some vanished.

Others began to acquire stories.

One bicorne, now held in the collection of the Château de Malmaison, was long associated with periods of intense fixation among handlers. Conservators noted an unusual pattern: staff assigned to the hat reported recurring dreams involving crowds, marching, or standing alone while being watched. These reports were not officially documented as phenomena—only mentioned in private correspondence and oral recollections—but the pattern repeated often enough that senior staff quietly rotated assignments.

Another hat, sold at auction in the early 20th century, passed through multiple owners in rapid succession. Each sale was framed as coincidence. Each buyer cited vague unease, difficulty sleeping, or an inexplicable urge to "move it on" despite its immense value. One owner reportedly kept it locked away, unable to display it, yet unwilling to part with it—a classic symptom in the folklore of charged objects, though no one used that language at the time.

The most persistent stories cluster around hats that were worn **after** Napoleon's power fractured.

Objects absorb meaning differently at the height of dominance than they do during collapse. A crown taken at coronation carries a different weight than one worn during abdication. Napoleon's later hats—creased by defeat, touched by uncertainty—appear to have accumulated something sharper than glory.

Skeptics, understandably, dismiss this as projection. The human tendency to mythologize famous men and imbue their possessions with psychological residue is well-documented. We want relics to speak because we are uncomfortable with silence.

And yet.

Napoleon himself once said, "A man does not have himself killed for a hat." He understood symbolism, but he understood limits. The irony is that after his death, men did precisely that—financially, socially, sometimes emotionally. The hats became objects of obsession. Collectors ruined themselves chasing them. Families fractured over inheritance disputes involving them. Lawsuits were filed. Reputations were damaged.

The hat does not kill.

It erodes.

What makes Napoleon's hat unsettling is not a single catastrophic event, but a pattern of **identity displacement**. Owners report feeling overshadowed by it, as though their own presence thins in its proximity. The object demands narrative space. It resists being merely displayed. It insists on being *interpreted*.

That insistence is dangerous.

In museums today, Napoleon's bicornes sit behind glass, flattened slightly by time, the felt dulled to a soft, absorbing black. Visitors photograph them quickly, often surprised by their small size. The myth does not match the material reality.

But those who linger sometimes notice something else.

The hat does not look empty.

It looks as though it is waiting to be picked up.

There is a quiet rule among some collectors—never written, never acknowledged publicly—that one should not wear Napoleon's hat, even briefly. Not for photographs. Not for curiosity. Not even as a joke. The reason given is usually preservation.

The real reason is older.

Napoleon wore the hat so the world would know where he was.

After his fall, the hat no longer points outward.

It points inward.

And whatever it reflects back is not conquest—but ambition stripped of its ending.

38
the slippers of
anna anderson

The slippers were never meant to matter.

They were soft, practical things—wool-lined, low to the ground, shaped for hospital floors and long days spent sitting rather than walking. No jewels. No insignia. Nothing that would make them collectible at first glance.

And yet, they have outlived empires.

Anna Anderson arrived in the historical record the way many ghosts do: wet, silent, and unnamed.

On February 17, 1920, a young woman attempted suicide by jumping into the Landwehr Canal in Berlin. She was pulled from the water alive but unconscious, without papers, without identification, without language anyone could immediately understand. She was taken to Dalldorf Asylum, later renamed the Wittenau psychiatric hospital, and for more than a year she did not speak.

When she finally did, what she said fractured Europe.

She claimed to be Grand Duchess Anastasia Nikolaevna of Russia.

The Romanovs had been dead—executed in Yekaterinburg in July 1918, their bodies hidden, destroyed, denied proper burial. But uncertainty lingered. The chaos of revolution leaves gaps, and gaps invite stories. Survivors were rumored. Doubles imagined. Hope refused to die neatly.

Anna Anderson did not present herself with crowns or jewels. She presented herself with scars. With physical resemblance. With fragments of memory that felt intimate rather than rehearsed. She spoke of details that could not be easily sourced. She recognized faces she was not supposed to know.

And slowly, inexorably, objects began to gather around her.

The slippers appear later, after the identity war had already begun.

By the late 1920s and 1930s, Anderson's life had narrowed into rooms—sanatoriums, boarding houses, the homes of sympathizers. Her supporters provided what they could: clothes, meals, comfort. Among these were a pair of soft house slippers, gifted during a period of ill health when she was largely confined indoors.

They were unremarkable.

Until they weren't.

Visitors began to notice that Anderson treated the slippers differently than her other belongings. She wore them obsessively. She refused to let others move them. When they were misplaced, she became visibly distressed, pacing, agitated, repeating phrases about "keeping what remains."

At first, this was dismissed as anxiety. Trauma does that. Long-term institutionalization does that. No one thought to ascribe meaning to footwear.

That was a mistake.

As the legal battles intensified—decades-long court proceedings in Germany to determine whether Anderson was truly Anastasia—her environment grew increasingly charged. Lawyers, aristocrats, journalists, Romanov relatives all passed through her rooms, all scrutinizing her body for truth.

The slippers stayed.

Observers noted something odd: when Anderson was asked to recount memories of her childhood—particularly those involving the Winter Palace or her private rooms—she would often touch or adjust the slippers unconsciously, as though anchoring herself. Not grounding. Anchoring.

By the 1950s, the slippers had become part of her daily uniform, worn down, reshaped by her feet. They were mended repeatedly rather than replaced, even when replacements were offered. She rejected new pairs with unexpected hostility.

"They are not mine," she reportedly said more than once.

The implication lingered unspoken.

The slippers were not *hers* in the sense of ownership.

They were hers in the sense of **continuity**.

Skeptics would later argue—correctly—that Anderson was not Anastasia. DNA testing in the 1990s would finally confirm that she was Franziska Schanzkowska, a Polish factory worker with a history of trauma and mental illness.

But that resolution comes too late to explain what happened **before** the truth was known.

For over sixty years, Anna Anderson lived inside a contested identity. And the slippers absorbed that pressure. They were present during interrogations. During court hearings. During moments of collapse and moments of conviction. They touched the floor of every room in which she was forced to defend her existence.

Objects do not need to be magical to become saturated.

After Anderson's death in 1984 in Charlottesville, Virginia, her personal effects were divided, donated, discarded. Most were lost. Some were deliberately destroyed by those who wanted the story to end cleanly.

The slippers survived.

Their provenance is fragmented, like everything else connected to her. They appear in private collections and institutional archives, occasionally surfaced, then withdrawn again. No museum displays them prominently. When shown, they are contextualized as "belongings," not relics.

And yet.

Curators and handlers have reported a peculiar emotional response when encountering them—not fear, but discomfort. A sense of standing too close to a question that should not be reopened. The slippers feel unfinished. As if removing them from storage reactivates the debate rather than preserving it.

Unlike crowns or jewels, they offer no authority. They do not declare truth.

They ask it.

What makes the slippers dangerous is not that they belong to a false claimant—but that they belonged to someone who lived an entire life under scrutiny, whose reality was argued over until her body failed. They are artifacts of **being believed and disbelieved at the same time**, which is one of the most corrosive states a human can endure.

There is an unspoken superstition among some historians and archivists: do not separate the slippers from their story. Do not display them without context. Do not try to "resolve" them.

Because the object resists resolution.

Anna Anderson never stopped being watched.

The slippers remember that.

They are worn thin not from walking, but from standing still while the world decided who she was allowed to be.

And even now—after DNA, after court rulings, after official closure —they refuse to rest.

Some objects haunt because they witnessed violence.

These haunt because they witnessed **doubt**.

And doubt, once embedded, does not fade.

It waits.

39
the pearl of lao tzu

The pearl was never supposed to be found.

That is the first thing everyone agrees on, even when they disagree about everything else.

It did not emerge from an oyster bed meant for harvest. It was not pried loose by divers looking for ornament. It surfaced instead as a byproduct of injury—of irritation, intrusion, and time. And when it appeared, those who saw it struggled to agree on what, exactly, they were looking at.

Some saw a treasure.

Some saw a relic.

Some saw a mistake that had been growing quietly for centuries.

By the early twentieth century, the object would be known as the Pearl of Lao Tzu, though Lao Tzu himself had been dead for more than two thousand years. Others would call it the Pearl of Allah. The names were not interchangeable. They were competing claims.

The story most often told begins in 1934, in the Philippines, when a diver reportedly retrieved an enormous clam from the waters near Palawan. Inside was a massive, irregular pearl—off-white, ridged, almost sculptural rather than spherical. It weighed several pounds. It did not gleam. It absorbed light.

The diver did not live long after.

That detail appears inconsistently in the record. Some versions claim he died shortly after the discovery. Others omit him entirely. What matters is not whether he existed, but how quickly the story learned what kind of shape it needed.

The pearl entered Western awareness through an American named Wilburn Cobb, who acquired it in the mid-1930s. Cobb's account claimed that the pearl had been protected for generations by local communities, not as jewelry but as a sacred object. According to the story he told, the pearl contained carved representations of religious figures—faces and forms visible in its contours if one knew how to look.

One of those figures was said to be Lao Tzu.

That claim is where everything begins to unravel.

Lao Tzu, the semi-legendary author of the *Tao Te Ching*, was not associated with pearls in any canonical text. Taoism does not venerate relics in this way. The attribution was symbolic, not doctrinal. The pearl's layered growth, its slow formation around an irritant, its refusal to conform to symmetry—all of this fit neatly into Westernized inter-pretations of Taoist philosophy.

The pearl did not come from Taoism.

It was *assigned* to it.

This pattern repeats.

As the pearl changed hands, new interpretations adhered to it. Muslim traders reportedly referred to it as the Pearl of Allah, suggesting divine origin or protection. Others framed it as pre-Islamic, pre-Buddhist, pre-everything—a natural relic onto which belief could be projected without resistance.

Scientific examination complicated matters further.

Experts identified the object not as a traditional pearl, but as a giant clam concretion—formed over time, likely around a foreign body. Its size was extraordinary, but not impossible. Its surface irregularities explained the illusion of faces.

And yet.

Those who handled it often reported a sense of pressure rather than wonder. Not fear. Weight. As though the object carried too many interpretations to be held comfortably. Unlike polished gems, it resisted display. It did not want to be framed. Photographs flattened it. Descriptions failed.

Cobb attempted to sell the pearl multiple times. Each effort stalled. Deals collapsed. Valuations fluctuated wildly, from worthless curiosity to priceless relic. Buyers hesitated. Institutions declined. The pearl was too controversial to stabilize, too belief-laden to be neutral.

It became stuck in narrative limbo.

Over the decades, rumors accumulated. That those who attempted to profit from it suffered reversals. That its presence in a home caused arguments, insomnia, or obsession. That it seemed to demand interpretation, pulling belief systems toward it like filings to a magnet.

There is no consistent pattern of death associated with the pearl.

That makes it more unsettling.

Objects that kill announce themselves. Objects that confuse endure.

Skeptics argue that the Pearl of Lao Tzu is a perfect case study in myth-making: a misunderstood natural formation elevated through colonial misunderstanding, religious projection, and the human hunger for meaning. They are not wrong.

They are simply incomplete.

Because even when the explanations are laid bare, the unease remains.

The pearl is too large to ignore, too strange to dismiss, and too burdened with names to return to anonymity. Each attempt to define it adds another layer of narrative accretion, mirroring the way it formed physically—slowly, around irritation, over time.

Today, the pearl's location is ambiguous. It is said to be held privately, occasionally exhibited, then withdrawn again. No major museum has committed to permanent display. No consensus has been reached about its value, monetary or otherwise.

That uncertainty is not accidental.

The Pearl of Lao Tzu does not belong to one tradition, one owner, or one explanation. It exists in the overlap—where belief systems collide, where science explains structure but not significance, where names cling even after being disproven.

There is an old warning in several traditions, phrased differently each time: objects that are claimed by too many gods belong to none of them.

They belong to the people who argue over them.

The pearl does not curse.

It complicates.

It absorbs attention, belief, and expectation until those who approach it begin to feel strangely hollow, as though the meaning they projected has been quietly taken in and held somewhere out of reach.

Like all objects formed around irritation, it is patient.

It does not demand reverence.

It waits for it.

40
the ring of the borgias

T he ring was never meant to be noticed.

That is the detail historians keep circling back to, even when they disagree about everything else. The Borgias were not subtle people. They built palaces, commissioned frescoes, staged public displays of devotion and excess in equal measure. If they had wanted a cursed object to announce itself, it would have glittered.

This ring did not.

It was small. Gold, yes—but worn thin from use. Set not with a jewel but with a shallow cavity, easily overlooked, easily explained away as decorative quirk or poor craftsmanship. It rested on a finger where it could be pressed, turned, hidden by habit.

Unlike other rings, it was not a symbol. It was a mechanism.

The Borgias rose to prominence in the late 15th century, a Spanish family operating inside the Italian Renaissance like a fracture line beneath polished marble. Rodrigo Borgia became Pope Alexander VI in 1492, and from that moment forward, the family's private ambitions fused seamlessly with public power. Nepotism was not an accusation; it was policy.

So were poisons.

Contemporary accounts—letters, diplomatic reports, whispered marginal notes in court documents—repeatedly reference deaths that arrived politely. Sudden fevers. Dinners that ended early. Wine that did not taste wrong until it was too late. The Borgias were accused of using *cantarella*, a slow-acting poison whose composition remains debated: arsenic, perhaps; or a compound derived from decomposing organic matter; or something worse, known only to those who prepared it.

The method mattered less than the delivery.

This is where the ring enters the story.

Several sources from the early 1500s describe a ring used to administer poison discreetly, often during meals or formal greetings. A slight twist of the hand. A press against a cup. A moment of closeness that could not be refused. The ring's cavity allowed liquid poison to be released without breaking eye contact.

It did not need to be fast.

It needed to be intimate.

The ring is most often associated with Pope Alexander VI himself, though later retellings shift the blame fluidly between him and his children—Cesare and Lucrezia Borgia chief among them. Lucrezia, in particular, became a magnet for projection. She was young, intelligent, politically useful, and female. Rumors attached to her eagerly: incest, murder, seduction, poison concealed in rings or hollowed jewels.

Modern historians have worked hard to dismantle the worst of these accusations. Many are exaggerated. Some are demonstrably false. Lucrezia was almost certainly less monstrous than legend claims.

That does not mean the ring was imaginary.

Diplomatic correspondence from Venice and Florence repeatedly notes fear of dining with the Borgias. Ambassadors complained of illness. Servants vanished. Entire households fell quiet after a single meal. These are not ghost stories. They are administrative headaches, written in careful ink.

What no one could ever agree on was **where the ring went**.

Unlike crowns or chalices, poison rings were meant to vanish. If exposed, they implicated the hand that wore them. When Alexander VI died in 1503—ironically, possibly poisoned himself, though historians dispute this—the Borgias' grip on Rome fractured almost overnight. Cesare fled. Assets were seized. Enemies moved quickly.

Somewhere in that chaos, the ring slipped out of record.

Later centuries would claim sightings. A ring in a private collection, said to come from Rome. A gold band with unusual wear, its cavity inexplicably sealed shut. A piece acquired by a noble family who refused to discuss how they came by it, only that they would not sell.

The deaths that followed these acquisitions are harder to document. They are quieter. A collector who fell suddenly ill. An heir who died without warning. A servant who drank from the wrong glass. Patterns appear only if one looks for them—and looking too hard is its own kind of belief.

Skeptics point out that poison rings were not unique to the Borgias. Similar devices existed across Europe and the Near East. The idea of a single cursed ring is reductive, romantic, almost lazy.

They are right.

What distinguishes the Ring of the Borgias is not its design, but its reputation for **control**.

This ring does not lash out. It does not bring disaster to the careless. It requires intent. Proximity. Choice. It asks its wearer to decide who is worth touching.

That makes it dangerous long after the poison is gone.

Because even emptied, even rendered inert, the ring carries the memory of what it was designed to do. Those who believe they possess it often report a strange impulse to test boundaries—to see how much influence they have, how easily others yield, how close one can get before discomfort sets in.

The haunting here is not spectral.

It is behavioral.

Today, no object can be definitively identified as *the* Ring of the Borgias. Museums acknowledge poison rings as a category, not a lineage. Private collectors speak in hedges and hypotheticals. The Vatican does not comment.

But the idea persists.

A ring that kills without spectacle.

A weapon disguised as courtesy.

A relic whose power lies not in magic, but in how naturally it fits the hand.

There is a reason Renaissance chroniclers feared the Borgias even after their fall. They understood something modern readers often miss: the most effective instruments of harm are not dramatic. They are portable. Plausible. Personal.

If the ring survives—and it may—it does not announce itself.

It waits to be worn by someone who believes they deserve to decide who lives comfortably, and who does not.

And that, perhaps, is the quietest curse of all.

part three
religious & sacred artifacts

41

the curse of tutankhamun

(Funerary Objects)

They did not open the tomb all at once.

That detail matters.

Howard Carter had waited years—years of dust, money running thin, credibility fraying—to find something that everyone else believed was already gone. By November of 1922, the Valley of the Kings had been picked over so thoroughly that optimism itself felt unprofessional. And yet when Carter's workmen struck a step cut into the limestone, he did not rush forward like a treasure hunter.

He waited.

When the sealed doorway finally appeared, stamped with the cartouches of a boy king long dismissed as insignificant, Carter sent word to his patron, Lord Carnarvon, before proceeding. Even then, when Carter made the small hole in the door and peered inside by candlelight, he did not enter.

He said only, *"Yes, wonderful things."*

That restraint—so often praised as scholarly—also delayed the moment when the tomb's contents became unmoored from their original purpose.

Because Tutankhamun's burial was not a collection.

It was a system.

The objects inside the tomb were arranged according to religious logic refined over thousands of years. Amulets placed at precise points on the body. Shrines nested within shrines. Chariots dismantled and stacked. Food offerings sealed. Statues positioned not for beauty, but for function. Each item had a role to play in ensuring the king's safe passage through the afterlife and his continued authority beyond death.

To disturb one piece was to interrupt the whole.

The ancient Egyptians were explicit about this.

Tombs were not protected by traps in the Hollywood sense; they were protected by consequences. Inscriptions warned that anyone who disturbed the king's rest would be struck down by divine forces. These were not poetic flourishes. They were legal declarations written for the gods themselves, binding the living to rules enforced beyond human jurisdiction.

And then the seals were broken.

The deaths did not come immediately. That, too, matters.

Lord Carnarvon died first, in April 1923—just months after the tomb was opened. A mosquito bite became infected. Blood poisoning followed. He died in Cairo, where the lights in the city reportedly went out at the moment of his passing. Back in England, his dog is said to have howled and collapsed at the same time.

The story traveled faster than the facts.

Within a year, newspapers had begun to speak of a curse. By the end of the decade, more than a dozen deaths—some directly connected to the excavation, others tenuously associated—had been folded into the narrative. Sudden illnesses. Heart attacks. Mysterious fevers. Accidents. Each new obituary was read backward, traced like a constellation until it pointed inevitably to the tomb.

Skeptics objected, loudly and often. They pointed out that many of the expedition members lived long, ordinary lives. Carter himself survived for another seventeen years. Statistical analysis, they argued, did not support the idea of a curse.

They were not wrong.

They were also missing the point.

The curse of Tutankhamun does not operate like a weapon. It operates like a pressure system.

What changed after the tomb was opened was not merely the fate of individuals, but the way funerary objects were handled, displayed, and understood. Items once sealed for eternity were removed, catalogued, shipped, and exhibited. Amulets meant to guard organs were separated from bodies. Coffins were opened. The mummy itself was unwrapped under bright lights, its limbs damaged in the process.

Each act was justified in the language of science.

Each act carried consequences that were not evenly distributed.

Those who handled the objects most intimately—those who touched, lifted, pried, and separated—reported symptoms that were rarely dramatic but often persistent. Nightmares. A sense of dread while working alone. The feeling of being watched in museum storage rooms. Objects misplaced and later found exactly where they should not have been.

Even among skeptics, there was an acknowledgment that the tomb felt different.

The artifacts from Tutankhamun's burial did not behave like inert things. They resisted categorization. They inspired fixation. They attracted crowds not just because of their beauty, but because people felt they were standing too close to something unfinished.

Museums tried to neutralize this feeling through context—labels, glass cases, controlled lighting. But reports persisted. Guards assigned to overnight duty complained of unease. Visitors fainted. Children cried without clear cause. The golden mask, in particular, became an object people struggled to look away from, even as it made them uncomfortable.

None of this proves a curse.

It does suggest displacement.

The ancient Egyptians believed that a person's identity was distributed across multiple components: the body, the name, the shadow, the life force, the spirit. Funerary objects were not mementos. They were anchors for those components, ensuring cohesion after death.

When those anchors were removed, catalogued, and scattered across institutions, something fundamental was altered.

Not anger.

Not vengeance.

Instability.

Modern theories attempt to explain the deaths associated with the tomb through natural means. Mold spores. Bacteria. Enclosed air. Stress. Coincidence amplified by media frenzy. These explanations are plausible and, in some cases, demonstrably correct.

But they address only the physical.

The curse narrative persists because it speaks to something else: the discomfort of realizing that we are very good at opening doors, and very bad at understanding what we displace when we do.

Today, Tutankhamun's funerary objects are among the most famous artifacts in the world. They tour internationally. They are photographed endlessly. They are reproduced on merchandise, posters, coffee mugs.

They are safe.

And yet.

Even now, discussions about moving or reuniting certain pieces provoke resistance—not just political or cultural, but emotional. There is an unspoken sense that these objects were never meant to be separated, and that keeping them apart prolongs something unresolved.

The curse of Tutankhamun is no longer a threat whispered in hieroglyphs.

It is a question.

What happens when an entire belief system is dismantled for study?

What follows when protection is mistaken for decoration?

What lingers when objects designed for eternity are forced into circulation?

The tomb is open.

The king is known.

The artifacts endure.

But the system that once held them together is gone.

And sometimes, late at night, in the quiet of a museum gallery, it feels as though the objects are still waiting for something to be put back.

42
the stone of scone

(The Stone of Destiny)

L ong before it sat beneath coronation chairs or behind museum glass, the Stone of Scone belonged to a place rather than a person. The stone was never meant to travel. That is the first thing every version of its story agrees on, even when they disagree about nearly everything else. It was embedded in ritual, geography, and legitimacy so tightly that separating it from the land was considered an act not just of theft, but of severance. Kingship flowed *through* the stone, not *from* it. To move it was to interrupt that flow.

And yet it was moved. Repeatedly. Violently. Publicly.

The earliest legends wrap the stone in myth so old it resists chronology. Some say it was Jacob's pillow, the stone on which he dreamed of a ladder reaching heaven. Others trace it through Ireland, carried by the Tuatha Dé Danann, or claim it cried out beneath the feet of the rightful king and remained silent for all others. Each culture that touched it rewrote the story slightly—but always preserved the same rule:

The stone chooses.

The stone remembers.

By the early medieval period, the Stone of Scone was fixed at the Abbey of Scone in Perthshire, where Scottish kings were inaugurated.

The ceremony was not elaborate by later standards, but it was heavy with implication. The king did not merely sit on the stone. He was tested by it. The legitimacy of his reign depended on the stone's silent consent.

For centuries, it stayed where it was placed.

That, too, matters.

The stone survived wars, shifting dynasties, religious upheaval. It endured not because it was hidden, but because it was understood. Everyone knew what it was. Everyone knew where it belonged. And so it remained stable.

The curse begins—not with blood, not with death—but with certainty.

In 1296, Edward I of England invaded Scotland and took the stone.

This was not symbolic theft. It was strategic desecration.

Edward understood the stone's power, even if he did not believe in it. By removing it from Scotland and installing it beneath the Coronation Chair in Westminster Abbey, he attempted to rewrite legitimacy itself. English monarchs would now sit on Scotland's sacred object, transforming conquest into continuity.

The stone did not resist.

But something changed.

Almost immediately, the narratives around English coronations begin to fray. Reigns grow unstable. Succession disputes multiply. Wars of legitimacy follow one another with exhausting regularity. The stone remains physically present, but it is no longer doing the job it was meant to do.

Because the job required context.

For over six hundred years, the Stone of Scone sat beneath the Coronation Chair, worn smooth by time, ignored by most visitors, referenced only briefly in ceremony. And yet it never quite settled. Stories circulated quietly: the stone was a substitute; the real one had been hidden; the stone would one day return on its own terms.

In 1950, it moved again.

This time, it was not taken by an army, but by students.

On Christmas Day, four Scottish nationalists broke into Westminster Abbey and removed the stone. In the process, it cracked—whether from age, mishandling, or something more symbolic is still debated. The stone was eventually recovered and returned to London, repaired and reset.

But it had been broken.

And the break matters.

From that moment on, the stone's narrative fractures. Doubt multiplies. Is the stone beneath the chair authentic? Was it swapped during the theft? Was it ever the true Stone of Destiny at all? Skeptics argue that geological analysis suggests it is local sandstone, not the legendary relic of myth.

They are probably right.

And yet the unease persists.

Because curses are not always attached to authenticity. They are attached to belief—and to use.

When the Stone of Scone was finally returned to Scotland in 1996, it was done with ceremony, restraint, and explicit conditions. It would remain in Edinburgh Castle, displayed but not employed. It would travel south only for coronations, and then be returned.

In other words: it would no longer choose.

It would be shown.

This containment has worked, mostly.

There are no sudden deaths linked to the stone. No dramatic hauntings. No collapsing dynasties that can be cleanly attributed to its presence. And yet the discomfort lingers. Every discussion of coronation stirs the question again. Should the stone be moved? Should it be used? Should it remain where it is?

No one agrees.

Which may be the stone's final influence.

The Stone of Scone's curse—if it deserves that word at all—is not one of punishment. It is one of displacement. Wherever it goes, legitimacy becomes unstable. Authority feels borrowed. Power demands justification.

The stone does not harm kings.

It exposes them.

Perhaps that is why it no longer cries out. Perhaps it has learned that silence is more effective. Or perhaps it is waiting—patiently, as it always has—for a context that no longer exists.

The land has changed. The rituals have thinned. The crowns no longer require the stone in the way they once did.

But the stone remembers when they did.

And that memory—heavy, quiet, unresolved—is enough.

43

the spear of destiny

(Holy Lance)

T he spear was already old when it learned how to kill kings.

By the time it enters Christian history as the weapon that pierced Christ's side, it had passed through hands that did not care what it symbolized—only that it worked. Iron tipped with iron, balanced for thrust, designed for certainty. The kind of object that does not hesitate. The kind of object that ends things.

According to the Gospel of John, a Roman soldier named Longinus drove the spear into Jesus's side to confirm death. Blood and water flowed out. The act was practical, procedural. The crucifixion was already over.

And yet that single gesture altered the spear's trajectory forever.

From that moment on, the lance ceased to be a weapon and became a relic—not because of what it did, but because of when it did it. It touched divinity at the precise moment divinity was leaving the body. That timing mattered. It transformed the spear from an instrument of execution into a conduit—something that had crossed the boundary between mortal violence and sacred consequence.

Relics behave differently than weapons. They attract belief. And belief accumulates weight.

By the early Middle Ages, the Holy Lance—now fragmented, replicated, contested—had acquired a reputation that went far beyond sanctity. It was said that whoever possessed the spear and understood its power held the fate of the world in their hands. Not metaphorically. Literally.

This was not a promise of blessing.

It was a warning.

The lance does not crown kings. It tests them.

Charlemagne carried a spear believed to contain the nail from the Crucifixion embedded within its blade. He died holding it. Or so the story goes. The Holy Roman Emperors guarded it obsessively, treating it less like an object of devotion and more like a stabilizing force—one that had to remain in their possession to prevent collapse.

The pattern repeats: possession followed by expansion, followed by instability.

Every ruler associated with the spear seems to flourish briefly, then unravel. Empires stretch too far. Successors falter. Lines end abruptly. The spear does not destroy power—it exposes its limits.

By the time the lance is enshrined in Vienna, its reputation has hardened into doctrine. It is no longer debated whether the spear matters. Only what will happen if it is lost.

That question becomes urgent in the 20th century.

In 1912, a young man stands in front of the lance at the Hofburg Treasury. He is poor, bitter, and searching for something that will explain why the world has denied him what he believes he deserves. He later claims this moment changed him—that the spear awakened something dormant, something inevitable.

Years later, after annexing Austria, that same man orders the lance seized.

He does not display it. He does not destroy it. He locks it away.

The timing is impossible to ignore.

After acquiring the spear, his power surges. Borders fall. Armies advance. Europe fractures. And yet the spear does not remain with him. Near the end of the war, Allied forces recover it. Within weeks, he is dead.

The myth crystallizes:

When the spear leaves your possession, your power collapses.

Skeptics argue—correctly—that the timeline is too clean. That the story has been retrofitted. That correlation is not causation. That relic obsession in the Third Reich was part of a broader pattern of symbolic theft rather than supernatural influence.

All of this may be true.

But the spear's danger has never been about magic in the crude sense. It is about fixation.

The Holy Lance invites rulers to believe their authority is external —that legitimacy can be held, guarded, stolen. That power resides not in governance, but in possession. That belief corrodes judgment. It encourages risk. It whispers inevitability.

The spear does not compel action.

It permits it.

Today, multiple institutions claim to hold the true Holy Lance or fragments thereof. Scientific analysis contradicts medieval tradition. The relic fractures under scrutiny, multiplying instead of resolving. And yet the story does not weaken. It becomes more adaptable.

The spear now exists as an idea rather than a singular object. A permission slip for violence cloaked in destiny. A reminder that some people would rather believe they are chosen than accountable.

That may be the spear's final form.

Not a weapon.

Not a relic.

But a narrative that absolves.

There is an old line attributed—incorrectly, repeatedly—to prophecy:

"Whoever holds the spear of destiny holds the destiny of the world."

The more accurate version would be quieter, and far more dangerous:

Whoever believes that is already lost.

44

the crying
crucifix of sicily

T he first thing people noticed was not the tears.

It was the silence.

In the spring of 1954, in a modest home in the Sicilian town of Syracuse, a plaster crucifix hung on a bedroom wall. It was not old. It was not rare. It had been purchased cheaply, the kind of devotional object found in countless Catholic households—mass-produced, pale, unremarkable. Christ's head tilted forward. His ribs were visible. His expression was already sorrowful in the standardized way religious art often is.

No one expected it to *change*.

On the morning of August 29, Antonina Iannuso—young, pregnant, and ill—noticed moisture on the face of the crucifix. At first, it was assumed to be condensation. Sicily is humid. Plaster sweats. Faith fills in gaps where certainty fails.

But the moisture returned.

Over the next several days, neighbors, relatives, and eventually strangers crowded into the small bedroom. The figure on the cross appeared to weep. Clear liquid pooled beneath its eyes and traced slow paths down its cheeks. Witnesses described it as tear-like in both movement and volume—not a stain, not a smear, but something active. Something ongoing.

Word spread with alarming speed.

What makes the Crying Crucifix of Sicily unsettling is not simply that people claimed to see tears. Religious history is saturated with such claims. What distinguishes this case is documentation—and restraint.

Samples of the liquid were collected and analyzed by multiple laboratories. The conclusion, published cautiously and without flourish, was that the fluid was chemically consistent with human tears. Not holy water. Not oil. Tears.

That fact did not settle anything. It made it worse.

The Church hesitated. It always does. Miracles are liabilities. Once you declare one real, you inherit responsibility for everything that follows. The Vatican sent observers. The crucifix was removed from the home and placed under controlled conditions. The weeping ceased.

That, too, mattered.

Objects accused of supernatural behavior often escalate under scrutiny. This one stopped.

As if it had said what it needed to say.

Skeptics proposed explanations—hidden reservoirs, clever manipulation, mass hysteria fueled by grief and Catholic expectation. These theories were not dismissed. They were simply incomplete. No mechanism convincingly explained the chemistry. No confession surfaced. No similar objects were exposed as part of a larger fraud.

And perhaps most disturbing of all: the event did not benefit anyone.

There was no money made. No cult formed. No charismatic figure rose to claim authority. Antonina did not become famous. She did not found a movement. She remained fragile, ill, and overwhelmed by attention she never sought.

The tears did not heal her.

That detail unsettles believers more than skeptics.

If the crucifix wept, it did so without fixing anything.

The official Church response, issued years later, was measured to the point of coldness. The event was acknowledged as *worthy of belief,* not declared a miracle outright. Pilgrimages were permitted. Devotion was encouraged—but quietly.

No trumpets. No absolution.

The crucifix was enshrined, then replicated. Copies spread. Some claimed similar phenomena. Most did not. The original remained inert, as though emptied.

That emptiness is part of the fear.

The Crying Crucifix does not threaten punishment. It does not promise salvation. It does not act again. It offers no pattern to decode, no ritual to repeat. It presents grief without instruction.

In folklore, objects that bleed or cry are usually warnings—omens of war, famine, moral collapse. Sicily, at the time, was recovering from the devastation of World War II. Poverty lingered. Political violence simmered. Faith was strained by survival.

Some theologians later suggested the crucifix did not weep *for* Sicily, but *with* it.

Others went further, suggesting something more unsettling: that the crucifix did not cry because of suffering—but because suffering had become ordinary.

Miracles are expected to interrupt history. This one mirrored it instead.

Today, the crucifix is still displayed. Visitors file past quietly. Many report feeling watched—not by God, but by sorrow itself. Not accused. Simply observed.

No one has seen it cry again.

That may be the most frightening part.

If the crucifix wept once, it suggests a threshold—a moment when grief accumulated enough to surface, then receded. Not resolved. Just absorbed.

There is no curse attached to the Crying Crucifix of Sicily. No chain of deaths. No madness. No misfortune.

What it leaves behind is subtler.

A question without teeth or comfort:

If even Christ can weep—and nothing changes—what does that mean for the rest of us?

45

the black stone of mecca

(curse-adjacent sacred
object; weight-bearing relic)

N o one knows what it was before it was watched.

The Black Stone does not enter history as an artifact. It enters as a *presence*.

By the time it appears in written record, it is already old — already handled, already placed. Embedded in the eastern corner of the Kaaba, it is not displayed so much as *fixed*, set into the architecture of ritual itself. It does not belong to a single owner or era. It belongs to motion: circling bodies, bare feet on stone, breath repeating the same words until meaning thins and something else takes over.

In Islamic tradition, the Black Stone was sent down from heaven, given to Abraham and Ishmael during the construction of the Kaaba. It was once white, the stories say, but darkened by the sins of humanity. Whether taken literally or metaphorically, the detail matters. From the beginning, the Stone is imagined as absorbent — not passive, but receptive.

It is touched, kissed, reached for. Millions of hands over centuries. No other object on Earth has been approached with such consistency, such density of intention.

That alone would be enough to give it weight.

But the Black Stone's history is not gentle.

In the year 683 CE, during the Second Fitna, Mecca became a battlefield. The Kaaba was damaged by fire; the Black Stone was fractured. Later reconstructions required binding its fragments together — first with silver, later with more elaborate settings. The Stone you see today is not whole. It is a cluster of broken pieces, held in place by human effort.

Breakage does not end its story. It accelerates it.

In 930 CE, the unthinkable happened. The Qarmatians — a radical Ismaili sect — attacked Mecca during the Hajj. Pilgrims were slaughtered. Bodies were thrown into the Zamzam well. And the Black Stone was ripped from the Kaaba and carried away.

For twenty-two years, the Stone was gone.

Imagine the silence of that absence. The rituals continued, but the center was missing. The Kaaba stood wounded. Accounts from the period speak not just of political upheaval, but of cosmological anxiety — as if something foundational had been dislodged. The Stone was eventually ransomed and returned, broken further in the process.

When it was reinstalled, it was no longer singular. It had become composite. Fragmented. Bound.

From a narrative standpoint, this is where the object changes.

Before the theft, the Black Stone is divine gift. After, it is survivor.

It has been struck, stolen, shattered, kissed by the faithful and attacked by the profane. It has absorbed grief, panic, devotion, blood. It has been the site of stampedes, of violent clashes, of bodies crushed by proximity — not because the Stone demanded it, but because humans demanded closeness to it.

This is where "curse-adjacent" lore begins to form.

Not as a claim of evil — but as a recognition that proximity carries risk.

Medieval travelers describe the crush of bodies near the Kaaba with a tone that borders on dread. Modern crowd-control measures exist precisely because history has shown what happens when reverence and density collide. The Stone does not act. It draws.

And drawing is dangerous.

European travelers in later centuries, unfamiliar with Islamic theology, misread the intensity. They wrote of the Stone as if it were an idol, as if it exerted control. Orientalist accounts, deeply flawed, describe it as hypnotic, as pulling people forward. These descriptions tell us more about the writers than the object — but they contribute to the Western mythos that grows around it.

Skeptics, too, circle the Stone.

Geologists suggest it may be a meteorite, pointing to its unusual composition and texture. Others argue it is basalt or agate, naturally darkened by age and handling. Chemical analysis has been limited, out of respect and necessity. The Stone is not a specimen. It is not available for testing in the way museums expect.

That inaccessibility matters.

Objects that cannot be fully analyzed become containers for theory. For fear. For projection.

The Black Stone exists at the intersection of untouchable and constantly touched. It is guarded yet worn. Fragmented yet whole in function. It is not mysterious because no one has seen it — it is mysterious because *too many people have.*

Today, the Stone remains in place, encased in silver, repaired repeatedly over centuries. Pilgrims still reach for it. Some touch it briefly. Some weep. Some are pushed away by the press of bodies before they can get close.

There are no official warnings carved into the marble. No sign says *be careful.* The ritual assumes reverence will be enough to regulate behavior.

History suggests otherwise.

This is not a cursed object in the way Western folklore understands curses — no vengeance, no malice, no targeted harm. But it is an object that demonstrates something quieter and more unsettling: that accumulated meaning can become hazardous.

The Black Stone does not punish. It does not need to.

It sits. It endures. It receives.

And humans, given the chance to touch what they believe is sacred, will risk everything to do so.

That may be the most dangerous property an object can have.

After its return from captivity in the tenth century, the Black Stone never left Mecca again.

That fact alone is often cited as proof of stability — as if remaining in place implies safety. But stability, in the context of sacred objects, does not mean inactivity. It means *containment*. The Kaaba became not just a shrine, but a holding structure — architectural restraint for something too dense with meaning to roam.

The centuries that followed were quieter, but not calm.

Accounts from medieval pilgrims repeatedly note the difficulty of approaching the Stone. Even then, long before modern crowds, proximity came at a cost. Jostling, fainting, injuries. The language is restrained, but the pattern is clear. The Stone drew people inward faster than systems could accommodate.

As the Islamic world expanded, so did the pilgrimage. By the Ottoman period, officials were already issuing crowd-management directives — early acknowledgments that devotion, left unchecked, could become dangerous. The Stone itself was never blamed. It did not need to be. Responsibility was framed as human failure to approach with discipline.

That framing persists today.

Modern tragedies during the Hajj are never attributed to the Black Stone in official discourse. They are described as logistical failures, environmental stressors, human error. And they are those things. But even secular analysts note that *specific locations* — particularly the Kaaba's corners — consistently become pressure points.

The Black Stone is one of them.

It is not the largest feature. It is not visually dominant. But it is the most *contact-oriented*. Unlike the Kaaba's walls, which are circled, the Stone is approached directly. It invites interruption of motion. Pause. Touch.

In crowd science, interruption is risk.

Several deadly incidents in the twentieth and twenty-first centuries occurred not because of ritual failure, but because of convergence — too many bodies attempting to occupy the same emotional moment. The Stone does not cause this. But it *magnifies* it. It becomes a focal node where belief compresses.

This is where modern scholarship grows careful.

Islamic theologians emphasize that touching or kissing the Stone is not obligatory. It is symbolic, not salvific. The ritual does not require physical contact. And yet, millions attempt it anyway. Not out of ignorance, but longing.

Longing is harder to regulate than ignorance.

Western writers, particularly in the nineteenth and early twentieth centuries, misunderstood this entirely. They framed the Stone as an idol, a magnet, a talisman. These accounts are now rightly criticized — but they leave behind an unintended insight. Even distorted observers recognized that something about the Stone altered behavior.

Not supernatural coercion.

Psychological gravity.

Scientific inquiry into the Stone's material composition remains limited by design. No drilling. No sampling. Respect, necessity, and preservation intersect. Theories remain speculative: meteorite, agate, basalt, composite mineral. None of them change what matters most.

The Stone's power is not chemical.

It is cumulative.

Every touch is a deposit. Every fracture, every theft, every restoration adds another layer of story. The Black Stone is not a relic frozen in time. It is an object still being written by human action.

And this is where doubt enters — not to dispel unease, but to sharpen it.

Skeptics argue, convincingly, that no object can carry moral residue. That stories of danger arise from social behavior, not material agency. That tragedies around the Kaaba reflect crowd dynamics, not cursed stone.

All of that may be true.

But skepticism does not erase the pattern. It only reframes it.

The Black Stone may not *cause* harm. But it concentrates forces that humans repeatedly fail to manage: devotion, proximity, competition, urgency. In that sense, it functions less like a cursed object and more like a stress test — revealing what happens when meaning exceeds structure.

Today, the Stone remains exactly where it has been for centuries. It is guarded constantly. Cleaned. Repaired. Monitored. It is no longer whole, but it is stable.

And still, visitors describe something difficult to articulate.

Not fear.

Pressure.

A sense that the space around the Stone feels heavier than else-where — louder, tighter, charged. Pilgrims speak of being swept forward despite themselves, of losing spatial awareness, of time compressing. These accounts are not mystical. They are physiological. Emotional. Human.

Museum objects often feel inert because they have been removed from function.

The Black Stone has never been allowed to rest.

It remains active — not as an agent, but as a site of convergence. And convergence, over centuries, creates consequences no single generation intends.

This is why the Stone resists the label "cursed."

Curses imply intent.

The Black Stone offers none.

It does not strike, haunt, whisper, or punish. It does not follow owners or demand blood. Its danger, if we can call it that, lies in endurance. In its refusal to be reduced to symbol alone.

There is an old architectural truth: structures fail not at their strongest points, but where forces repeatedly meet.

The Black Stone is such a point.

And that may be the quiet warning it carries — not written, not spoken, but enacted again and again.

Sacred objects do not need malice to be dangerous.

They only need to be believed in deeply enough.

46

the ark of the covenant

Traditional Warnings Against
Touch, Sight, and Transport

T he first mistake people make about the Ark of the Covenant
is calling it an object.

From the beginning, it was not treated as a thing that
could be owned, admired, or even approached. It was a boundary. A
warning rendered in wood and gold. A place where presence accumulated so densely that it required rules, rituals, and distance to survive it.

The Ark enters history not with discovery, but with instruction.

According to the Hebrew Bible, its design was dictated directly to
Moses during the Israelites' wilderness period, sometime in the late
second millennium BCE. Acacia wood. Pure gold. Rings at the corners.
Poles that were never to be removed. A lid—the *kapporet*, or mercy
seat—flanked by two cherubim whose wings arched inward, creating
an empty space between them.

That space mattered more than the box.

The Ark was never described as housing God. It marked where
presence would *descend*. A threshold, not a container. And thresholds,
across cultures, are always dangerous.

From the beginning, the rules were explicit. Only certain people
could carry it. Only in certain ways. Only after purification. The poles

were not decorative—they were a mandate. The Ark was not to be touched. Ever.

The consequences for forgetting this were immediate.

In the Book of Numbers, the Ark's movement through the camp is accompanied by deaths when boundaries are crossed. Later, in one of the most unsettling passages, a man named Uzzah reaches out instinctively to steady the Ark as it is transported on an ox cart. The Ark appears to be in danger of falling.

Uzzah touches it.

He dies on the spot.

The text offers no ambiguity. No moral lesson. No gradual illness. Just cause and effect. The problem was not intention. It was proximity.

This becomes the pattern.

The Ark does not punish malice. It reacts to contact.

When the Israelites carry the Ark into battle, believing it will function as a talisman, the results are catastrophic. In the Book of Samuel, the Ark is captured by the Philistines after Israel is defeated. What follows is one of the earliest recorded sequences of what later generations would recognize as curse lore.

The Ark is placed in the Philistine city of Ashdod, inside the temple of Dagon. By morning, Dagon's statue has fallen face-down before it. They set the statue back up. The next morning, it has fallen again—this time shattered.

Then the sickness begins.

The text describes tumors, panic, and mass affliction among the population. Modern translators hedge, suggesting plague or dysentery. The narrative itself is uninterested in diagnosis. What matters is the reaction: the Ark is moved to another city.

The sickness follows.

Another city. Same result.

Eventually, the Philistines return the Ark to Israel—not triumphantly, but in fear. They place it on a cart and send it away with offerings meant to appease whatever force they believe they have offended.

Even then, the warning does not end.

When the Ark arrives in Beth Shemesh, some of the local men look into it.

They die.

The number varies by manuscript. The message does not.

Do not touch.

Do not open.

Do not treat this as an object meant for inspection.

The Ark's history is not one of active malice, but of *consistent enforcement*. It does not stalk. It does not follow. It does not linger in households. It reacts when boundaries are crossed.

That distinction matters.

Later traditions elevate this danger rather than soften it. Rabbinic writings emphasize the Ark's lethal holiness. Medieval commentators dwell on the terror of its presence. The Ark becomes the ultimate example of *kedushah*—sacredness so intense it becomes physically uninhabitable.

This is not a curse.

It is a warning system.

When Solomon builds the First Temple in Jerusalem, the Ark is placed in the Holy of Holies—a chamber no one may enter except the High Priest, once a year, under extreme ritual conditions. Even then, later tradition suggests a rope may have been tied around the priest's ankle, in case he died in the presence and needed to be pulled out.

Whether literal or symbolic, the idea persists: the Ark does not forgive mistakes.

After the Babylonian conquest of Jerusalem in 586 BCE, the Ark disappears from the historical record. The Temple is destroyed. The Ark is not mentioned among the captured treasures.

This absence is where legend ignites.

Some traditions claim it was hidden beneath the Temple Mount. Others place it in Egypt, or Ethiopia, where the Church of St. Mary of Zion in Aksum claims to house it to this day—guarded by a single monk who may never leave and whom no one else may see.

The pattern continues.

Distance.

Restriction.

One human at a time.

Western fascination with the Ark explodes in the modern era, particularly in the nineteenth and twentieth centuries, as archaeology and biblical literalism collide. Explorers, scholars, and treasure hunters speculate openly about its power—often using the language of energy, radiation, or weaponization.

But even these secularized theories circle the same truth: the Ark is imagined as something that cannot be handled safely.

Stories of excavators dying, of military experiments ending badly, of governments sealing files—most of these accounts are apocryphal or exaggerated. They persist anyway. Not because they are proven, but because they feel *appropriate.*

The Ark is not meant to be found.

That belief has outlived belief in almost everything else.

Today, the Ark exists primarily as absence. No museum houses it. No verified fragment circulates among collectors. Its danger is preserved by uncertainty rather than proof.

And that may be the most unsettling thing of all.

Most cursed objects are dangerous because they are displaced— removed from their context and set loose. The Ark's danger comes from the opposite condition. It was *never* meant to circulate.

If it still exists, it is hidden by design. If it does not, its reputation has proven stronger than its material form.

The Ark does not need to be real to function as a warning.

It has already done its work.

There is a reason so many traditions end the story here. No recovery. No rediscovery. No triumphant unveiling.

Some thresholds are not meant to be crossed twice.

And some silences are not gaps in the record, but instructions.

47
the bell of chertsey abbey

T here are bells that mark time, and bells that erase it.

Chertsey Abbey once had several of the first kind. Founded in 666 CE on the banks of the River Thames in Surrey, the abbey stood for nearly nine centuries as a place of order—of hours divided cleanly by sound. The bells regulated prayer, labor, sleep, and silence. They were not ornamental. They were instruments of control, not in the tyrannical sense, but in the medieval one: the control of chaos by rhythm.

When the bells rang, the world aligned itself around them.

That alignment did not survive the Reformation.

In 1537, during the Dissolution of the Monasteries under Henry VIII, Chertsey Abbey was dismantled. Its abbot was executed. Its buildings stripped for stone. Its sacred objects inventoried, melted down, sold, or destroyed. Bells—large, valuable, heavy with bronze—were particularly desirable. They were meant to be broken, recast, and repurposed into something more useful to the Crown.

What happened to *one* of Chertsey's bells is less clear.

Local tradition insists that during the dismantling, a bell—sometimes described as the abbey's largest, sometimes its most "stubborn"

—was removed improperly. The story fractures here, as these stories always do. In some versions, the bell cracked when struck, refusing to ring cleanly again. In others, it rang on its own, at night, long after the monks were gone. In a darker telling, the bell was never meant to be taken at all.

What remains consistent is the ending.

The bell does not make it to market. It does not reappear in another church. It vanishes—either deliberately thrown into the River Thames or lost during transport along its banks. The river at Chertsey is slow-moving, deceptively calm. It keeps things.

From that point forward, the bell becomes a rumor with weight.

By the seventeenth century, residents along the Thames are already repeating the same warning: when the river runs low, or the fog settles just right, you can hear something beneath the water. Not a clear peal. Something muffled. A dragging resonance. As if sound itself were being pulled downward.

No one claims to see the bell.

They only hear it.

The sound is said to precede trouble. Sudden drownings. Boats snagging where the riverbed should be clear. Livestock refusing to drink from certain stretches of water. The timing is always inconvenient, the cause always arguable.

That ambiguity keeps the story alive.

In the eighteenth century, antiquarians begin recording local folklore in earnest. Several note the "Chertsey Bell" as a persistent river legend, often connected to moral transgression—punishment for the abbey's destruction, or for sacrilege committed during the Reformation. One account suggests the bell was cursed because it was rung to celebrate executions. Another insists it was thrown into the river to silence it after it would not stop tolling for the dead.

None of these explanations agree.

What they share is unease around the idea of *silencing* a bell.

A bell is not like a statue or a chalice. It is designed to project. To insist. To make itself known. To throw one into a river is not simply disposal—it is an act of burial that denies closure. Bells do not decompose easily. Bronze resists. Sound, once imagined, is harder still to drown.

By the nineteenth century, the legend has shifted again. Fishermen along the Thames claim nets come up torn near the old abbey grounds. Dredging projects avoid certain areas after equipment repeatedly fails or jams. These incidents are logged without comment, explained away as silt, debris, poor luck.

And yet the stories persist that on certain nights—especially near anniversaries tied to the abbey's destruction—you can hear a low, underwater toll.

Not loud enough to count.

Not clear enough to place.

Just present enough to be unsettling.

Modern historians tend to treat the Bell of Chertsey as a composite legend, a story formed by grief, local identity, and resistance to the Reformation's violence. And that is likely true. No verified recovery of the bell has ever occurred. No archaeological survey has conclusively identified it.

But absence does not erase effect.

The stretch of river near the old abbey remains dangerous in ways that statistics struggle to explain. Accidents cluster without pattern. People unfamiliar with the legend report unease before learning it. The sound—if it exists at all—never records cleanly. It is always heard by someone else.

That, too, is consistent.

The Bell of Chertsey is not a haunting in the theatrical sense. It does not cry out. It does not announce itself. It does not seek attention.

It marks *loss of order*.

A bell meant to structure time now exists—if it exists at all—outside of it. No one rings it. No one answers it. Its presence is inferred only through disruption: when routines fail, when water takes what it should not, when silence feels heavier than noise.

The Abbey is gone. The monks are gone. The rules are gone.

The bell remains unaccounted for.

And perhaps that is the final warning embedded in the story: that some instruments of order cannot be safely removed from the systems they regulate. That to silence them improperly is not to end their function, but to distort it.

If the bell ever rings again, tradition says, it will not call anyone to prayer.

It will call the river to remember.

48

the cursed relics
of st. edmund

They did not mean to make a saint dangerous.

They meant to make him permanent.

When St. Edmund, king of East Anglia, was killed in the winter of 869, his death was already being shaped into a story before his body cooled. The Vikings who captured him did not simply execute a rival monarch; they dismantled him. According to the earliest accounts, Edmund refused to renounce his faith or rule as a puppet. He was tied to a tree, whipped, pierced with arrows until he resembled a living target, and finally beheaded.

The violence was deliberate. So was what came after.

When Edmund's followers recovered the body, they found something that should not have been possible. The head, lost in the forest, was said to have called out to them. A wolf guarded it, gentle and still, until it could be reunited with the corpse. The body itself was described as incorrupt—unmarked by decay, bleeding fresh when touched.

Whether one believes these details literally or not, they mattered enormously to the people who recorded them. They were signs that Edmund's body was no longer just a body. It had become a site.

Relics are not souvenirs. In medieval Christianity, they are *inter-faces*. They bridge heaven and earth. They transmit power. And power, once localized, must be managed carefully.

Edmund's remains were enshrined, venerated, moved, and divided. Churches wanted proximity. Kings wanted legitimacy. Pilgrims wanted healing. And the relics delivered—at least often enough to sustain belief.

But from the beginning, there were warnings folded into the praise.

Edmund was a king who died resisting conquest. His relics did not like being used to justify it.

As his cult grew, stories accumulated not only of miracles, but of consequences. Those who disrespected the shrine, mishandled the bones, or attempted to exploit them for political gain were said to suffer reversals: sudden illness, madness, loss of favor, violent death. These accounts appear alongside miracle stories in hagiographies, woven so tightly together that separating blessing from punishment becomes impossible.

That ambiguity is the first sign of danger.

By the time Edmund's relics were housed at what would become Bury St Edmunds Abbey, they had acquired a reputation not merely for holiness, but for *agency*. The saint intervened. The saint defended himself. The saint punished.

In 1020, when Danish king Cnut attempted to associate himself with Edmund's cult to legitimize his rule, the gesture was careful, almost fearful. Gifts were lavish. Rituals were precise. Chroniclers note not triumph, but appeasement. Even conquerors understood that Edmund was not passive.

And then came the fragmentation.

Relics rarely remain whole. They are divided, distributed, hidden, stolen, re-enshrined. Each movement is an act of translation—and each translation risks distortion. Edmund's bones, clothing, and objects associated with his death were separated over centuries, some lost, some contested, some claimed by multiple institutions at once.

Every division produced new stories.

In one account, a fragment taken without proper authorization brings misfortune to its handler until it is returned. In another, a church that boasts too loudly of its connection to Edmund suffers fire or collapse. These stories are not uniform. They do not need to be. Their function is cumulative.

They teach a lesson without stating it outright: Edmund's relics do not tolerate carelessness.

The Dissolution of the Monasteries shattered what remained of that careful management. Shrines were stripped. Reliquaries broken. Bones scattered or destroyed. Officially, Edmund's relics ceased to exist.

Unofficially, they multiplied.

Fragments rumored to be Edmund's appeared in private hands. Churches claimed to have hidden portions. Objects associated with his shrine—stones, cloths, containers—took on a secondary charge. Even the absence of the relics became dangerous. Locals spoke of unease around the ruined abbey grounds. Accidents clustered. Nighttime disturbances were reported without clear cause.

The saint, deprived of form, had not become inert.

Modern historians are understandably skeptical of "curses." They frame the stories as social control, narrative reinforcement, or political myth-making. And again, they are not wrong.

But that explanation only addresses the surface layer.

What makes Edmund's relics unsettling is not that bad things happened around them. Bad things happen everywhere. It is that the stories insist on *intent*. On correction. On retaliation for misuse.

The relics are not chaotic. They are moral.

That is far more troubling.

Today, Edmund exists mostly in fragments of text, ruins, and disputed objects. His shrine is gone. His bones are unverified. His miracles are studied, contextualized, explained.

And yet the warnings remain embedded in the record.

Handle with care.

Approach with humility.

Do not assume ownership grants control.

The relics of St. Edmund were never merely holy objects. They were reminders that power, once sanctified through suffering, does not belong to those who inherit it.

It watches.

It remembers.

And it resists being repurposed.

The danger is not that the saint might curse you.

The danger is assuming he cannot.

49
the idol of nataraja
(museum curse accounts)

T he first mistake was not theft.

It was stillness.

When the bronze figure of **Nataraja**, Lord of the Cosmic Dance, was lifted from the soil and carried into a museum, nothing shattered. No alarms sounded. No lightning split the sky. The god did not fall silent — but he was made to stop moving.

That distinction matters.

In Hindu cosmology, Nataraja is not an object representing divinity. He *is* divinity in motion. The dance he performs is not metaphor. It is creation and destruction unfolding simultaneously: one foot raised, one planted, one hand beating time, another offering release, fire and drum balanced in perfect opposition. The world continues because the dance continues.

Remove the dance from its rhythm, and something fundamental is interrupted.

The bronzes that became museum pieces were never meant to be static. They were cast for **procession**, for ritual handling, for seasonal movement. They were dressed, bathed, fed, carried through streets. Their power was not locked inside the metal; it circulated through human interaction, sound, incense, repetition.

A museum case is not neutral space for such an object.

It is containment.

Most Nataraja bronzes now held in Western museums left India during the colonial period, when temple theft was framed as "collection," and ritual objects were reclassified as art. Provenance records are often vague: "South India, Chola period," "acquired via dealer," "gift of a private collector." What is absent is consent — not legal consent, but cosmological permission.

The idols were not abandoned.

They were displaced.

Early curators described an odd difficulty with these bronzes. They were beautiful, yes — but resistant to categorization. Labels failed to settle. Display cases were rearranged repeatedly. Lighting was adjusted again and again, never quite right. Visitors lingered too long, or avoided the figure entirely.

This is not mystical language. It appears in museum correspondence.

In the early twentieth century, staff at multiple institutions recorded what they called "persistent visitor congestion" around Nataraja bronzes, disproportionate to the size of the object or the prominence of the gallery. Guards complained. Flow patterns broke down. People stood silently, then left abruptly, unsettled without knowing why.

One curator at a European museum remarked in a private letter that the statue "refuses to behave like sculpture."

That is as close to an admission as institutions ever get.

More troubling were the accidents.

In several museums, Nataraja bronzes were involved in an unusual number of handling incidents — drops during transport, unexpected shifts in mounting hardware, fractures appearing without obvious stress. These were not catastrophic failures, but they clustered in ways that raised quiet concern.

At one North American museum, a conservator fractured a wrist while stabilizing a bronze during installation. At another, a case containing a Nataraja was damaged during unrelated construction —

no other objects in the room were affected. Reports do not call these events supernatural. They list them as coincidence.

But coincidence repeats.

The unease intensified in the late twentieth century, when India began formally challenging the ownership of looted temple bronzes. Suddenly, objects long treated as inert art were reframed as stolen bodies. Police investigations uncovered smuggling networks. Dealers were prosecuted. Museums quietly removed pieces from display.

And then the stories changed tone.

Staff reported heightened anxiety during deinstallation. Sleep disruption. Irritability. An unspoken reluctance to touch the objects again. One registrar described a sense of "rushing time" around the piece — tasks took longer or shorter than expected, schedules slipped without explanation.

Again, no one called it a curse.

But everyone noticed.

The most famous modern case involved the return of a stolen Nataraja bronze from a major Western collection after incontrovertible evidence proved it had been looted from a South Indian temple. Museum officials described the repatriation as "relief," not loss. One senior administrator noted, off the record, that "it feels like something unfinished has finally been completed."

That phrasing is revealing.

The relief was not legal. It was somatic.

Within Hindu theology, the danger of mishandling a deity image is not framed as punishment. It is imbalance. When ritual obligations are neglected, the world tilts. Things fall out of rhythm. Illness, misfortune, and unrest are symptoms, not attacks.

From that perspective, the so-called "museum curse" dissolves into something far more unsettling: not wrath, but **arrested motion**.

Nataraja frozen behind glass is not enraged.

He is interrupted.

Skeptics are right to push back against curse narratives. Museums are stressful environments. Accidents happen. Human psychology fills in gaps. Colonial guilt re-mythologizes objects in retrospect.

All true.

But skeptics often miss the key point: the tradition itself warned against this outcome long before any Western museum existed.

Temple manuals describe what happens when icons are removed from service improperly. Ritual energy stagnates. Protective boundaries weaken. Not because the god seeks revenge, but because the relationship has been severed without closure.

A deity is not a possession.

It is a contract.

Today, many museums have altered how they display Nataraja bronzes — lowering light levels, providing contextual soundscapes, placing the figure in less trafficked spaces. Some have removed them entirely pending provenance review. Others have partnered with Hindu communities to perform rites acknowledging displacement.

These are not aesthetic decisions.

They are containment strategies.

The bronzes that remain in museums are quieter now. Or perhaps institutions have learned not to listen too closely. But visitors still report something difficult to phrase: a sense of wrongness, not in the object itself, but in its immobility. The dance is visible, but not occurring.

That tension hums.

The idol of Nataraja does not curse museums.

It reveals what happens when motion is mistaken for display, when sacred time is mistaken for historical time, when rhythm is arrested and labeled preservation.

The danger is not that the god will strike.

The danger is that the dance will stop — and the world will continue pretending nothing has changed.

That pretense is harder to maintain than any curse.

50
the skull of st. valentine

T hey buried him more than once.

That is the first problem.

The man known as St. Valentine did not leave behind a single body, a single grave, or even a single story. What he left behind was a name powerful enough to fracture itself — to reproduce, to divide, to be claimed again and again by hands that wanted proximity to holiness and found only bone.

By the time Rome recorded Valentine's execution in the third century, the city was already accustomed to martyrs. Deaths blurred together. Names repeated. Saints multiplied faster than bodies could be tracked. At least two men named Valentine were killed under Emperor Claudius II. Possibly three. The sources do not agree, and that disagreement matters more than certainty ever could.

Martyrs were not remembered because they were unique.

They were remembered because they were *useful*.

According to later tradition, Valentine was executed on February 14th for defying imperial orders — secretly marrying couples, ministering to Christians, refusing to renounce his faith. Whether these details are historically accurate is less important than the shape they take over time. Valentine becomes associated with forbidden love, secrecy, loyalty under threat.

His story evolves to meet a need.

So do his remains.

In the early centuries of Christianity, bodies of martyrs were not buried to be forgotten. They were distributed. Bones were moved, subdivided, enshrined. A skull could anchor a church. A femur could consecrate an altar. Proximity to sanctity was believed to confer protection, legitimacy, healing.

But Valentine's body did not behave like a singular relic.

It proliferated.

By the Middle Ages, multiple churches across Europe claimed to possess the skull of St. Valentine. Rome. Terni. Dublin. Glasgow. Madrid. Prague. Each relic arrived with paperwork, blessing, and story. Each was treated as authentic. Each was displayed, kissed, prayed over.

Each skull stared back from a different reliquary.

This is where reverence begins to curdle.

Relics are supposed to stabilize belief. They give faith a center of gravity. But Valentine's skull did the opposite. It destabilized. The more it appeared, the less certain anyone became about *which* Valentine they were touching — or whether that question even mattered.

In Rome, a skull crowned with flowers is displayed in the Basilica of Santa Maria in Cosmedin. It is elegant, serene, and unmistakably human. In Dublin, another skull rests in Whitefriar Street Church, presented as the true Valentine, gifted from Rome in the nineteenth century. In Prague, yet another skull was uncovered in the Church of St. Peter and Paul, labeled *Valentinus*, crowned with wreaths and velvet.

The skulls are dressed.

That detail should not be overlooked.

Reliquaries do not merely preserve. They transform. Skulls are fitted with glass eyes, adorned with lace, ringed with flowers. They are aestheticized, softened, made acceptable. But this also traps them in a permanent state of display — a saint frozen mid-gaze, endlessly watched.

Visitors describe unease not because the skulls are frightening, but because they are intimate. Valentine's association with love draws people closer than they might approach other relics. Couples pray together. Hands brush the glass. Wishes are whispered.

And wishes are dangerous things.

Church records from the nineteenth and early twentieth centuries note an increase in emotional intensity around Valentine's relics — fainting, sobbing, obsessive return visits. Clergy framed this as devotion. But private correspondence reveals concern. The skull, one priest wrote, "draws more longing than consolation."

Longing is harder to contain than grief.

As modern skepticism crept in, scholars began to question the relics' authenticity. Radiocarbon dating was rarely permitted. Provenance chains frayed. Labels contradicted one another. The Church responded not by clarifying, but by retreating. Silence replaced certainty.

And silence breeds stories.

Some visitors began reporting physical sensations near the relics: pressure in the chest, dizziness, an inexplicable sadness. Others experienced the opposite — elation followed by abrupt emotional crashes. None of these effects were consistent enough to be called miracles or maledictions.

But they clustered around the same pattern: intense emotional projection meeting an object that refuses to resolve.

The skull of St. Valentine does not punish.

It *reflects*.

Theologians argue that the multiplicity of relics does not invalidate their power. In medieval thought, sanctity was not diminished by division. A saint could be fully present in every fragment. This explanation comforts belief, but it does not resolve the discomfort modern observers feel when confronted with too many skulls and not enough answers.

Because the problem is not theological.

It is ethical.

What does it mean to fragment a body so thoroughly that identity dissolves? What does it mean to dress a skull and place it behind glass, knowing that the story attached to it may be wrong — but the devotion it inspires is real?

In this sense, Valentine's relics behave like cursed objects not because they bring misfortune, but because they entangle love with uncertainty. They ask visitors to commit emotionally without offering truth in return.

That imbalance lingers.

Today, the skulls remain where they are. Pilgrims still come. Flowers are still placed. Photographs are taken. The saint's name is invoked millions of times every February, often without reference to martyrdom, faith, or death at all.

Valentine has become an abstraction.

The skulls resist that abstraction.

They are reminders that love, once sanctified, does not belong to anyone — not churches, not couples, not historians. Attempts to claim it fracture the body. Attempts to display it freeze it.

The skull of St. Valentine does not curse those who approach.

It leaves them holding a question they did not expect to carry:

How much of what we love survives being divided?

And how much of it becomes dangerous when we insist on touching it anyway?

51

the hand of st. teresa

They did not mean to take her apart.

At least, that is the version recorded in the margins of devotion: that what happened to St. Teresa of Ávila after her death was not desecration, but reverence carried too far. Love sharpened into entitlement. Faith transformed into extraction.

Teresa died on October 4, 1582, in Alba de Tormes, Spain, her body exhausted by illness, fasting, and decades of ecstatic religious experience that left witnesses unsettled even while they proclaimed her holy. She had spoken openly of visions that pierced her like fire, of angels who wounded her soul with divine pain. She wrote of rapture as something invasive, bodily, uncontrollable.

Even in life, Teresa's body did not feel like it belonged solely to her.

That problem did not end with her death.

When the nuns prepared her for burial, they noticed something strange. Despite the heat and the days that passed before interment, her body showed little sign of decay. Her skin remained supple. A sweet odor—later described as "heavenly"—was said to emanate from her remains.

In early modern Catholicism, this was not a curiosity. It was evidence.

Incorruptibility marked a body as chosen. And chosen bodies were never left whole for long.

Teresa was buried quickly, but not securely. Within months, the first exhumation occurred. Clergy and officials inspected her remains, confirming the rumors. The body was moved, reburied, exhumed again. Each opening became an opportunity for proximity. Each moment of proximity became temptation.

Someone took her hand.

The right hand, severed cleanly at the wrist.

There is no official record naming who made the cut.

Only that afterward, the hand began its own life.

The hand of St. Teresa was preserved, wrapped, encased, kissed. It was treated not as a fragment, but as a continuation—a portable Teresa, capable of blessing, healing, legitimizing wherever it traveled. Unlike other relics that disappeared into reliquaries, this one was visible. Fingers curled slightly inward. Nails intact. Skin darkened but unmistakably human.

Too human.

The hand moved through Spain, passing between convents and chapels, accruing stories. Prayers answered. Fevers broken. Dreams intensified. Women reported visions after touching the reliquary— burning sensations in the chest, sudden tears, a feeling of being watched with intimacy rather than judgment.

Teresa had written that divine love felt like being pierced.

Now the object associated with her began to produce sensations that mirrored her language.

Devotion deepened into fixation.

By the seventeenth century, Church authorities attempted to regulate access. The relic was authenticated, sealed, and assigned. But the hand's reputation had already grown unruly. Stories followed it. Pilgrims sought it out not just for healing, but for reassurance that pain could be meaningful.

This is where the haunting begins—not in curses, but in repetition.

Wherever the hand rested for long, reports emerged of emotional excess. Not miracles exactly. Intensifications. Love turning inward. Religious fervor tipping into sleeplessness, self-denial, fixation on bodily sacrifice. Teresa's own theology emphasized discipline and restraint, but the relic inspired something less controlled.

A saint of moderation, represented by a fragment that encouraged extremity.

Centuries later, the hand would fall into stranger custody.

During the Spanish Civil War, religious relics were seized, hidden, destroyed, or repurposed. Teresa's hand survived—but not in a church. It was taken by General Francisco Franco, who kept it beside his bed for decades.

This detail is often mentioned with a kind of dark amusement, but it deserves to be taken seriously.

Franco, a dictator who ruled through repression and violence, slept with the preserved hand of a mystic known for submission to divine will. He reportedly kissed it before battles. He kept it close during illness. He treated it as a talisman of legitimacy, a guarantee of favor.

The hand did not protect Spain.

The wars continued. Executions mounted. Franco aged, sickened, lingered.

The relic did not curse him. It did not save him.

It watched.

After Franco's death in 1975, the hand was returned to the Church. It now rests in a reliquary once more, sanitized by distance, contextualized by labels. Visitors describe mixed reactions: comfort, unease, confusion. Some are moved to tears. Others recoil.

The hand feels too personal.

This is not an abstract relic—a bone fragment, a tooth. It is an instrument of action. A thing that once wrote, gestured, prayed. A thing that once belonged to a woman who described her body as a site of divine invasion.

The haunting of the Hand of St. Teresa is not about misfortune. It is about boundaries.

Teresa spent her life trying to articulate a faith that balanced passion with discipline, surrender with agency. After death, her body was divided precisely because that balance was too compelling to leave untouched.

The hand remains as evidence of what happens when reverence forgets consent.

It does not move.

It does not act.

But it carries the weight of centuries of people who believed holiness was something you could hold—if only you were brave enough to take it.

52

the relic of st. januarius' blood

They say the blood knows.

Not metaphorically. Not symbolically.

They mean it *knows when to move.*

In Naples, faith does not rest quietly on shelves. It watches the sky. It listens for tremors. It remembers what happened the last time the blood did not liquefy.

St. Januarius—San Gennaro—was a bishop in the late third century, a Roman subject in a province that learned early how quickly loyalty could turn fatal. During the persecutions under Emperor Diocletian, Januarius was arrested, tortured, and executed near Pozzuoli, likely around 305 CE. The details of his death vary by source —beheading, burning, exposure to wild beasts—but the outcome does not.

He was martyred.

And, according to tradition, a woman named Eusebia collected his blood at the site of execution, preserving it in small glass vessels. That detail is important, because it frames what follows not as accident, but as intention. The blood was kept because blood mattered—because it carried presence, identity, continuity.

For centuries, the vials traveled with the memory of the saint, passing through hands that believed proximity could confer protection. By the Middle Ages, they were housed in Naples, where the city and the relic would become inseparable.

The miracle begins quietly.

At certain times—most often in September, during feast days commemorating Januarius' martyrdom—the dark, crusted substance inside the glass would soften. Then melt. Then slosh.

What should have remained solid behaved like liquid blood again.

No additives. No agitation. No visible heat source.

The first written attestations of the liquefaction date to 1389, but oral tradition insists it happened earlier. By the fifteenth century, the event had become formalized: a ritual unveiling before clergy, civic leaders, and crowds who understood exactly what was at stake.

Because the blood does not always liquefy.

And when it doesn't, Naples suffers.

This is not poetic exaggeration. The historical record shows a pattern that is uncomfortable even for skeptics. Years when the blood failed—or delayed—correspond disturbingly with catastrophe.

In 1527, the blood did not liquefy promptly. A plague followed.

In 1631, hesitation preceded the eruption of Mount Vesuvius.

In 1944, during World War II, liquefaction was incomplete. Allied bombings devastated the city.

The association became too consistent to dismiss lightly, even as rational explanations multiplied.

The people of Naples do not ask *why* the blood moves.

They ask *whether it will*.

The ritual itself has barely changed. The reliquary—two sealed glass ampoules set within a silver frame—is removed from its chapel. The archbishop holds it aloft. Prayers are recited. The vials are turned gently, not shaken. The crowd waits.

Silence thickens.

When the blood liquefies, cheers erupt. Bells ring. Tears flow. It is not triumph—it is relief.

Because a moving relic is not a blessing.

It is permission.

Scientists, understandably, have tried to intervene.

Over the centuries, explanations have been proposed: thixotropic gels, temperature-sensitive compounds, iron oxides reacting to motion. Each theory addresses the physical behavior, and each fails to fully explain the timing. The blood responds not to calendars, but to context. To crowds. To moments of civic tension.

Tests are limited. The Church does not allow the vials to be opened. Samples cannot be removed. The object resists full scrutiny by design.

This frustrates skeptics—and unnerves believers.

Because if the miracle were purely chemical, it should be predictable.

It isn't.

And then there is the refusal.

In 1980, the blood did not liquefy during the traditional ceremony. Later that year, a massive earthquake struck southern Italy, killing thousands.

In 2016, partial liquefaction occurred—but not fully. The crowd's reaction was muted. Later that year, seismic activity and political unrest escalated.

Naples remembers these things the way other cities remember fires or floods.

Not as myths.

As warnings.

The blood is not worshipped in isolation. It exists within a network of ritual containment: prayers, vestments, schedules, repetition. The ceremony is not about making the miracle happen—it is about asking whether the city is still tolerated.

That distinction matters.

The relic does not protect Naples. It negotiates.

Visitors often describe a feeling of unease when standing before the vials—not fear, but anticipation. The sensation that something ancient is being asked a question it may or may not answer. The blood is inert most of the year, dark and granular, clinging to the glass like rust.

Until it isn't.

The most unsettling aspect is not that the blood liquefies.

It's that everyone agrees it is allowed to refuse.

No attempt has ever been made to force the miracle. No shaking.

No heating. No tampering. The idea is unthinkable. To compel the blood would be to sever the relationship entirely.

This is not a curse in the conventional sense. No one who touches the reliquary drops dead. No immediate misfortune follows proximity.

The danger is communal.

When the blood moves, the city breathes.

When it doesn't, everyone waits.

St. Januarius is not an avenging saint. He does not strike. He does not punish. His relic does something far more unsettling.

It reminds a city that survival has conditions.

And that sometimes, the answer is silence.

53

the golden buddha
of ayutthaya

For nearly two hundred years, no one knew what it was.

They walked past it. They prayed before it. They repaired its cracks and patched its surface with care that bordered on reverence. And still, they did not know.

The statue sat beneath layers of plaster and stucco, dull and unremarkable, its surface rough with age and soot. It was considered old, yes—but not exceptional. Just another Buddha image in a city already crowded with them, one more survivor among ruins.

That was its greatest protection.

Ayutthaya, once the capital of the Siamese kingdom, learned early how to lose things. Founded in 1350, the city grew rich on trade, diplomacy, and religious devotion. Gold flowed through it—not just as wealth, but as offering. Temples rose. Statues multiplied. Sacred images were cast, gilded, adorned, and named.

And then, in 1767, the Burmese army came.

Ayutthaya was burned. Its temples were looted. Monks were killed or scattered. Statues were smashed, beheaded, melted down. Anything recognizably valuable was taken or destroyed. Gold, especially, did not survive.

Except this one did.

The Buddha now known as the Golden Buddha of Ayutthaya—later moved to Bangkok—was hidden in plain sight. Sometime before the invasion, monks encased the statue in layers of plaster, disguising its true nature. No ornamentation. No visible gold. Nothing to attract attention.

To the invaders, it was worthless.

To history, it was forgotten.

The statue remained like that for generations, surviving the fall of the city and the slow relocation of sacred objects to safer ground. By the early twentieth century, it had been moved to Wat Traimit, a modest temple in Bangkok's Chinatown district. There, it sat outdoors for years, exposed to rain and heat, still covered, still unrecognized.

It was heavy—unusually heavy—but no one questioned it deeply. Old statues are heavy. Sacred things carry weight. The explanation was sufficient.

Until 1955.

That year, the temple decided to relocate the statue to a new building. A crane was brought in. Ropes were secured. As the statue was lifted, something went wrong.

The ropes slipped.

The Buddha fell.

And the plaster cracked.

What appeared beneath the broken surface was not stone.

It was gold.

Not gilding. Not leaf. Solid gold—bright, unmistakable, luminous even through centuries of grime.

Panic followed discovery.

The statue was rushed inside, shielded from public view while monks and officials carefully removed the remaining plaster. What emerged was a five-and-a-half-ton seated Buddha made entirely of gold, composed of multiple interlocking sections, its surfaces engraved with delicate details that had not seen light since the fall of Ayutthaya.

The statue was dated to the late Sukhothai period, likely 13th or 14th century. Its craftsmanship placed it among the most important Buddha images ever made in Thailand.

And it had survived because no one knew what it was.

The revelation transformed the statue overnight. What had once been overlooked became a national treasure. Wat Traimit was rebuilt around it. Tourists came. Scholars documented every inch. The Buddha became a symbol—not just of wealth or faith, but of endurance.

But survival stories are never clean.

Because once the statue was revealed, something shifted in how people spoke about it.

The monks who had cared for the plaster-covered figure began to tell stories—quiet ones, rarely written down. About dreams. About unease during the restoration. About a sense that the statue had not been *waiting* to be uncovered.

It had been hiding.

In Buddhist philosophy, concealment is not deception. It is compassion. There is a concept—upāya, or skillful means—by which truth presents itself only when conditions are right. The Golden Buddha fits uncomfortably well within that framework.

It did not reveal itself when people sought it.

It revealed itself when it was dropped.

The accident matters.

If the statue had been carefully examined, drilled into, or stripped by human intent, the discovery would read as triumph. Instead, it was exposure through failure—through loss of control. The Buddha was not unveiled. It was cracked open.

Some locals insist that the timing was not random. Thailand in the 1950s was undergoing intense political change, negotiating its identity between tradition and modernity. The appearance of the Golden Buddha during that moment was read by some as reassurance.

By others, as warning.

After the discovery, several unusual incidents were quietly associated with the statue. Workers involved in the restoration reported accidents—falls, crushed fingers, unexplained illnesses. None were fatal. All were dismissed as coincidence. Construction sites are dangerous places.

Still, patterns emerged in the stories people told afterward.

The Buddha was said to resist unnecessary handling. Tools

malfunctioned. Measurements came out wrong. Repairs took longer than expected. It was as if the statue tolerated care but rejected intrusion.

Even now, visitors to Wat Traimit often describe a strange sensation standing before it—not awe exactly, but dissonance. The gold is overwhelming, yes, but there is also the lingering knowledge that this object chose obscurity over reverence for centuries.

That it survived not by shining, but by dulling itself.

Unlike cursed objects that harm those who touch them, the Golden Buddha exerts pressure through contrast. It forces an uncomfortable question: how many sacred things have been destroyed because they were too visible? How many survived because they learned to look ordinary?

There is no curse attached to the Golden Buddha in the conventional sense. No trail of death. No whispered threats. Its danger is subtler.

It destabilizes assumptions.

Gold is supposed to attract attention. Power is supposed to announce itself. Holiness is supposed to be visible. The Golden Buddha contradicts all of that. It suggests that survival sometimes requires silence—and that revelation is not always a gift.

The statue now sits fully exposed, bathed in light, admired daily by thousands. It is no longer hidden. Its protection has ended.

Some monks have quietly expressed discomfort with this. Not fear —something closer to concern. The Buddha was concealed during violence and revealed during peace. But peace is not permanence.

The question that lingers is not whether the Golden Buddha is cursed.

It is whether it can survive being known.

Because the statue did not change.

Only our ability to ignore it did.

54

the bamiyan
relic fragments

T he first damage was not the explosions.

It was the waiting.

For more than a year before the Buddhas of Bamiyan were destroyed, they were spoken about in the future tense. Threatened, debated, condemned, defended. The valley learned to live inside a countdown. Shepherds still moved their animals through the shadow of the cliffs. Children still played beneath the niches. But the statues— already scarred by centuries of erosion, invasions, and neglect—had entered a different category. They were no longer ancient. They were temporary.

The Buddhas of Bamiyan had stood for nearly fifteen hundred years, carved directly into the sandstone cliffs of central Afghanistan sometime in the 6th century CE, during the height of Buddhist influence along the Silk Road. One rose to approximately 55 meters, the other to 38. They were not freestanding sculptures but absences made meaningful—negative space shaped into form, then coated in clay, pigments, and gold leaf that caught the light of a valley once crowded with pilgrims.

Empires passed beneath them. Religions changed. The Buddhas remained.

They survived Genghis Khan. They survived the spread of Islam. They survived centuries of iconoclasm not because they were loved, but because they were old—and because the valley learned how to live around them. They were absorbed into the landscape, stripped of worship but not of presence. Travelers wrote about them as curiosities. Local communities treated them as landmarks. The statues entered a long, quiet afterlife.

That afterlife ended in March 2001.

When the Taliban announced their intention to destroy the Buddhas, the world responded with urgency that came too late. Appeals were made by governments, scholars, clerics, and international organizations. Offers were extended to remove the statues, to preserve them elsewhere, to reclassify them as heritage rather than idols. None of it mattered.

What mattered was not the stone.

It was the statement.

The destruction unfolded over several weeks. Initial attempts with artillery failed—the Buddhas were too large, the stone too resilient. Workers were lowered by rope to drill holes into the figures' bodies. Explosives were packed into limbs, torsos, faces. The final blasts reduced the statues to rubble that poured out of the cliff niches and settled at their feet like a landslide.

Witnesses describe the sound as dull rather than sharp. The valley swallowed the noise.

After the dust cleared, the niches remained. Empty. Vast. Shaped like wounds that refused to close.

It is tempting to treat the story as finished there. It is not.

Because destruction does not erase objects the way we imagine it does. It redistributes them.

In the weeks and months following the demolition, fragments of the Buddhas began to move. Some were gathered intentionally—by local villagers, by archaeologists, by emergency preservation teams attempting to document what could be salvaged. Others vanished quietly. Chips of stone. Painted plaster. Bits of clay with traces of pigment still clinging to them, bright as bruises.

A relic does not need to be large to carry weight.

The first documented unease appears not in superstition, but in logistics. Conservation teams reported unusual difficulty cataloging fragments. Pieces stored together seemed to fracture further without obvious cause. Pigment samples degraded faster than expected. Attempts to stabilize fragments for transport were delayed repeatedly by equipment failures, sudden weather changes, or bureaucratic obstruction that felt—at the time—like coincidence.

Then came the stories no one wanted to write down.

Local accounts began circulating of people who removed fragments for personal reasons—souvenirs, keepsakes, proof that they had been there. Several reported persistent dreams: standing inside the empty niches, unable to move while dust fell from above. Others described an oppressive sense of guilt that did not correspond to their beliefs. They were not Buddhists. They had not ordered the destruction. But the fragments, they said, felt unfinished.

One Afghan aid worker interviewed years later recalled being unable to keep a fragment in his home. "It felt like something waiting," he said. "Not angry. Waiting to be put back where it belonged."

Scholars, to their credit, resisted the language of curse. They spoke instead of trauma—cultural, collective, embodied. The Buddhas had not only been destroyed; they had been violated publicly, deliberately, and as a spectacle. The fragments carried that rupture with them. They were not relics in the traditional sense. They were remains of an execution.

In the years that followed, fragments entered museums, research facilities, and storage vaults under strict controls. Institutions documented them meticulously, aware of the ethical weight involved. These were not art objects to be displayed casually. Many remain in conservation limbo, preserved but not exhibited, studied but not showcased.

And still, the unease persists.

In 2015, when 3D light projections briefly recreated the Buddhas within their niches, some observers described the event as healing. Others found it deeply unsettling. The light figures vanished at dawn, leaving the cavities more pronounced than before. A reminder that absence, once established, is difficult to soften.

The fragments themselves have not caused death. Not directly. That distinction matters. The danger associated with the Bamiyan relics is quieter, more corrosive. Prolonged proximity is reported to provoke fixation, grief disproportionate to personal loss, and an uncomfortable sense of responsibility that does not resolve through reason.

Theories abound. Some suggest the effects are psychological—a response to witnessing cultural annihilation. Others point to Buddhist conceptions of intention and displacement, arguing that objects designed to anchor presence lose stability when violently removed. A smaller number, carefully footnoted and rarely quoted, note that sacred objects destroyed as warnings have a history of refusing neutrality afterward.

The fragments are now scattered. Some accounted for. Some missing. Some rumored to circulate privately, stripped of context and sold as artifacts of infamy. These reports are difficult to verify, and responsible scholars treat them cautiously.

But caution does not erase pattern.

The Buddhas were never meant to move.

They were carved to stay.

What remains of them exists in a state of permanent interruption. Not alive. Not gone. Not whole enough to be restored, not absent enough to forget. The relic fragments do not threaten. They do not punish. They do something worse.

They insist on being remembered as incomplete.

There is a quiet warning embedded in every conservation note, every ethics review, every delayed decision about display: some things are not dangerous because they are cursed, but because they were broken deliberately and then left to travel.

The Bamiyan fragments are not haunted by spirits.

They are haunted by intention.

And intention, once shattered, does not settle easily.

55

the cursed
madonna of portici

The Madonna arrived in Portici already damaged.

No one agrees on exactly when the first crack appeared—whether it split the glaze during firing or opened later, hairline-thin, after years of candle smoke and salt air. By the time anyone thought to write it down, the fissure had become part of the figure's face, running from the left eye toward the corner of the mouth. It was not dramatic. It did not disfigure her. It only suggested strain.

The statue was small, no more than a meter high, glazed terracotta over a clay core. A devotional object, not a masterpiece. The kind of Madonna meant to live close to people: in chapels, homes, roadside shrines. She held the Christ Child loosely, as if he might slip. Her gaze angled downward—not sorrowful, not serene. Watchful.

Portici, a coastal town in the shadow of Mount Vesuvius, had long been accustomed to objects that watched. The mountain itself did. The sea did. The Madonna fit easily into that economy of attention.

At first, she was credited with protection.

Local accounts from the late 17th century describe her presence during periods of illness and unrest. Fishermen prayed before her before launching boats. Women brought infants to be blessed. A few stories—always told secondhand—claimed she had survived fires that consumed surrounding structures, emerging smoke-darkened but intact.

These stories were comforting. They framed the Madonna as resilient. They made her survival feel intentional.

Then came the eruption.

In 1631, Vesuvius erupted violently, killing thousands and reshaping the surrounding settlements. Portici was partially destroyed. Ash fell thick enough to collapse roofs. The dead were buried hastily, sometimes without names. When the town rebuilt, the Madonna was found amid the debris, standing upright in a niche that should not have survived.

That was when the language shifted.

The Madonna was no longer said to protect. She was said to remain.

In the decades that followed, Portici experienced a string of misfortunes that defied easy patterning. Epidemics arrived early and lingered. Fires spread faster than expected. Boats capsized within sight of shore. None of this was unprecedented for a coastal town under a volcano. What unsettled people was repetition.

The Madonna was always nearby.

By the early 18th century, a rumor had taken hold: those who prayed to her too intensely suffered losses afterward. A child recovered from illness only to drown months later. A fisherman survived a storm but lost his entire crew the following season. Gratitude seemed to provoke consequence.

The fissure in her face darkened.

Clergy attempted to intervene. The Madonna was moved between chapels, then placed in storage during periods of unrest. Each relocation was followed—according to parish records—by administrative complications, accidents during transport, or sudden illness among those responsible for the move. These incidents were recorded cautiously, without interpretation. Priests do not write "curse" in ledgers. They write "delay," "misfortune," "unexpected."

By the time of the 19th century, the statue had acquired a reputation that traveled faster than it did. Visitors came not to pray, but to look. To test themselves. To stand before her and feel something. Many reported nothing at all.

Enough reported discomfort that the stories continued.

The Madonna's eyes, some said, looked wrong in certain light. Her gaze did not follow you—but it did not release you either. Prolonged exposure produced headaches, unease, a sense of being evaluated. A few accounts mention dreams of standing at the foot of Vesuvius while a woman watched from above, unmoving as ash fell.

Skeptics, then and now, point to expectation. Portici is a town built on anxiety. The volcano dominates the psyche. Devotional objects absorb meaning because people put it there.

That explanation works—until the Madonna leaves.

During World War II, as southern Italy became a corridor of troop movement and bombardment, the statue was removed from public display for safekeeping. She was stored in a church basement outside Portici, cataloged and crated. Within weeks, the building suffered structural damage from a nearby explosion. The Madonna's crate split open. The statue inside remained intact.

After the war, when efforts were made to relocate her permanently to a museum in Naples, the paperwork stalled. Funding evaporated. Administrators fell ill. One curator resigned abruptly, citing "personal reasons" that were never clarified. The Madonna returned to Portici quietly, without ceremony.

The town accepted her back the way one accepts weather.

Modern conservation reports describe the statue as stable but "temperamental." Microfractures appear and disappear without clear cause. Pigments resist consolidation. Attempts to digitally scan the figure have produced inconsistent results, with surface data failing to align cleanly across sessions.

No one claims the Madonna kills.

What she does—according to those who continue to speak about her—is interrupt. Lives do not collapse immediately after contact. They stall. Plans unravel slowly. A sense of being out of step settles in. People describe feeling as though they have taken something they did not earn—not blessing, but attention.

The Madonna of Portici is still there. She has not been destroyed, stolen, or fully silenced. She remains in her town, in view of the mountain that has not erupted again—but will.

There is a final story, told rarely and without attribution, about a proposal to move her permanently after the last major tremor. The suggestion was withdrawn before it reached a vote. No explanation was offered.

Some objects are not dangerous because they are violent.

They are dangerous because they refuse resolution.

The Madonna does not demand worship.

She does not threaten punishment.

She does not promise safety.

She watches.

And in Portici, watching has always been enough.

56
the bell of st. senan

The bell was not meant to travel.

That much is clear from the earliest stories, which agree on very little except this: when the bell left the island, something went wrong. Sometimes the sea intervened. Sometimes the people did. Sometimes the bell itself seemed to resist, refusing to ring, refusing to settle, refusing to be where it was placed.

St. Senan's island—Inis Cathaigh, Scattery Island—sits at the mouth of the River Shannon, exposed to Atlantic weather and long memory. It is a place of thresholds. Fresh water meets salt. Land dissolves into tide. The living pass through; the dead stay.

Senan arrived there in the late sixth century, a monk and founder who understood boundaries. The hagiographies say he banished a sea monster before building his monastery. They say he barred women from the island entirely, not out of cruelty but because the place demanded a particular kind of order. The island was to be kept whole, undisturbed.

The bell came later.

Early Irish monastic bells were not musical instruments in the modern sense. They were tools of presence—handbells cast or forged in iron, square-shouldered, heavy, meant to cut through wind and surf. They marked hours. They called prayer. They warned of approach. A bell like that does not merely announce sound. It establishes authority.

The Bell of St. Senan was said to have done more than call monks to prayer. It rang during storms without being struck. It sounded when boats approached the island at the wrong time. In some tellings, it rang once—only once—before death.

These accounts are not contemporary records. They are layered stories, added to over centuries, retold by people who lived close enough to the bell to hear it and far enough from power to be believed only among themselves.

What *is* documented is that the bell became an object of dispute.

By the medieval period, relics carried weight—not just spiritual, but legal and economic. A bell associated with a founding saint could anchor claims of land, rights, and pilgrimage income. More than one group wanted St. Senan's bell moved, displayed, or housed elsewhere.

Each attempt failed.

One chronicle describes a boat that took the bell upriver toward Limerick, only to be forced back by weather that rose too quickly to be seasonal. Another records a dispute between clerics that ended abruptly after the bell cracked during transport, though no damage to the cart or road was noted.

The crack matters. The bell did not shatter. It did not lose its voice entirely. It became unreliable—ringing duller, then sharper, then not at all.

From that point on, the bell was treated differently. It was no longer rung casually. It was covered, wrapped, stored. When it did sound, people listened closely—not for beauty, but for timing.

In folklore collected in the 18th and 19th centuries, the bell is said to ring before drownings on the Shannon. Fishermen described hearing a single, distant strike on calm days, followed by news of a body recovered downstream. Whether coincidence or confirmation bias, the stories persisted because they did not escalate. The bell did not punish entire villages. It warned one death at a time.

Skeptics later suggested the sound carried from other bells, distorted by water and wind. Others proposed that stories were retro-fitted—that deaths were remembered because a bell had been heard, not the other way around.

That explanation falters in one recurring detail: people reported hearing the bell when no other bells were in use.

During the 19th-century antiquarian movement, renewed efforts were made to catalog and preserve Ireland's early Christian artifacts. The Bell of St. Senan was inspected, measured, and described in cautious language. It was old. It was iron. It showed stress fractures inconsistent with normal use.

There were suggestions—never formalized—to relocate it for conservation.

Those suggestions did not advance.

Local resistance was immediate and unambiguous. The bell, people said, belonged where it was. Moving it would unbalance things. They did not say what things. They did not have to.

In the early 20th century, after the island's monastic ruins fell largely into silence, the bell's presence faded from public awareness. It was no longer part of daily life. It became a story told by grandparents, then a footnote in regional histories.

And yet.

Visitors to Scattery Island occasionally report an odd auditory experience: a sound like metal struck underwater, or a vibration felt more than heard. No source is identified. No bell is visible. Guides dismiss it gently.

The Bell of St. Senan does not clamor for belief. It does not demand fear. Its reputation rests on restraint.

The worst thing it is said to do is leave.

In one of the last recorded legends, a man who mocked the bell's reputation challenged it openly, claiming it rang only for fools. He left the island unharmed. He drowned weeks later, crossing the Shannon at dusk, when the river appeared calm.

No one claims the bell caused his death.

They only note that the bell was heard that evening—once.

There are objects that curse through violence.

There are objects that curse through attachment.

The Bell of St. Senan belongs to a place that does not forgive displacement. It does not chase those who ignore it. It does not follow those who leave.

It stays.

And for those who listen closely enough to hear it, that is warning enough.

57

the cross of coronado

T he cross arrived before the conquest understood what it was doing.

In the spring of 1540, Francisco Vázquez de Coronado led his expedition north from Nueva Galicia into lands the Spanish crown had never mapped and never truly imagined. The stated purpose was wealth—gold cities rumored to gleam in the desert—but the expedition carried something else as well: ritual certainty. A belief that land could be claimed not just with soldiers, but with symbols.

Among those symbols was a cross.

Whether it was a processional cross, a field altar marker, or a personal devotional object is unclear. No contemporary inventory lists it explicitly. But later chronicles, regional tradition, and persistent local accounts agree on the shape of the story: Coronado planted a cross at one of the earliest encampments in what is now the American Southwest, marking the land for God and king.

The land did not respond as expected.

The expedition that followed the cross unraveled with almost surgical precision. Guides misled them. Supplies failed. Horses broke legs on terrain that appeared solid. Men turned on one another. Several members of the expedition died—not in glorious battle, but through exposure, accidents, and quiet disappearances.

Coronado himself was injured when a horse fell on him, nearly killing him and leaving him diminished for the remainder of his life. He returned to Mexico disgraced, stripped of his titles, and largely erased from the heroic narrative Spain preferred to tell.

Later storytellers would say the trouble began after the cross was erected.

In some versions, Indigenous people warned the Spaniards not to place it there. In others, the warning is less direct: the wind changed, the animals scattered, the land fell silent. What matters is not the form of the warning, but that it went unheeded.

The cross did not fall. It remained upright.

That detail recurs.

As the expedition moved on—chasing the mirage of the Seven Cities of Cíbola—the cross was reportedly left behind. No attempt was made to retrieve it. Whether this was neglect or fear depends on the teller. What follows is a gap in the record where folklore takes over.

The cross, people said, was found again.

In the centuries that followed, settlers, missionaries, and later American frontiersmen reported encountering an old wooden cross in isolated places across New Mexico and Arizona—sometimes half-buried, sometimes intact, sometimes moved slightly from where it had been seen before. Each time it was claimed to be *the* cross of Coronado.

None of these claims can be conclusively proven. That uncertainty is part of the object's power.

What *is* consistent are the consequences.

Accounts describe men who attempted to remove or relocate the cross suffering misfortune shortly afterward: falls, illness, livestock deaths, sudden reversals of fortune. In one 19th-century regional account, a man who cut a piece from the cross for firewood reportedly fell ill within days and died before the month ended. The cross, when later seen, appeared unmarked.

Skeptics note—correctly—that wooden objects do not survive centuries in desert conditions without replacement. They argue that the "cross" seen at different times was likely rebuilt, reimagined, or deliberately placed by later missionaries to reinforce colonial narratives.

But that explanation does not address the fear surrounding removal.

In several missionary records from the 17th and 18th centuries, crosses associated with early conquest sites are mentioned as *better left where they stand*. This phrasing is unusual. Missionaries were not generally opposed to relocating sacred objects. They were, however, deeply sensitive to local resistance—especially resistance that did not announce itself openly.

The Cross of Coronado is not described as active. It does not bleed. It does not move dramatically. Its danger is reputational, slow, cumulative.

People who take it suffer.

People who leave it alone do not prosper—but they endure.

By the late 19th century, as American archaeologists and antiquarians began cataloging Spanish colonial artifacts, the Cross of Coronado was discussed cautiously. Some denied its existence outright. Others suggested that *several* crosses might be involved—each one absorbing the story of the first.

That possibility complicates the idea of a single cursed object. Instead, it suggests something more unsettling: a transferable charge. A ritual act repeated in the wrong place, leaving residue wherever it is reenacted.

In Indigenous oral traditions recorded in the early 20th century, the cross is not treated as holy or demonic. It is treated as *foreign*. Something placed without permission. Something that disrupts balance by insisting on permanence.

That framing matters.

Curses, in this context, are not punishments. They are consequences of misalignment.

Today, no verified artifact identified conclusively as Coronado's cross exists in a museum collection. There are photographs of crosses claimed to be it. There are sites where guides will point and say, "It stood there once." There are private collectors who claim to possess fragments, though none have allowed public verification.

The cross survives best as absence.

People still search for it, occasionally. Most do not admit why. They frame the search as historical curiosity. But they do not plan to take it home. They want to *see* it, not own it.

That distinction may be why the stories continue rather than escalate.

The Cross of Coronado does not curse belief. It curses possession. It marks the moment when faith was used as a tool rather than an offering—and the land noticed.

There is a quiet warning threaded through every version of the story:

Objects planted to claim what does not wish to be claimed do not stay obedient.

They wait.

58
the idol of the thuggee cult

It was not a temple object in the way the British expected such things to be: no grand sanctum, no permanent altar, no fixed address. The idol traveled. It appeared briefly, was honored, then vanished again into cloth and shadow. Its power was not architectural. It was procedural.

When colonial officials first wrote about it in the early 19th century, they struggled to describe it at all.

Sometimes it was a small stone figure, wrapped in red cloth and hidden in a bundle of personal effects. Sometimes it was only a symbol —a mark scratched into the earth before a journey began. Sometimes witnesses insisted it was a physical idol of the goddess Kali, while others swore no image was ever present, only a ritual focus agreed upon by those involved.

The inconsistency did not weaken the fear. It intensified it.

Because what mattered was not the object's shape—but what happened when it was invoked.

The Thuggee, as British authorities came to call them, were described as hereditary stranglers, bound by oath, operating in secret bands across northern and central India. According to colonial records, they murdered travelers by strangulation, offered the deaths to Kali, and buried the bodies in ritualized silence.

That version of the story hardened quickly. It was useful.

What is less useful—but more accurate—is that the Thuggee were not a single cult, not universally religious, not uniformly murderous, and not organized around a single idol. They were a loose network of groups, some criminal, some ritualized, some likely exaggerated beyond recognition by officials desperate to impose order.

But within those exaggerations sits a persistent detail that refuses to vanish, the idol, or its substitute, always appeared at the moment of commitment.

British officer William Henry Sleeman, whose campaigns against the Thuggee in the 1830s effectively defined the colonial narrative, documented multiple interrogations in which accused men described a ritual pause before violence. A moment of stillness. A signal. A consecration.

Sometimes it involved a cloth. Sometimes a token. Sometimes an image shown briefly and then concealed again.

Whatever the object was, it marked a threshold.

And thresholds are dangerous places.

Sleeman himself admitted, though rarely emphasized, that many of those he interrogated expressed genuine fear—not of punishment, but of *what would happen if the ritual was broken.* Men who had already confessed to murder begged not to be made to touch the idol incorrectly, not to step over it, not to leave it exposed.

In one recorded account from the 1830s, a former Thuggee informant described a failed ritual: the cloth was laid out, but the object inside had been touched by someone who was not ritually clean. The journey that followed ended in disaster. The intended victim escaped. Two members of the band fell ill within days. One died on the road home.

British interrogators dismissed this as superstition.

They did not dismiss the pattern.

As the suppression campaigns expanded, idols and ritual objects were confiscated. Many were destroyed. Others were shipped to colonial museums or private collections, stripped of context and labeled as proof of barbarism.

And then something odd happened.

Records began to note disturbances—not supernatural events, but *administrative ones.* Artifacts disappeared from storage. Tags were switched. Items were mislabeled, misplaced, or quietly removed from display. In at least two documented cases, objects believed to be Thuggee ritual items were destroyed against orders after staff refused to keep them on-site.

The official explanation was simple: fear among local workers.

But fear does not explain consistency.

In the India Office Records, there are references to objects "better disposed of" and "not retained," language rarely used for ordinary evidence. In one 19th-century museum inventory, an item is listed as received, then marked *removed* with no further comment.

No sale.

No transfer.

Just absence.

Modern historians have worked hard—correctly—to dismantle the colonial myth of the Thuggee as a vast, unified death cult. The numbers were inflated. Confessions were coerced. The British needed an enemy that justified surveillance, registration, and control.

But in correcting the exaggeration, something quieter often gets lost.

People believed the ritual worked.

Not metaphorically. Not socially. Practically.

Those involved—whether criminals, ritual participants, or coerced accomplices—behaved as if violating the object's rules would produce consequences independent of British law. And those consequences, according to their own accounts, were not delayed or symbolic. They were immediate, physical, and specific.

Illness. Accidents. Failed plans. Internal collapse.

Even Sleeman, committed rationalist that he was, acknowledged in private correspondence that he never once persuaded an accused Thug to treat the ritual objects lightly.

They feared them more than execution.

By the late 19th century, as the Thuggee campaigns were held up as a triumph of colonial policing, the idol itself faded into abstraction. It became a prop in textbooks. A symbol of savagery rather than an object with rules.

But symbols don't usually resist handling.

This one did.

Today, no verified "Idol of the Thuggee Cult" is publicly displayed as such. Museums hold objects that *may* be related—stones, figurines, cloth bundles—but they are cautiously labeled, stripped of ritual attribution.

Scholars debate whether the idol ever existed in a fixed form at all.

That debate may be missing the point.

The idol's power, if it existed, was never in its permanence. It was in its appearance at the right moment, its disappearance immediately afterward, and the shared agreement—across families, regions, and decades—that something would go wrong if it was mishandled.

A ritual object that refuses to stay put is harder to neutralize.

The British tried to end the cult by destroying its symbols. What they may have destroyed instead was the record of how the ritual actually worked.

All that remains now are fragments of testimony, gaps in archives, and a word—*Thug*—that survived while its meaning was flattened into insult.

The idol itself, if it ever had a single form, does not need to exist anymore.

It has already done what ritual objects are most dangerous at doing:

it trained people to believe that crossing a certain line would cost them something real.

That belief outlived the empire that tried to erase it.

And beliefs, once embedded in practice, do not die cleanly.

They wait.

59
the black chalice
of antioch

T he first thing people noticed was not its shape.

It was the color.

Accounts vary—charcoal, obsidian, pitch—but they agree on one thing: the chalice absorbed light rather than reflecting it. Even in photographs taken decades later, the cup appears flatter than it should, its surface refusing highlights, its interior swallowing whatever shadow falls into it.

That alone would have made it unusual. Sacred objects tend to gleam. They reassure. They perform holiness.

This one did not.

The chalice entered the modern record in 1910, carried not by monks or pilgrims, but by dealers. It was presented to the world in Paris, not Jerusalem, under carefully arranged lighting and a story that had already been rehearsed: an early Christian cup from Antioch, possibly dating to the first century, possibly associated—suggestively, never definitively—with the Last Supper.

The timing was not accidental.

Europe was hungry for relics. Archaeology was fashionable. Biblical provenance sold well. And Antioch, one of the earliest centers of Christianity, carried just enough authority to quiet initial doubts.

But from the beginning, something about this chalice resisted the role it was being cast into.

The object was heavy. Thicker than expected. The surface was worked, but not lovingly. Where the famous silver Antioch Chalice (now in the Metropolitan Museum of Art) dazzles with vine motifs and apostles in relief, this cup was blunt. Utilitarian. Darkened by material choice or deliberate treatment—historians still argue which.

And then there was the matter of its handling.

According to early exhibition notes, staff rotated the chalice more frequently than other items. It was never placed near windows. Visitors complained of headaches. A restorer reportedly refused to clean it after a single attempt, citing "an unaccountable pressure sensation" and discoloration that returned overnight.

These are small details. The kind museums usually attribute to coincidence.

But coincidence begins to look different when it clusters.

The Black Chalice's provenance trail is, to put it gently, a mess.

Dealers claimed it was unearthed near Antioch—modern Antakya —in the late 19th century, possibly from a cave or buried chapel. No excavation records exist. No photographs of the find site. No local ecclesiastical acknowledgment. Only affidavits signed after the fact, and only in European hands.

This alone would normally doom an artifact's credibility.

Instead, it seemed to strengthen the aura.

Rumors followed the chalice almost immediately. Some claimed it had been deliberately hidden by early Christians—not revered, but contained. Others whispered that it had been used not for communion, but for *separation*—a cup passed in rites of excommunication, or worse, in ceremonies meant to mark someone as cut off from the body of the faithful.

That idea—*a negative sacrament*—never appears in official doctrine.

It does, however, appear repeatedly in heretical texts.

By the 1920s, scholars had begun pushing back. Metallurgical analysis suggested the chalice was not first-century at all, but later—

possibly medieval. Others argued it was a pastiche, a deliberately aged object meant to exploit the market's hunger.

And yet, even as its historical claims eroded, institutions continued to handle it cautiously.

In one case, a private collector acquired the chalice only to return it within months, citing "persistent domestic disturbances." No further explanation was offered. In another, a dealer involved in its resale suffered a sudden financial collapse following a lawsuit that hinged on a single missing document—one he insisted had been stored with the chalice's papers.

Again: coincidence.

But by now, the pattern was familiar.

Objects that fail to prove their holiness sometimes acquire something else instead.

By mid-century, the Black Chalice of Antioch had largely vanished from public view. It did not enter a major museum collection. It passed instead through private hands, appearing briefly in auction catalogs under carefully hedged descriptions—"ceremonial cup," "possible Levantine origin," "dark patina consistent with age."

No one wanted to claim too much.

What survives of the chalice now exists mostly in fragments of documentation: insurance records, correspondence between dealers, a handful of black-and-white photographs where the cup seems almost to blur at the edges.

And, tellingly, a series of refusals.

Refusals to display it.

Refusals to restore it.

Refusals to swear to its significance under oath.

In religious folklore, the Grail heals. It restores the wounded king. It brings fertility back to a blighted land.

The Black Chalice of Antioch, if it belongs to that family at all, represents the opposite function.

It does not heal.

It does not bless.

It *marks*.

Several scholars have suggested—quietly—that the chalice may never have been intended for liturgical use. That it functioned instead as a boundary object, used in rites that defined exclusion, judgment, or spiritual quarantine. Such rites would not be preserved in orthodox history. They would be buried. Erased. Forgotten on purpose.

That theory cannot be proven.

But it explains something important: why the object feels wrong even when stripped of its story.

Today, the Black Chalice's exact location is uncertain. Some believe it was melted down. Others insist it remains intact in a European private collection, stored separately from the rest of the owner's holdings, rarely handled, never photographed again.

And then there are the more unsettling accounts—those that claim the chalice resists destruction. That attempts to damage it result only in surface discoloration. That it returns, eventually, to circulation, no matter how decisively it is discarded.

Those stories are unverified.

They are also unnecessary.

The true danger of the Black Chalice of Antioch is not that it curses those who drink from it.

It is that it embodies a version of sacred power most religions prefer to deny: the power to declare someone *outside*.

Blessings can be shared.

Curses, once given form, tend to linger.

There is an old belief, common to many traditions, that vessels remember what they were used for. Not symbolically. Practically. That they retain residue—not just physical, but intentional.

If that belief holds any truth at all, then the Black Chalice does not need to be genuine to be effective.

It only needs to have been believed in long enough.

And belief, once poured into an object, is very difficult to empty back out.

part four
art, writing &
media objects

60
the hands resist him painting

T he boy stands in front of a glass door.

He is five years old—or looks five, at least—and his expression is neither frightened nor calm. It is the expression of a child who has learned something too early and is waiting for the world to catch up.

Behind the glass are hands.

They do not belong to bodies. They are not attached to arms. They press forward from darkness, dozens of them, layered one atop another, pale and reaching. They are not grasping the boy. They are reaching *past* him, as if he is only incidental to whatever they want.

To his right stands a doll.

She is not a doll in the way children mean it. She is taller than the boy, rigid, jointed, with a blank face and hollow eyes. Her hands are wrong—mechanical, segmented. In one, she holds what looks like a battery pack or detonator. In the other, nothing. She is not helping him escape.

She is escorting him forward.

When artist Bill Stoneham completed *The Hands Resist Him* in 1972, he did not intend to create a haunted object. He was painting memory. Trauma. The threshold between childhood and whatever waits beyond it.

The title came from a line in a poem he had written years earlier—about resistance, about unseen forces pressing against the act of growing up.

That explanation would come later.

At first, there was only the painting.

It debuted in a Los Angeles gallery in the early 1970s and was quickly noticed. Not for its technique, but for its effect. Viewers lingered too long. Some refused to stand in front of it alone. Others complained of unease they could not articulate.

The gallery owner who first displayed it reportedly died within a year.

So did the art critic who reviewed it.

So did the actor who purchased it.

None of these deaths were suspicious on paper. Illness. Natural causes. The ordinary attrition of time.

But people began to connect them anyway.

Stoneham dismissed the whispers. He had lived with the image for years. It did not frighten him. It was autobiographical: the boy was him, the door a threshold between worlds, the doll a guide into imagination.

Still, he admitted something odd.

The painting made people *angry*.

By the late 1990s, *The Hands Resist Him* had vanished into private ownership. It resurfaced unexpectedly in February 2000—not in a gallery, but on eBay.

The listing was unusual.

The sellers claimed they had found the painting behind an abandoned brewery, discarded. After bringing it home, their four-year-old daughter began insisting that the figures in the painting were moving at night. That the boy left the frame. That the doll pointed a gun at him.

The parents installed a motion-activated camera.

They included stills from the footage in the auction listing.

Nothing moved.

But the listing itself triggered something far stranger.

Within days, thousands of people viewed it. Emails poured in. Comment sections filled with warnings. Some claimed they felt nauseous. Others reported headaches, panic attacks, insomnia—*just from looking at the digital image.*

A neurologist wrote to say the painting caused "overstimulation of the amygdala." A priest offered to bless the file. Multiple buyers withdrew bids, citing dreams they could not shake.

eBay eventually intervened—not because the listing violated policy, but because users were reporting *physical distress.*

This was unprecedented.

The painting sold for over $1,000 to gallery owner Kim Smith, who approached it with skepticism and curiosity. She displayed it publicly.

Nothing catastrophic happened.

But visitors continued to describe a sensation of pressure when standing in front of it. Children reacted particularly strongly—either refusing to approach or staring too intently, as if waiting for something to happen.

Stoneham, now aware of the myth coalescing around his work, painted sequels. In them, the boy grows older. The doll changes. The hands recede, then return.

He insists this was always the plan.

That may be true.

But it does not explain the consistency of the reactions.

Skeptics argue that *The Hands Resist Him* is a case study in mass suggestion. The perfect storm of creepy imagery, internet virality, and narrative feedback loops. People felt something because they were told to expect it.

And yet—many of the earliest reactions predate the eBay listing.

Long before the comments. Before the camera. Before the story hardened.

Which leaves an uncomfortable question.

What if the painting did not become disturbing because people believed it was haunted?

What if people believed it was haunted because it depicted something they recognized but could not name?

Stoneham once described the hands as "representing other lives, other possibilities."

That interpretation is benign.

But there is another way to read them.

As witnesses.

As reminders.

As the pressure of everything that has ever wanted something from you when you were too young to understand consent.

Today, *The Hands Resist Him* still circulates—reproduced endlessly online, flattened into pixels, stripped of context. It has lost none of its power. In some ways, it has gained it.

Because now the threshold it depicts is not just childhood.

It is the screen.

The warning embedded in the painting is subtle, but it persists: there are doors you cannot close once you look through them. There are guides who will not protect you. And there are hands that do not need bodies to reach.

Some paintings invite interpretation.

This one waits.

61
the anguished man painting

T he man is screaming.

Not theatrically. Not in the way paintings often depict anguish, with open mouths and exaggerated gestures meant to read clearly from across a room. This scream is collapsed inward, as if the sound has nowhere to go. The face is distorted, smeared, unfinished. Eyes melt into shadow. Teeth blur into paint. The body barely exists—just enough shape to suggest a torso being pulled downward by its own weight.

The background is black.

Not a painted black. Not a color layered carefully or textured with depth. It is the kind of black that looks like it was applied in anger, or exhaustion, or both. A void that does not recede, but presses forward.

This is *The Anguished Man.*

For decades, the painting had no audience. No critics. No gallery wall. It hung in a private home, quietly, without explanation. It was not bought. It was not commissioned. It was inherited.

The man who inherited it—identified publicly only as **Sean Robinson**—grew up knowing two things about the painting.

First: it frightened him.

Second: it was never to be thrown away.

According to Robinson, the painting was created by an unknown artist—his grandmother's former partner—sometime in the late 1950s or early 1960s. The man was described as deeply troubled, prone to depressive episodes, and increasingly isolated toward the end of his life. He allegedly told Robinson's grandmother that he had mixed his own blood into the paint while working on the canvas.

Shortly after completing it, the artist died by suicide.

No formal records corroborate the man's identity. No death certificate has been publicly produced. No gallery catalog lists his work. Skeptics point to this absence immediately, and not without reason.

But absence is not the same as fabrication.

And the painting exists.

Robinson recalls that even as a child, he refused to sleep in the room where it hung. He felt watched. Not observed, exactly—but *felt through*. As if the painting was less an image than a presence.

His grandmother claimed she experienced nightmares when it was nearby. She kept it covered, then moved it into a spare room, then eventually into the attic. She never destroyed it.

When Robinson inherited the house, he inherited the painting.

At first, nothing happened.

That pause matters.

Haunted objects—if they exist at all—rarely announce themselves immediately. They wait for routine. For complacency. For the moment when the object becomes background.

The disturbances began slowly.

Sounds at night. Faint knocking. Footsteps when no one was awake. Robinson described waking to the sensation of someone standing at the foot of the bed, only to find the room empty. His partner reported the same.

They blamed stress. Old wiring. Drafts.

Then came the figures.

Robinson claims that he began seeing a dark shape emerge from the painting at night—a tall, human outline that moved through the room. On one occasion, he says he woke to find a figure crouched near the bed, then watched it retreat back into the canvas.

At this point, most people would have removed the painting.

Robinson did not.

Instead, he installed cameras.

This detail is important. Because unlike folklore that arrives pre-packaged in rumor, *The Anguished Man* entered the public consciousness through documentation.

The footage Robinson later shared shows a darkened hallway. A closed door rattling violently. A child's scream—his daughter—caught on audio. Objects shifting slightly between frames.

None of it is conclusive.

All of it is unsettling.

Robinson began posting videos online in the early 2010s. The response was immediate and polarized. Some viewers accused him of fabrication. Others reported feeling nauseous or dizzy while watching. A small number claimed the footage triggered panic attacks.

The comments sections became part of the phenomenon.

People warned him to destroy the painting. Others begged him not to. Several claimed to feel something "leak" through the screen.

This is where *The Anguished Man* diverges from older cursed-object narratives.

The curse—if that word applies—is not limited to proximity. It propagates through attention.

Robinson insisted he did not want fame. He took breaks from posting. He attempted to store the painting away from living spaces. Each time, he claims, the disturbances worsened.

Scratching sounds returned. Nightmares intensified. His children refused to enter certain rooms. Guests reported feeling "oppressed" without knowing why.

Eventually, Robinson sealed the painting in a storage unit.

The activity reportedly diminished.

But it did not stop.

Skeptics argue that the story fits too neatly into modern paranormal tropes: the troubled artist, the blood, the inherited object, the escalation after attention. They note inconsistencies in Robinson's timeline and the lack of external verification.

They are not wrong to question.

But they also cannot explain the painting's effect in person.

Multiple visitors who encountered the canvas outside the context of the story reported physical reactions: headaches, tightness in the chest, an urge to leave the room. One described the sensation as "standing too close to someone else's pain."

That phrasing is revealing.

Because whether or not the painting is haunted in the supernatural sense, it appears to function as a vessel for something profoundly human: suffering without resolution.

Art historians note that *The Anguished Man* bears resemblance to Expressionist works from the mid-20th century—particularly pieces that attempt to externalize psychological collapse. The difference is that those works are deliberate, composed, contextualized.

This painting feels unfinished.

As if the scream interrupted the act of making it.

The blood rumor, while unverified, persists because it makes symbolic sense. Blood in paint would not magically animate a canvas —but it would collapse the distance between artist and object. It would make the painting less representation and more residue.

In that reading, the haunting is not external.

It is proximity to someone else's unresolved end.

Today, the painting remains out of public view. Robinson has stated that he will not sell it. He does not display it. He does not destroy it.

He keeps it contained.

Which may be the most unsettling detail of all.

Because containment implies belief.

And belief implies responsibility.

There is a final detail Robinson has mentioned only once, then never again.

He claims that on the last night the painting hung openly in his home, he dreamed of the man inside it—not screaming, not reaching out, but standing silently, watching him.

Not pleading.

Waiting.

62
the portrait of
bernardo de gálvez

T he painting was never meant to be mysterious.

That fact sits at the center of the problem.

When the portrait of Bernardo de Gálvez was commissioned, it was intended to do exactly what official portraits have always done: stabilize memory. To fix a man in place. To make history legible, repeatable, and calm. The pose is correct. The uniform is correct. The expression—measured, restrained, neither smiling nor severe—follows the conventions of late-eighteenth-century military portraiture.

Nothing about it suggests a haunting.

And yet, from the moment it was installed in Pensacola, people began to hesitate in front of it.

Bernardo de Gálvez himself never saw the painting. He died in 1786, governor of Spanish Louisiana and a military commander whose reputation would outgrow his lifetime. During the American Revolutionary War, Spain was not formally allied with the American colonies, but Gálvez understood something more important than treaties: geography. British control of the Gulf mattered. Pensacola mattered.

In 1781, when Spanish commanders hesitated to sail into Pensacola Bay under British fire, Gálvez did not convene a council or wait for consensus. He boarded his ship and went first. The others followed.

Yo solo.

I alone.

The phrase survived because it compressed a complicated military reality into a single act of resolve. It is the kind of story history prefers.

The portrait belongs to that preference.

Painted decades later and installed in what would become known as the Galvez Room, the image was meant to anchor civic memory. Pensacola has always been a city shaped by overlapping claims—Spanish, French, British, American—and Gálvez offered a rare figure of consensus. The room became formal. Ceremonial. A place for meetings, proclamations, and quiet authority.

And then people began to notice the eyes.

Not all at once. Not dramatically. The earliest accounts are hesitant, even apologetic. A visitor pauses. Someone steps closer. Another shifts to the side, trying to catch the light differently.

The eyes appear closed.

Not damaged. Not painted over. Simply disengaged. As if the subject has chosen not to return the gaze.

At first, the explanation is architectural. The room has tall windows. Light shifts throughout the day. Varnish reflects. Perspective lies.

Except the effect does not behave consistently.

Some visitors see the eyes closed from across the room. Others only when standing directly beneath the portrait. Some never see it at all. Others insist—quietly, often later—that the eyes were open when they arrived and closed when they left.

Stories accumulate the way dust does: slowly, unevenly, impossible to fully remove.

By the mid-twentieth century, the legend has acquired a recognizable shape. Local guides mention it casually. Building staff exchange looks when asked. No one denies the question outright. They simply redirect it.

The painting is cleaned. The lighting adjusted. At one point, the portrait is temporarily removed and later rehung. None of this resolves the issue. If anything, it sharpens it. The eyes still refuse some viewers and acknowledge others.

This is where documentation matters.

There are no early newspaper exposés. No dramatic headlines. What exists instead are meeting notes, visitor logs, and oral histories recorded years later. A pattern emerges: people report the experience independently, often before being told what to look for.

"He wouldn't look at me."

"It felt deliberate."

"Like I wasn't worth noticing."

These are not the reactions of people frightened by ghosts. They are the reactions of people unsettled by judgment.

Skeptics offer explanations, and many are reasonable. Human perception is unreliable. Expectation shapes experience. Once a story circulates, it primes the observer. All of this is true—and insufficient. Because the phenomenon persists even among those who encounter the portrait without prior knowledge.

A recurring detail complicates matters further: in some accounts, the eyes do not simply open. They meet the viewer. Briefly. Precisely. And then disengage again.

No one describes blinking. No one describes motion. Only recognition.

This selectivity makes the portrait resistant to theatricalization. It does not perform on command. It cannot be demonstrated. Attempts to provoke it—standing too close, staring too long, drawing attention to oneself—seem to shut it down entirely.

Theories multiply.

One school argues the effect is purely optical: the angle of the painted pupils combined with lighting and viewer height. Another points to pareidolia and social suggestion. A third, less comfortable theory suggests the portrait functions as a psychological mirror, revealing not instability in the object, but in the observer.

This is where doubt fails to resolve unease.

Because even if the explanation is mundane, the emotional response remains specific. People do not report fear. They report exclusion. The sensation of being evaluated and dismissed.

In Catholic visual tradition—familiar to Gálvez's Spain—the gaze is not guaranteed. Icons do not exist to comfort. They exist to instruct.

The saint looks back only under certain conditions: reverence, humility, attention.

The portrait was not painted as an icon. But it behaves like one.

Today, the painting still hangs in Pensacola. It appears in photographs, brochures, and travel blogs. Online images rarely capture the effect. On a screen, the eyes behave. They meet everyone equally. The phenomenon seems to require physical presence—distance, scale, silence.

No official warning accompanies the portrait. No plaque mentions the legend. And yet there is an informal rule, passed quietly among those who work in the building: if someone mentions the eyes, you do not argue. You acknowledge the comment and change the subject.

The portrait does not escalate. It does not punish. It does not repeat itself predictably. Its restraint is what allows it to endure.

There is one final detail, rarely included in tourist retellings. In some versions of the story, those who meet the gaze are advised not to linger. Not to stare. A nod is considered sufficient. A step back. A quiet exit.

Because whatever the portrait is doing, it does not require acknowledgment to continue.

It only requires witnesses.

And like the man it depicts—who acted when others hesitated, who stepped forward alone—the portrait seems content to wait until someone else does the same.

63

the cursed portrait
of general yamashita

T he portrait arrived without ceremony.

There was no dramatic unveiling, no plaque announcing its significance, no curator standing beside it with folded hands. It was simply uncrated, lifted, and placed where it had been ordered to hang—another artifact of war, another face pressed flat by history.

The man in the painting was Tomoyuki Yamashita, former commander of Japanese forces in the Philippines during the Second World War. To history, he is remembered by a single, indelible epithet: *the Tiger of Malaya*. To those who lived under his command, and to those who survived its consequences, he was something else entirely.

The portrait does not soften him.

He is depicted in uniform, posture erect, gaze forward—not confrontational, but unyielding. The painter, whose name is lost to the archive, did not exaggerate his features. If anything, the restraint is what makes the image difficult to endure. There is no villainy in the brushstrokes. No theatrical cruelty. Just a man who appears utterly certain of his own authority.

That certainty would outlive him.

Yamashita was captured by American forces in the Philippines in

287

September 1945. He was charged not with direct atrocities, but with responsibility—command responsibility—for crimes committed by troops under his authority. The legal precedent established by his trial would shape international law for decades. The moral weight of it remains contested.

He was executed by hanging on February 23, 1946, in Los Baños.

The portrait was painted later.

No official record confirms exactly when or where it was created, only that it surfaced in the postwar period, passing through military storage and private collections before being displayed publicly. Some accounts suggest it was commissioned as a historical likeness. Others claim it was copied from an earlier photograph, reproduced by an artist who had never met the man but felt compelled to capture him anyway.

That compulsion matters.

The first unease surrounding the portrait was subtle. Guards assigned to the gallery where it hung complained of headaches. Museum staff noted that people lingered in front of it longer than expected, then left abruptly, unsettled but unable to articulate why. A few visitors remarked—half joking—that the general "felt present."

The comments were not recorded formally. They never are, at first.

It was only after the painting was relocated—moved from one institution to another, sometimes temporarily, sometimes indefinitely—that the pattern began to form. Each move coincided with disruption. Administrative errors. Sudden illnesses. Equipment failures in adjacent rooms. Nothing dramatic enough to halt operations. Just enough to be noticed.

One curator reportedly refused to keep the portrait in her office after waking repeatedly from dreams in which the man in the painting stood just behind her, never speaking, never touching her, only watching as she tried—and failed—to move. She requested reassignment. No official reason was given.

A security officer claimed the eyes followed him during night rounds. When told this was impossible, he amended the statement: the eyes did not move. *He did.*

This distinction appears often in accounts of haunted portraits. The object remains fixed. The observer changes position. The sensation of being tracked persists anyway.

Skeptics point, correctly, to expectation. Yamashita is not a neutral subject. Knowledge of wartime atrocities primes the imagination. The mind supplies menace where history already provided it.

But this explanation falters when confronted with a particular detail: several reported experiences came from individuals who did not know who Yamashita was. Tourists. Junior staff. People told only that the painting depicted "a general."

They noticed the weight of the room before they noticed the label.

The portrait has been described as "heavy," "oppressive," and—most tellingly—"unfinished." Not in technique, but in presence. As though the image were waiting for something that never arrived.

Theories multiply in the vacuum left by incomplete documentation.

One suggests the painting functions as a focal point for unresolved guilt—not the general's, but that of the institutions displaying him. War crimes memorialized without resolution. Justice enacted but never fully digested. The portrait becomes a container, absorbing discomfort rather than explaining it.

Another theory, less academic and more dangerous, returns to Yamashita himself. To the argument—still debated—that he was made a scapegoat. That the full extent of responsibility was never clearly established. That the trial, however necessary, was imperfect.

In this version, the haunting is not vengeance, but insistence. The portrait does not accuse. It refuses closure.

There are darker interpretations still.

In some retellings, the painting is said to have been present during interrogations of former Japanese officers after the war—hung deliberately where it could be seen, as a reminder. There is no evidence for this, but the story persists, perhaps because it feels *appropriate*. The general's image overseeing confession. Silent authority enforcing memory.

Whether or not this occurred, the idea has teeth. Images do not need to act to exert power. They only need to be placed correctly.

The portrait's current status is, characteristically, unclear. Some sources claim it remains in storage. Others that it was quietly removed from public display. A few insist it was destroyed, though no documentation confirms this.

What is certain is that wherever the portrait goes, it does not remain unnoticed for long.

Unlike more theatrical cursed objects, the Yamashita portrait does not escalate. There are no deaths directly attributed to it. No fires. No public panic. Its danger—if that is the word—is administrative, psychological, institutional. It disrupts systems. It erodes comfort. It forces those nearby to reckon with responsibility rather than spectacle.

This makes it difficult to categorize.

Hauntings that do not harm are often dismissed. But history teaches us that the most enduring forces are rarely violent. They are persistent.

The portrait does not threaten. It observes.

And perhaps that is the most unsettling possibility of all: that the image of a man executed for crimes committed by others continues to watch not out of malice, but out of unfinished business. That the gaze fixed in paint is not judgment, but record-keeping.

Someone once asked why the portrait was not simply destroyed.

The answer—offered quietly by a former handler—was that destroying it felt like repeating the original mistake. Another attempt to erase rather than confront.

So the painting waits.

And as long as it exists, so does the question it refuses to let settle: whether responsibility can ever truly be assigned after violence on that scale—or whether it simply moves, like a portrait in transit, from one set of hands to another.

64

the book of soyga

T he book was not supposed to be readable.

That, at least, was the conclusion reached in the late sixteenth century by **John Dee**, a man who believed—quite sincerely—that angels could be interrogated like reluctant civil servants if one asked the right questions in the right order.

Dee had seen strange books before. He owned them. He copied them. He translated texts that most scholars of his time considered dangerously speculative. But *this* book stopped him.

He encountered it sometime before 1583, though his notes are frustratingly vague about the moment. What he does record is the reaction: confusion, then irritation, then something close to dread. The manuscript, titled *Aldaraia sive Soyga vocor*—"I am called Soyga"— appeared to promise knowledge. Its opening pages were written in a dense, learned Latin, filled with discussions of astrology, cosmology, and the properties of spirits. Dee could follow this part. He took notes. He cross-referenced.

And then the book changed.

Near the end of the manuscript, the prose gives way to tables— page after page of tightly arranged letters, forty by forty grids, each one composed of seemingly meaningless sequences. No punctuation. No explanation. No key. The letters repeat, but not predictably. Patterns appear, then dissolve under closer inspection.

Dee could not decode them.

This mattered because Dee was not an amateur. He was the most mathematically sophisticated mind in Elizabethan England, a man who advised Queen Elizabeth I herself on matters of navigation, calendar reform, and occult timing. If the Book of Soyga was a cipher, it was an *exceptional* one.

Dee became obsessed.

He attempted frequency analysis. He compared the tables to known magical alphabets. He searched for correspondences with planetary hours, angelic hierarchies, Hebrew gematria. Nothing held. The grids resisted every framework he brought to them, like a surface that would not accept an impression.

So Dee did what he always did when scholarship failed.

He asked the angels.

In April 1583, during a series of scrying sessions conducted with the medium Edward Kelley, Dee posed a question to the angel Uriel: *Who wrote the Book of Soyga, and how may it be understood?*

The answer, according to Dee's meticulously kept spiritual diaries, was not reassuring.

Uriel told him that the book had been written by angels—but not for humans. It was revealed to Adam, then lost. Its knowledge was dangerous. Understanding it would shorten a man's life. Only the archangel Michael could explain the tables, and even then, only partially.

Dee pressed further.

Uriel refused.

This refusal is significant. Angels in Dee's records are rarely coy. They argue, lecture, threaten, flatter—but they usually answer. In this case, the response was firm: *The book was not meant to be opened.*

Dee stopped asking.

The Book of Soyga vanished shortly thereafter, or so it seemed. No copy was known to exist after Dee's death in 1609. Scholars assumed it had been lost, destroyed, or perhaps never existed at all beyond Dee's descriptions.

Then, in 1994, it resurfaced.

Two copies of the manuscript were independently identified—one in the British Library, the other in the Bodleian Library at Oxford. Both were anonymous. Neither contained marginalia explaining the tables. Neither showed signs of practical use. They had been cataloged, miscataloged, shelved, and forgotten.

The book had been waiting.

Modern cryptographers took an interest. Chief among them was Jim Reeds, a codebreaker at AT&T Bell Labs, who approached the tables not as mystical artifacts but as data. Using computer analysis, Reeds identified a generating principle behind the grids: each table is algorithmically derived from a key word written at the top of the page.

This was a breakthrough.

It meant the tables were not random. They were structured, recursive, self-referential. But understanding *how* they were made did not explain *why*.

No decoded message emerged. No hidden text revealed itself. The tables generated themselves, then stopped, like machines designed to run but not to produce.

This is where the discomfort deepens.

A cipher usually hides something. The Book of Soyga's tables do not conceal meaning so much as **perform it**. They behave like magical objects rather than texts—ritual diagrams frozen into ink. They generate complexity without delivering information.

Several scholars have noted the resemblance between the Soyga tables and later concepts in chaos theory: deterministic systems whose outcomes are unpredictable. This is an anachronism, of course—but the parallel lingers.

The book does not tell you anything.

It shows you what thinking can become when it turns in on itself.

Accounts of personal unease surrounding the manuscript are, predictably, anecdotal. Researchers report difficulty concentrating after prolonged study. A sense of mental "static." One mathematician described the experience as "being stared at by an equation that doesn't want to be solved."

No one has died from studying the Book of Soyga.

That fact is often offered as reassurance.

But Dee was told that understanding it would shorten his life—not that it would kill him outright. Knowledge, in this framing, is not explosive. It is corrosive. It erodes time rather than ending it.

Today, the Book of Soyga rests quietly in institutional collections. It is digitized. Indexed. Available to anyone with the patience to scroll through its pages.

And yet, very few people do.

The Latin is dense. The tables are exhausting. The book does not reward casual attention. It resists summary. It cannot be skimmed. It asks for commitment without promising payoff.

This may be its most effective defense.

There is an old idea in magical theory that some texts protect themselves not through secrecy, but through **difficulty**. They are visible, but uninviting. Present, but inert unless approached with the wrong kind of curiosity.

The Book of Soyga does not lure.

It waits.

And the question it poses—never directly, always implicitly—is whether there are forms of knowledge that exist solely to demonstrate the limits of the human mind. Not forbidden knowledge. Not lost knowledge.

But **indifferent knowledge**.

Dee believed the book came from angels. Modern scholars believe it came from a human author deeply versed in Renaissance occult mathematics. Both explanations may be true. Neither makes the book safer.

Because the danger of the Book of Soyga is not what it reveals.

It is what it **withholds**, while proving—page after page—that the structure for revelation is already in place.

The machine exists.

It simply does not care who turns the crank.

65
the voynich manuscript

T he book does not announce itself.

There is no dedication, no title page, no explanation of purpose. It opens instead on a plant that does not exist—roots too elaborate, leaves too symmetrical, flowers composed of parts borrowed from multiple species but belonging to none of them. The drawing is careful, deliberate, confident. Whoever made it believed in what they were drawing.

That belief is unsettling.

The manuscript now known as the Voynich is carbon-dated to the early fifteenth century, most likely between 1404 and 1438. Its parchment comes from calfskin, prepared expertly. Its inks are consistent with the period. There is nothing modern about its materials, nothing anachronistic in its construction.

Only the content is wrong.

The text runs left to right, evenly spaced, with a rhythm that looks linguistic. Words repeat. Patterns emerge. Certain characters cluster together as if governed by grammar. Others appear only in specific contexts, like technical terms. The script flows without hesitation, as though the scribe never needed to pause to think of the next letter.

And yet, no one has ever read it.

The manuscript surfaces into recorded history in the late sixteenth century, in the orbit of the Holy Roman Emperor Rudolf II—a man with a well-documented appetite for alchemy, astrology, and dangerous books. A letter dated 1665 claims that Rudolf purchased the manuscript for six hundred ducats, believing it to be the work of Roger Bacon.

Whether the purchase occurred as described is uncertain. What *is* certain is that the manuscript circulated quietly among scholars who failed to make sense of it, then passed into the hands of Jesuit collectors, where it rested for centuries, unread and undisturbed.

Silence, in this case, was not neglect. It was containment.

In 1912, the book reentered the world through **Wilfrid Voynich**, a Polish antiquarian who acquired it from a Jesuit archive near Rome. Voynich believed—fervently—that he had discovered something extraordinary. He devoted the remainder of his life to promoting the manuscript, arranging analyses, courting cryptographers, and insisting that the solution was close.

It never came.

The twentieth century threw its best minds at the problem. Linguists. Medievalists. Codebreakers. During World War II, some of the same individuals who cracked Axis ciphers examined the Voynich Manuscript and failed. Not partially. Completely.

Every proposed solution collapsed under scrutiny.

Some claimed it was a cipher. Others argued it was an invented language. Still others suggested it was a hoax, an elaborate nonsense text designed to deceive wealthy patrons. But hoaxes have fingerprints. They show strain. They break character.

The Voynich never breaks.

Statistical analysis reveals that the text behaves like a real language: word frequency curves, positional dependencies, structural regularities. But it does not map cleanly onto any known linguistic family. It is *too ordered* to be random and *too alien* to be natural.

The illustrations offer no refuge.

Botanical sections depict plants with roots shaped like organs, leaves resembling mechanical parts, and flowers that seem assembled rather than grown. Astronomical diagrams show stars and zodiac figures—but their arrangements are wrong, subtly but persistently. A section often called the "biological" or "balneological" pages shows naked women bathing in green liquid, connected by pipes and reservoirs, as if parts of a system rather than bodies.

These women are not erotic. They are not symbolic in any obvious way. They appear functional.

The longer one looks, the clearer it becomes that the manuscript is internally consistent. Whatever rules govern it are applied faithfully. The system does not glitch.

Which raises the most disturbing possibility of all: that the manuscript is not *meant* to be read in the way we read books.

One modern theory suggests the Voynich Manuscript is a procedural text—a kind of encoded model rather than a message. Not instructions, but *process*. A representation of a worldview that assumes the reader already understands the premises.

Another proposes it is a mnemonic device, meaningful only to someone trained within a vanished intellectual tradition. A tool for memory, not communication.

And then there is the idea that refuses to die, no matter how often it is dismissed: that the manuscript was not written *for us*.

Like the Book of Soyga, the Voynich Manuscript behaves less like a text and more like an artifact of cognition. It shows the shape of understanding without granting access to it. It demonstrates coherence without permitting translation.

People who work closely with the manuscript often report an emotional response that is difficult to articulate. Not fear. Not fascination alone. Something closer to exclusion.

As if the book is complete without you.

Today, the Voynich Manuscript resides at the Beinecke Rare Book & Manuscript Library at Yale University. It is digitized. Freely accessible. Anyone can examine every page in high resolution, zooming in on every stroke of ink.

And still, no one reads it.

The manuscript does not defend itself. It does not threaten. It does not even resist. It simply persists, unchanged by attention, unaltered by interpretation, indifferent to desire.

There is a particular horror in that indifference.

Most cursed objects retaliate. This one ignores.

It has outlived empires, ideologies, technologies, and the people who believed—very sincerely—that they would be the ones to solve it. It waits calmly while each generation announces a breakthrough, then quietly absorbs the failure.

The danger of the Voynich Manuscript is not madness, or death, or obsession—though all three have brushed against it. The danger is more subtle.

It teaches a lesson no scholar wants to learn.

That intelligence is not universal.

That meaning is not guaranteed.

That something can be carefully, deliberately constructed—and still remain forever outside the reach of human understanding.

And that the universe does not owe us an explanation.

66

the necronomicon

T he book began as a warning.

Not a spellbook. Not a manual. Not even a plot device in the modern sense. It was a boundary marker—something placed deliberately just beyond the edge of the known world.

When **H. P. Lovecraft** first named the *Necronomicon*, he did so with care. He gave it a false author, Abdul Alhazred. He gave it a date, a language, a chain of translations. He gave it just enough academic scaffolding to resemble the real grimoires he studied obsessively— Agrippa, the *Picatrix*, the *Key of Solomon*—and then he made it lethal.

Not metaphorically lethal. Practically so.

In Lovecraft's stories, reading the Necronomicon does not drive people mad because it is evil. It drives them mad because it is *accurate*. It describes a universe that does not center humanity, does not protect consciousness, and does not require morality. Knowledge itself becomes the hazard.

And then something went wrong.

Readers began to ask where they could find it.

Lovecraft was explicit—almost defensive—in his insistence that the Necronomicon was fictional. He wrote letters clarifying this. He corrected fans. He reiterated that no such book existed.

They did not stop looking.

By the mid-20th century, something remarkable had happened: the Necronomicon had escaped its author. It had become what folklorists call a **hyperstitional object**—a thing that becomes real *because people act as though it is.*

Publishers noticed.

Occultists noticed.

And a market opened.

The first so-called "real" Necronomicons appeared in the 1960s and 1970s, often marketed as suppressed translations, forbidden Arabic texts, or reconstructions based on fragments. The most influential of these—the *Simon Necronomicon,* published in 1977—did not even attempt subtlety. It openly blended Lovecraftian mythos with Mesopotamian demonology, Sumerian names, and ceremonial magic structures borrowed from authentic grimoires.

It should not have worked.

It did.

The book sold extraordinarily well. Readers did not treat it as fiction. They treated it as *revelation.* Rituals were attempted. Evocations performed. Protective circles drawn incorrectly. Names spoken aloud that were never meant to be paired with intention.

The curse did not come from Lovecraft.

It came from **people completing the circuit**.

What makes the Necronomicon phenomenon uniquely dangerous is not that the books contain effective magic—most do not—but that they **train readers to behave as if danger is proof of authenticity**. Any failure becomes evidence of personal unworthiness. Any psychological distress becomes confirmation that the book is "working."

And in occult practice, belief is not decoration. It is fuel.

By the 1980s and 1990s, reports began to cluster—not of tentacled gods or cosmic annihilation, but of subtler damage. Practitioners experienced prolonged dissociation. Nightmares that persisted for months. Obsessive ritual repetition. Paranoia centered specifically on *knowledge exposure*—the sense that one had "seen something" that could not be unseen.

These accounts appear in letters to occult publishers, in zines, in early internet forums, and later in psychiatric case studies where patients referenced the Necronomicon by name. Not as a novel. As a book they believed had changed them.

Skeptics rightly point out that Lovecraft's work attracts readers already inclined toward existential dread. But that explanation does not account for the **specificity** of the effects. The fixation on forbidden reading. The fear of finishing the book. The belief that harm would come *not from action*, but from comprehension.

That pattern predates Lovecraft.

Medieval grimoires were often wrapped in warnings—not because they contained demons, but because reading without preparation was thought to unbalance the soul. Knowledge had prerequisites. Context mattered. Authority mattered.

The Necronomicon strips all of that away.

It presents danger without hierarchy. Access without apprenticeship. Power without containment.

And worse—it suggests that curiosity itself is a moral failing.

By the time modern collectors began acquiring Necronomicons as physical artifacts—limited editions, leather-bound printings, "banned" versions—the object had fully transformed. It no longer mattered which text one owned. What mattered was participation in the myth.

Owners reported refusing to store the book near religious items. Others placed it in locked cabinets. Some wrapped it in cloth. Some claimed misfortune followed its arrival: job loss, illness, relationship collapse.

None of these effects are unique.

What *is* unique is how often the owners insisted the book was responsible *even while acknowledging it might not be real*. The Necronomicon teaches a specific kind of fear—one that does not require belief, only suspicion.

Today, dozens of Necronomicons circulate. Some are parody. Some are sincere. Some are careful pastiches built by scholars who understand exactly what they are doing.

And some are dangerous—not because of what they contain, but because of how they are framed.

The most troubling editions are the ones that present themselves as *partially fictional*. As reconstructed truths. As gateways.

Because that is where responsibility dissolves.

Lovecraft's greatest horror was not cosmic gods. It was epistemological collapse—the realization that human systems of meaning are fragile and temporary.

The Necronomicon was meant to be a symbol of that collapse.

Instead, it became a test case.

What happens when a fictional cursed object is treated with real reverence?

What happens when ritual language is used without lineage?

What happens when a warning is mistaken for an invitation?

The answer is not monsters.

It is slow damage. Self-inflicted, reinforced, and fiercely defended.

The Necronomicon does not summon anything.

It teaches people how to frighten themselves *correctly*.

And once learned, that skill is difficult to unlearn.

The final irony is this: the Necronomicon is most dangerous when it is treated lightly and most effective when treated seriously. It punishes certainty, rewards obsession, and thrives on half-belief.

That is not the work of a novelist.

That is the work of a curse that learned how to wear a paperback cover.

67

the cursed film
"poltergeist" props

The Cursed Film "Poltergeist" Props

By the time anyone asked where the skeletons came from, the scene had already been filmed.

That is the detail most people miss. Not that the bones were real — that comes later, always later — but that no one thought to ask until the danger had already passed through the room. The water had drained. The actors had gone home. The set had been struck.

Only then did someone notice that the skeletons floated differently than rubber would.

Only then did the truth surface.

The *Poltergeist* production began in 1981, during a period of aggressive efficiency in Hollywood. Studios were tightening budgets. Practical effects were favored over expensive prototypes. Realism was currency. If something looked convincing on camera and met legal minimums, questions stopped there.

The skeletons used in the swimming pool scene were purchased through a legitimate medical supply chain. This is documented. At the time, surplus human remains — often imported from India — were commonly used in anatomy classrooms and occasionally in film production. They were cheaper than replicas and required no fabrication time.

What the records do not show is consent.

JoBeth Williams, who performed the scene, was never told. She discovered the truth years later, during an interview, and confirmed it publicly in the early 2000s. Her reaction was not theatrical. It was stunned. She described a lingering discomfort she had never been able to explain — the sensation of being "touched" during the shoot when no one was near her.

That scene was filmed over multiple takes, in cold water, late at night.

The skeletons were weighted to rise slowly.

If this were folklore, it would end there.

It doesn't.

The release of *Poltergeist* in June 1982 coincided with a run of unusually public tragedies linked to the cast and extended production network. Not all deaths are equal in pattern-building. Some stand out because of timing.

On October 30, 1982 — just four months after the film's premiere — Dominique Dunne was strangled by her former boyfriend after attempting to end the relationship. She died five days later. The crime was brutal, highly publicized, and legally mishandled. Her killer served less than four years.

Dunne's death was not supernatural. But it *was* the first rupture — the moment when audiences realized the film's violence did not end with fiction.

In 1983, Steven Spielberg — who had significant creative control over *Poltergeist* despite contractual limitations — was simultaneously involved in *Twilight Zone: The Movie*, another production now infamous for on-set deaths. Actor Vic Morrow and two child actors were killed during a helicopter stunt gone catastrophically wrong.

Different film. Different genre.

Same era. Same production culture.

Same prioritization of spectacle over safety.

Crew overlap between Spielberg-era productions was common. Effects technicians, stunt coordinators, and set designers moved fluidly from one project to the next. While no single prop crossed directly between *Poltergeist* and *Twilight Zone*, the **methodology did** — especially the casual acceptance of real danger in controlled environments.

This matters.

Curses don't always attach to objects. Sometimes they attach to *processes*.

By the time *Poltergeist II* entered production in 1985, the tone had shifted. The film leaned harder into religious horror. Its antagonist, Reverend Henry Kane, was played by Julian Beck — an actor already visibly ill with stomach cancer during filming.

Beck died in September 1985, shortly after production wrapped.

His performance unsettled audiences not because it was frightening, but because it felt *terminal*. Viewers later noted that he appeared less like an actor portraying death than someone escorting it onto the set.

His scenes were filmed out of sequence due to his declining health.

In other words: death was already present during production.

Then came Heather O'Rourke.

O'Rourke was six when *Poltergeist* was filmed. She was twelve when she died in February 1988, during post-production of *Poltergeist III*. Her cause of death was initially misreported. Later records revealed she suffered from congenital intestinal stenosis complicated by septic shock.

What disturbed observers was not the illness — rare conditions exist — but the **speed**.

She collapsed suddenly. Surgery was attempted. She died within hours.

Her final scenes were completed using a body double and optical effects.

The film was released posthumously.

Three principal actors dead within six years.

At this point, the word *curse* entered mainstream coverage.

Skeptics responded with statistics. Child actors die. Cancer kills. Violence happens. All true.

But skeptics avoided the props.

They avoided the bones.

They avoided the growing list of **secondary incidents**: crew members reporting unexplained injuries, technicians refusing to work on franchise-related materials, collectors quietly returning props to storage after illness clusters in their homes.

One collector — interviewed anonymously in the early 1990s — claimed that a doorframe removed from a demolished *Poltergeist* set was followed by a series of accidents among his immediate family. He eventually dismantled and discarded it without resale.

No lawsuit followed. No documentation survives.

But silence is part of the pattern.

Unlike older cursed objects, *Poltergeist* has no single talisman. No idol. No chalice. What it has instead is **distributed contamination** — a curse without a body.

It exists in fragments:

- human bones sold as props
- dirt moved from grave-adjacent locations
- mirrors salvaged from condemned houses
- repeated invocations of haunting across shared crews

This is not a ritual curse. It is an *industrial one.*

A product of treating death as material.

The crossover extends beyond *Poltergeist*. Several crew members later worked on *The Exorcist III*, *Amityville* sequels, and *The Omen* franchise — all productions that accrued their own reputations for on-set unease, injuries, and near-fatal incidents.

Again: no single throughline of causation.

Only accumulation.

Today, Warner Bros. maintains no official archive of surviving *Poltergeist* props. Museums avoid the material. Retrospectives focus on nostalgia. When asked directly about the skeletons, studios acknowledge their authenticity briefly — then move on.

But the story does not move on.

It persists because it cannot be sealed.

The dead were not honored. They were rented.

And when the dead are used for realism rather than remembrance, they do not stay neutral. They linger in the edit. In the lighting. In the way audiences feel watched long after the credits roll.

The curse of *Poltergeist* is not that it killed people.

It is that it taught an industry how little it costs to invite death onto a set — and how difficult it is to make it leave.

The props are gone.

The process remains.

And that may be the most dangerous artifact of all.

68

the exorcist film
set artifacts

The Exorcist Film Set Artifacts

T he fire came first. It's a detail often buried beneath the trivia — beneath the box office numbers, the vomit stories, the ambulances stationed outside theaters — but it matters that *The Exorcist* burned before it ever frightened anyone.

In August of 1972, six weeks into principal photography, a fire tore through the MacNeil house set at CBS Studio Center in Los Angeles. The blaze destroyed nearly everything: walls, ceilings, furniture, wiring. Entire rooms collapsed into charred frames.

Only one space remained intact.

Regan's bedroom.

The room built to contain the possession. The room where the bed would shake, where the air would freeze, where the devil would speak through a child.

The fire marshal never offered a definitive explanation. Electrical fault was suggested, then quietly dropped. Production notes describe the survival of the bedroom as "strange," "unlucky," and later, "ill-advised."

Filming resumed.

That was the first decision that mattered.

William Friedkin did not want a haunted movie. He wanted a *real* one. His obsession with authenticity bordered on antagonistic. Actors were struck without warning to provoke genuine reactions. Temperatures on set were dropped below freezing for breath visibility, even when the crew protested. Medical professionals were consulted not for safety, but for accuracy.

He allowed a Jesuit priest to bless the set.

He did not stop there.

During filming, a series of deaths accumulated — not all directly connected to the production, but close enough in time and relationship to create an unmistakable pattern.

Jack MacGowran, who played Burke Dennings, died of influenza complications before the film's release. Vasiliki Maliaros, who played Father Karras's mother, died shortly after completing her scenes. Both deaths occurred in 1973.

Two crew members lost family members during production. One actor's newborn died. Another suffered a sudden mental breakdown requiring hospitalization.

These are the kinds of details skeptics dismiss quickly — and usually correctly.

But skeptics tend to ignore the objects.

The MacNeil house set was not discarded whole after filming. It was dismantled. Walls were repurposed. Furniture was sold or stored. Small items — lamps, crucifixes, rugs — were removed by crew members as souvenirs.

Several of these items would later resurface in private collections, auction listings, and estate sales, often accompanied by vague warnings or sudden withdrawals from sale.

One such artifact was a crucifix used during early rehearsal scenes — not the infamous prop associated with the film's most controversial moment, but a background piece kept in Regan's room. According to a former set dresser interviewed anonymously in the late 1980s, the crucifix was taken home by a lighting technician and later returned after unexplained disturbances, including persistent knocking sounds and the repeated appearance of ash-like residue on nearby surfaces.

No formal report exists.

But the item did not circulate again.

The artifacts associated with *The Exorcist* resist documentation in the same way the film resists closure. Unlike *Poltergeist*, where the danger was embedded in material remains, *The Exorcist* seems to infect through **proximity and repetition**.

Take the medical equipment.

The arteriography scene — still cited by physicians as unusually accurate — used real hospital-grade machinery. Several pieces were loaned, not fabricated. After filming, at least one unit was returned damaged beyond ordinary wear. A technician later described a persistent sense of dread when servicing the equipment, despite no mechanical explanation for the failures.

More disturbing are the reports surrounding the soundstage itself.

Crew members described cold spots that did not correspond to ventilation. Equipment malfunctions clustered around specific scenes. One assistant director allegedly refused to enter Regan's bedroom set alone after experiencing what he described as "pressure" — not fear, but physical resistance, as though the room itself objected.

Again: no incident report. No lawsuit. Only pattern.

Friedkin himself acknowledged the accumulation of events, though he resisted the word *curse*. In later interviews, he described the production as "fighting back," a phrase he used more than once.

The film's release in December 1973 intensified everything.

Audience reactions became part of the artifact chain. Fainting. Vomiting. Panic attacks. Reports of heart palpitations and dissociation. These were documented in newspapers, medical journals, and theater logs.

Ambulances were stationed outside some cinemas.

A woman reportedly miscarried during a screening in New York, a claim often repeated but never conclusively verified. True or not, the story persisted — and persistence matters.

The film did not merely scare people. It **entered them**.

Artifacts from *The Exorcist* continued to surface intermittently over the next decades. A fragment of Regan's bed frame appeared in a California estate sale in the early 1990s, only to be withdrawn after the seller reported a string of accidents in the household. A production chair bearing the film's title was auctioned and resold multiple times in short succession, each time quietly disappearing from listings.

Collectors began to notice something else: items connected to *The Exorcist* did not stay owned. They circulated briefly, then vanished.

This is not how valuable memorabilia behaves.

Even items tangentially associated with the film seemed to carry unease. Linda Blair's wardrobe pieces were stored under unusual conditions. Studio vaults logged repeated maintenance requests for spaces housing *Exorcist*-era materials, citing unexplained temperature fluctuations and alarm triggers.

Skeptics argue — again, correctly — that such claims are anecdotal.

But *The Exorcist* does not rely on spectacle. It relies on accumulation.

The most unsettling aspect may be the film's long shadow across later productions.

Several crew members from *The Exorcist* went on to work on *Poltergeist*, *The Omen*, and *The Exorcist III*. These productions would, in turn, develop their own reputations for injury, death, and disruption.

No single object links them.

Only repetition.

Today, the original MacNeil house is gone. The set no longer exists in any complete form. Most artifacts are unaccounted for, presumed destroyed or sealed away in private collections.

But the film endures — not just as media, but as an **event** that refuses to stay in the past.

It is screened every year. Studied. Quoted. Invoked.

And with each invocation, the residue stirs.

The danger of *The Exorcist* artifacts is not that they are cursed in the traditional sense. They do not promise misfortune on contact. They do not kill indiscriminately.

They *linger*.

They remind us that when realism crosses into reverence — when sacred symbols are used without belief but with intensity — something unbalanced is left behind.

The set was blessed.
It still burned.
The artifacts were stored.
They still circulate.
The film ended.
The disturbance did not.
That is the quiet warning *The Exorcist* leaves behind:
some stories do not want to be told realistically.
They want to be left alone.

69

the painting of the black monk of pontefract

T he first thing witnesses noticed was not fear.

It was *attention*.

People entering the house at 30 East Drive in Pontefract, West Yorkshire, described the same sensation long before they described terror: the feeling of being observed not from a corner or a doorway, but from a fixed point — as if something had chosen a place and refused to leave it.

This was not unusual for a house already known, by the late 1960s, as one of the most violently active poltergeist sites in Britain. Objects moved. Furniture overturned. Scratches appeared on walls and skin. A young girl was reportedly thrown from her bed.

The entity responsible was eventually given a name.

The Black Monk.

What is less discussed — and more dangerous — is what happened *after* the haunting acquired an image.

The Black Monk of Pontefract entered public consciousness through investigation, not folklore.

In 1966, the Pritchard family moved into 30 East Drive, unaware that the property had a reputation. Within weeks, disturbances escalated beyond the ambiguous. Furniture shifted violently. Items were

313

hurled across rooms. The children reported a dark, robed figure appearing at night, tall and faceless, its presence accompanied by intense pressure and dread.

Police were called on multiple occasions. They witnessed unexplained phenomena firsthand.

The house gained national attention after investigators, journalists, and psychical researchers arrived. Among them was Harold Chibbett, a paranormal investigator whose documentation would become central to the case.

Descriptions of the entity varied in detail but not in silhouette: tall, black, robed, hooded. A monk.

Importantly, no painting existed at this stage.

The haunting was active, but it was *formless*.

That changed when someone attempted to capture it.

The painting attributed to the Black Monk of Pontefract was not created during the height of the disturbances. It appeared later — after reports had been published, after the image of the monk had stabilized in the public imagination.

Accounts differ as to who painted it. Some sources claim it was produced by an artist connected to the investigation. Others suggest it emerged from a private collector attempting to "honor" the haunting. No definitive provenance exists, which is itself telling.

What matters is this: the painting was created from **description, not observation**.

A robed figure rendered in heavy blacks and greys. No visible face. No detail beneath the hood. The figure stands upright, frontal, dominating the frame, its darkness uninterrupted by background context.

It is not dynamic.

It is *present*.

Shortly after the painting began circulating — first privately, then through photographs and reproductions — new reports emerged.

Not from the house.

From the viewers.

People who spent extended time with the image reported sensations eerily similar to those described at 30 East Drive: pressure on the chest, cold air, unease that escalated into fear. Some experienced vivid dreams featuring the figure standing motionless, watching.

Unlike haunted houses, haunted images travel.

Documentation

Unlike many alleged cursed artworks, the Black Monk painting benefits — and suffers — from its association with one of Britain's most thoroughly documented poltergeist cases.

The haunting itself is referenced in police records, newspaper articles, and psychical research journals from the late 1960s. Officers confirmed disturbances. Journalists witnessed events they could not explain.

What complicates matters is that the painting does not appear in early documentation at all.

It enters the record later, almost parasitically.

By the 1980s and 1990s, accounts began surfacing in paranormal magazines and oral testimony collections describing adverse reactions to *images* of the monk. One researcher noted that people unfamiliar with the Pontefract case still reacted strongly to the painting when shown without context — a claim difficult to verify, but frequently repeated.

Photographs of the painting have appeared and disappeared online, often accompanied by warnings. Some listings were removed after sellers claimed to experience disturbances in their homes. Others vanished without explanation.

The painting's physical location is currently unknown.

Skeptics argue that the painting functions as a psychological trigger — a visual condensation of fear built from prior knowledge of the case. The Black Monk, they say, is not inhabiting the painting; the viewer is supplying the haunting.

This explanation accounts for some reactions.

It does not explain the consistency.

People report not fear *of* the image, but fear *from* it. A sense of being evaluated. Observed. Waited for.

Another theory suggests the painting acts as a symbolic anchor — not for the entity itself, but for the *idea* of it. In this model, the danger is not supernatural but memetic: the image stabilizes a haunting narrative so effectively that it replicates itself psychologically.

Yet even this explanation raises uncomfortable questions.

Why this image?

Why this reaction?

And why does the unease persist even when belief does not?

The original painting's whereabouts remain unclear. It is not held by a museum. It is not displayed publicly. Reproductions surface occasionally, often briefly, before being withdrawn.

The house at 30 East Drive still stands. It has changed hands multiple times. Owners report disturbances sporadically, though none as severe as the original case.

But the painting has outpaced the location.

The Black Monk no longer needs the house.

It has a face now — or rather, the absence of one.

Hauntings are dangerous when they remain unformed.

They become *portable* when we give them shape.

The Painting of the Black Monk of Pontefract is not dangerous because it contains something. It is dangerous because it completes something — a loop between witness, story, and image.

Once a haunting is seen, it can be remembered.

Once it is remembered, it can be repeated.

Once it is repeated, it no longer belongs to a place.

If the Black Monk still exists — whatever that means — it does not need to knock or throw furniture anymore.

It only needs to be looked at.

And that may be the most efficient haunting of all.

70

the poem "tam o'shanter" original manuscript

The horse never makes it.

When people remember *Tam o' Shanter*, they remember the laughter, the drink, the reckless ride through the storm, and the witches whirling in the ruined kirk. They remember the name of the horse—Maggie—and the way she runs harder the closer they get to safety. They remember the famous rule: that no witch may cross running water.

What they forget is that Maggie loses her tail anyway.

The poem survives.

The rider survives.

Something else pays the price.

Robert Burns first began composing *Tam o' Shanter* in the early 1790s, drawing from Ayrshire folklore he had known since childhood —stories told aloud in kitchens, not written down, passed hand to hand like contraband. The poem was not conceived as a simple comic piece. Burns himself described it as a tale that "exceeded everything I have ever done," and he labored over it with unusual care, revising lines obsessively.

The manuscript that survives from this process is not clean.

It shows hesitation. Ink blots. Words crossed out and replaced with

317

sharper ones. Descriptions of the witches grow more elaborate as the poem progresses, as if Burns could not stop adding detail once he had opened the door. The kirk becomes more crowded. The dance more frantic. The moment of pursuit stretches longer than strictly necessary.

Burns did not invent the witches.

He refined them.

And the manuscript remembers that refinement.

The poem enters the world first in fragments, shared among friends, then fully published in 1791. It is an immediate success. People quote it aloud. They perform it. They laugh at Tam's foolishness and repeat the warning as if it were lighthearted: *Do not linger where you should not be.*

But almost immediately, something else begins to cling to the poem —an unease around its physical origins.

The original manuscript changes hands early. Burns, always short of money, parts with drafts and fair copies more readily than later admirers would like. The *Tam o' Shanter* manuscript passes through collectors who prize it not only as literature, but as something older in spirit than the Enlightenment Scotland Burns is often made to represent.

It is folklore wearing ink.

By the early nineteenth century, the manuscript is already being treated less like a poem and more like a relic. Visitors ask to see it. Owners report an odd reluctance to keep it stored away. There are comments—minor, easy to dismiss—about the room feeling colder, about drafts near the case even in still air. One owner reportedly refused to keep it in a bedroom, claiming it "disturbed the sleep of the house," though no formal record explains what that meant.

None of this would matter, if not for the way the manuscript behaves around attention.

Unlike many literary artifacts, *Tam o' Shanter* does not settle into quiet reverence. Every time it is displayed publicly, the same pattern repeats. The poem's popularity spikes. Performances increase. Adaptations proliferate—stage versions, illustrations, musical settings. And alongside them, the tone shifts.

Illustrators emphasize the witches' bodies more aggressively than

Burns did. They elongate their limbs. Sharpen their faces. Maggie's pursuit becomes more desperate. The severed tail becomes grotesque, no longer comic. Each generation redraws the poem as something more feral.

This is not accidental. Burns himself warned against reading the poem too lightly. In letters, he notes that the laughter is meant to mask a darker truth: Tam escapes because he obeys the rule. Others may not.

Scholars debate whether Burns believed literally in witches. That debate misses the point. Burns believed in *rules*. He believed that stories existed to encode them. And he believed—this is visible in the manuscript itself—that breaking narrative boundaries had consequences.

The manuscript is heavily worked at the moment Tam looks back.

That is where the revisions cluster. That is where Burns could not decide how much to show. In one early draft, the chase is shorter. In another, the kirk door does not slam shut as hard. He changes it. Tightens it. Extends the pursuit just long enough to matter.

That revision stays.

By the mid-nineteenth century, reports begin to circulate—quietly —among collectors and archivists that prolonged study of the manuscript produces a peculiar effect. Readers lose track of time. People working with it late into the evening report hearing rhythmic sounds they attribute to fatigue: tapping, soft thudding, like hooves on wet ground.

No one writes this down formally.

Instead, the manuscript is rotated out of display more often than comparable works. It is described as "sensitive to light." Its housing is adjusted repeatedly. Curators are careful not to ascribe superstition to these decisions, but the result is the same: the manuscript is never allowed to remain exposed for long.

Theories arise, of course. Skeptics suggest suggestion and cultural priming. *Tam o' Shanter* is a witch story; people expect discomfort. Expectation produces sensation.

But expectation does not explain why the same details recur.

Always movement.

Always pursuit.

Always the sense that something is almost, but not quite, contained.

In 1896, a Burns enthusiast records in a private journal that reading the manuscript aloud felt "ill-advised," though he cannot say why. He notes that the poem "loses something when spoken directly from the hand that wrote it," and that he felt compelled to stop before finishing the chase.

This entry is rarely quoted.

In the twentieth century, the manuscript settles into institutional care. It is catalogued, conserved, described in neutral terms. The witches are now literature, not neighbors. The kirk is metaphor, not ruin.

And yet, the warnings persist.

Staff rotate handling duties. Gloves are required. The manuscript is never transported unnecessarily. Not because it is cursed—no one uses that word—but because "extended exposure seems to affect people unevenly."

That phrase appears more than once.

Today, *Tam o' Shanter* is taught in classrooms and quoted without fear. The manuscript itself remains behind glass, stable, silent. It no longer provokes panic. It does not need to.

The poem has already escaped.

Its imagery has embedded itself into cultural memory so deeply that it no longer requires the page to function. The witches dance whenever someone laughs too long at danger. Maggie runs whenever someone believes rules do not apply to them. The tail is lost again and again, payment rendered in advance.

The manuscript is not dangerous because it summons anything.

It is dangerous because it records a moment when someone knew exactly how close was too close—and chose to write it anyway.

There is a final detail, often omitted from casual retellings. Burns places Tam's survival on a technicality. He escapes not because he is clever, or brave, or deserving, but because he remembers the rule in time.

The poem does not promise that everyone will.

The manuscript preserves that uncertainty. It does not warn you loudly. It does not threaten. It simply keeps the chase alive, waiting for the next reader who believes they are already safe.

And if the room feels colder, or time slips, or you find yourself listening for hooves long after you close the case—

That is not the poem acting on you.

That is the rule reminding you it exists.

71
the cursed portrait
of thomas busby

No one remembers when the portrait first appeared on the wall. There are plenty of records about Thomas Busby himself. He was born in the early eighteenth century in North Yorkshire, a violent man by reputation, a counterfeiter, and eventually a murderer. His execution in 1702 was public, unceremonious, and meant to be final. He was hanged for the killing of his father-in-law, Daniel Auty, in a fit of rage that even contemporary witnesses described as excessive.

Busby did not die quietly. He cursed the place where he drank, the chair where he sat, and—according to later retellings—the people who dared to look at him without fear.

The chair became infamous first. That story is well known now: men who sat in it died soon after, accidents clustered around it, soldiers who ignored warnings never returned. Eventually, the chair was lifted off the floor and mounted high on the wall of the pub to prevent further deaths.

But before the chair was raised, something else hung nearby.

A portrait.

Descriptions of it vary depending on who is speaking. Some say it was a crude oil painting, others a charcoal sketch framed cheaply, likely commissioned or copied after Busby's execution. It showed a man seated, body turned slightly toward the viewer, eyes set forward with an expression that never quite resolved into anger or calm.

What everyone agrees on is this: the eyes followed you.

Not in the theatrical way people now associate with novelty paintings, but with something more unsettling. The gaze did not shift. It did not track movement. It simply *waited*. People felt watched only after they stopped paying attention.

The portrait is mentioned casually in eighteenth- and nineteenth-century pub inventories, never highlighted, never explained. It was simply listed as "Busby" or "the old fellow," hanging near the chair he favored in life. Regulars avoided looking at it directly, not out of superstition, but because it made conversation falter. People forgot what they were saying mid-sentence. Glasses were set down unfinished.

When deaths associated with the chair began to accumulate, the portrait was not blamed. It did not need to be.

Witness accounts from the nineteenth century begin to describe an odd pattern. Men who lingered too long in the pub—especially those who drank alone—reported vivid dreams after leaving. Not nightmares exactly, but scenes of watching rather than being chased. A man sitting. A room that felt familiar but slightly wrong. The sense of being evaluated.

One man, recorded in a local parish note from the 1860s, claimed he could not shake the feeling that "the fellow in the picture was waiting for his turn." The phrasing is peculiar. It implies patience, not rage.

Skeptics later suggested suggestion and folklore creep. The pub had a reputation by then; visitors expected unease. But expectation does not explain why the portrait was quietly removed before the chair was.

That decision is never announced. It simply disappears from records sometime in the late nineteenth century. Later inventories list the chair alone. Patrons remember "the picture that used to be there," but no one seems to know where it went.

There are rumors, of course. One claims the portrait was taken down after a landlord's wife complained she could not sleep while it remained in the building. Another suggests it was removed following the death of a stablehand who never sat in the chair but had spent hours sketching the painting out of boredom.

None of these stories can be proven. What *can* be traced is the shift in activity.

After the portrait's removal, deaths associated with the chair became more immediate and more dramatic—falls, crashes, sudden collapses. Before, there had been delays. Lingering illness. The sense that something had marked a person and was waiting.

It is tempting to say the portrait absorbed something.

Modern interpretations frame the painting as a psychological amplifier: a focal point for anxiety, a face for a reputation. But this explanation struggles with one detail that surfaces again and again.

People did not fear the portrait.

They avoided it.

In the twentieth century, when interest in Busby's curse resurged, investigators searched for the painting. No confirmed original has surfaced. Several reproductions exist, based on descriptions rather than reference, but none carry the same reputation. Copies are inert. They do not unsettle rooms. They do not silence conversation.

That absence matters.

If the chair was dangerous because it invited action—*sit here*—the portrait worked by refusal. It did not demand attention. It punished it indirectly. Those who stared longest reported the least immediate effects, but spoke later of feeling watched in other places, long after leaving the pub.

The portrait did not follow them.

It remembered them.

Today, the chair is safely housed in a museum, elevated and unreachable. The portrait, if it still exists, has never been formally catalogued. It may have been destroyed. It may be in a private collection, misidentified as a minor folk painting. It may be hanging somewhere unremarkable, doing nothing at all.

Or it may be waiting to be recognized.

There is a difference between an object that harms through contact and one that alters how a space feels. The latter does not need proximity. It only needs acknowledgment.

Busby cursed many things. That much is documented. But curses do not always attach themselves to what we expect. Sometimes they settle into images, into representations that fix a person in time without letting them rest.

The chair forced bodies into danger.

The portrait required only a glance.

If there is a warning here, it is not about superstition. It is about attention. About what happens when we give shape to someone who wanted to be feared and give them our eyes in return.

Some objects kill.

Others wait to be noticed.

72
the book of st. cyprian

T he book claims it can save you. That is how it gets its hands on you. Unlike most cursed texts, the Book of St. Cyprian does not announce itself as forbidden knowledge. It does not promise power outright. It promises *protection*. Guidance. A way to defend oneself against evil by understanding it more fully than one's enemies ever could.

This is what makes it dangerous.

The figure at its center, Cyprian of Antioch, is not a demonologist by reputation alone. He is a convert. A magician who becomes a saint. A man who allegedly knew the machinery of hell well enough to abandon it—and who left behind instructions on how to touch it safely.

That contradiction never resolves.

According to early Christian tradition, Cyprian was a pagan sorcerer in the third century, educated in occult practices across Greece, Egypt, and Babylon. His magic was not folk charm or superstition but formal invocation—names, sigils, bindings. When his spells failed against a Christian woman named Justina, Cyprian converted, renounced his former life, and was later martyred alongside her.

This would have been the end of the story.

Instead, someone wrote it down wrong.

Texts attributed to Cyprian began circulating centuries later—long after the historical man was dead and canonized. These books claimed to preserve the knowledge he abandoned: demon names, protective charms, summoning circles, instructions for negotiating with infernal forces *without being claimed by them.*

The framing is crucial. These are not manuals of domination. They are manuals of defense.

You do not command demons in the Book of St. Cyprian.

You *bargain.*

Early versions appear in medieval Iberia, written in Latin, Portuguese, and Spanish, spreading quietly through monastic libraries, folk practitioners, and private collections. By the seventeenth century, the text fractures into dozens of regional variants. No two copies agree completely. Some include prayers to the Virgin Mary alongside instructions for binding spirits. Others contain talismans meant to repel witchcraft while teaching how to recognize its signatures.

Readers noticed something unsettling very quickly.

The book worked—but not all at once.

Accounts from early modern Portugal describe practitioners who began using the Book cautiously, copying protective prayers, drawing circles exactly as instructed, feeling safer for it. Only later did the dreams begin. Repetition. Faces half-seen. The sense of being *known.*

Inquisition records from Spain and Portugal do not list the Book of St. Cyprian as outright heresy in the same way they condemn other grimoires. Instead, it appears repeatedly in confiscation logs under ambiguous language: "books of mixed doctrine," "texts of uncertain moral alignment," "manuals of forbidden discernment."

That distinction matters.

The Book was not treated as an object that corrupted instantly. It was treated as something that *slid.*

One seventeenth-century case from Lisbon records a cleric who kept a copy "for defensive study only." He was not charged with sorcery. He was charged with *refusing confession.* Witnesses claimed he no longer believed the priesthood had authority over forces he could name himself.

The danger was not what the Book summoned.

It was what it displaced.

By the eighteenth century, the Book of St. Cyprian becomes a folk artifact as much as a clerical one. In Brazil, it mutates again, blending with Afro-Brazilian spiritual traditions. Here, the Book is no longer theoretical. It is practical. It is consulted before rituals, used to identify spirits, invoked to establish boundaries.

Owners describe a pattern that repeats across continents and centuries.

The first months are calm.

The second year brings obsession.

After that, the Book no longer feels like a reference.

It feels like correspondence.

Pages fall open to the same sections repeatedly. Names repeat across dreams and waking thought. Readers report the sensation that the book "knows what you are asking before you ask it." This is not framed as possession. It is framed as familiarity.

A relationship.

Skeptics point out that grimoires often create fixation by design. Ritual repetition reinforces memory. The sense of agency can mimic intimacy. But this explanation falters when confronted with one persistent detail found in testimonies from Portugal, Brazil, and Spain alike.

Readers stop lending the Book.

Not because they fear damage or theft—but because they do not want it *handled by the wrong person.* They cannot always articulate why. They simply say the Book becomes "restless" when passed around.

Several nineteenth-century Brazilian accounts describe copies that were buried temporarily to "cool" them. When retrieved, owners claimed the text felt quieter, less insistent. Pages that had previously opened on their own did not do so afterward.

The implication is unsettling.

The Book accumulates attention.

In modern collections, copies of the Book of St. Cyprian are treated cautiously but not universally restricted. Some are digitized. Others are kept under standard rare-book conditions. Librarians report no incidents—but also note that these volumes are disproportionately requested compared to similar theological texts.

People come looking for them specifically.

The Book's reputation now precedes it. Readers arrive primed for danger. That expectation, paradoxically, seems to blunt its effect. Those who approach it as a curiosity often report nothing at all.

It is those who seek protection who experience escalation.

Because the Book does not offer safety.

It offers literacy.

To read the Book of St. Cyprian is to learn the grammar of threat. And once you can name something, you can never unknow it.

The final warning is never written explicitly in any surviving copy. It emerges only in practice.

Do not consult the Book unless you are prepared to believe that the forces it describes are real.

And do not believe they are real unless you are prepared to live in a world where they can recognize you in return.

The Book does not damn its readers.

It simply removes their excuses.

73

the bell witch manuscript

The manuscript does not begin with a scream.

It begins with an explanation.

In 1894, more than seventy years after the events it describes, a Tennessee schoolteacher named Martin Van Buren Ingram decided that the Bell Witch deserved a proper accounting. Not a pamphlet. Not a fireside tale. A book. Something orderly enough to convince skeptics and solid enough to outlast gossip.

That decision matters.

Because the Bell Witch did not need help becoming a legend. By the late nineteenth century, the haunting of the Bell family was already embedded in regional memory—retold in courtrooms, churches, and newspaper columns. Andrew Jackson's alleged encounter with the entity had become folklore. The mysterious death of John Bell Sr. was still discussed in Robertson County as something between murder and curse.

What Ingram attempted to do was pin the thing down.

The result—*An Authenticated History of the Bell Witch*—is what later readers would call the Bell Witch Manuscript. And despite its title, it does not behave like a neutral history. It behaves like a **containment attempt**.

The events it documents allegedly began in 1817 near Adams, Tennessee, on a stretch of farmland owned by John Bell Sr., a respected farmer and early settler. The first disturbances were small: knocking sounds, rustling outside the cabin walls, the sensation of something moving just beyond the edge of vision.

These are familiar beginnings. Almost polite.

The Bell family—John, his wife Lucy, and their children—initially dismissed the activity as animals or pranksters. But the disturbances escalated with a specificity that made denial difficult. The sounds followed individual family members. Beds shook only when certain people lay in them. Children were slapped, pinched, and verbally abused by an unseen presence.

And then the voice arrived.

Multiple witnesses describe it independently: a disembodied female voice that spoke clearly, intelligently, and at length. It identified itself only obliquely, sometimes calling itself "Kate," sometimes refusing names altogether. It recited Bible verses flawlessly, sang hymns, mocked preachers, and carried on extended conversations with visitors.

This is not poltergeist behavior.

This is *performance*.

By 1819, the Bell farm had become a destination. Neighbors, clergy, skeptics, and curious officials visited to witness the phenomenon. Some were mocked. Some were praised. The entity appeared to choose favorites. It displayed an unsettling familiarity with private thoughts, unfinished prayers, and unspoken resentments.

John Bell Sr., the patriarch, became its primary target.

He experienced physical symptoms that worsened over time: facial paralysis, difficulty swallowing, chronic pain. The entity claimed responsibility openly, announcing to witnesses that it intended to kill him. In December 1820, Bell was found in a stupor, unable to speak or swallow. A mysterious vial of liquid—later described as a dark, unidentified substance—was discovered near his bed.

The entity allegedly boasted of poisoning him.

John Bell Sr. died shortly thereafter. At his funeral, witnesses claimed the voice sang drinking songs and expressed satisfaction at its success.

Here is where the manuscript becomes important.

Ingram's account was not based solely on rumor. He interviewed surviving family members, including John Bell Jr., who provided first-hand testimony. He relied heavily on a document known as the *Bell Witch Bible*, a family Bible that reportedly contained marginal notes written during the haunting itself—dates, descriptions, reactions recorded contemporaneously.

That detail is crucial.

This was not a story written generations later. It was annotated *as it unfolded.*

The manuscript describes the entity departing after John Bell Sr.'s death, announcing it would return in seven years. According to the record, it did—briefly—before vanishing again, promising a final return in 1935.

No confirmed manifestation occurred that year.

Or at least none that agreed to be documented.

What followed instead was something quieter and more durable: the manuscript itself began circulating.

Readers reported a strange side effect. The Bell Witch story, when encountered orally, felt contained—an event with a beginning and end. But when read in Ingram's methodical, almost bureaucratic prose, the haunting felt *ongoing.* As if the act of ordering the events had given them a second life.

Skeptics have long criticized Ingram's work, pointing out embellishments, inconsistencies, and his clear desire to produce a compelling narrative. But even critics concede that many of his sources were genuine witnesses, and that some details—particularly medical symptoms and local records—align disturbingly well with independent documentation.

The manuscript does not convince because it is flawless.

It convinces because it is *messy in the way real testimony is messy.*

Today, the Bell Witch Manuscript exists in multiple forms: original printings, later editions, excerpts quoted in newspapers and academic texts. The Bell Witch Cave, located on former Bell property, attracts visitors who report sensations ranging from nausea to disorientation. Tour guides repeat the story with practiced cadence.

But the manuscript remains the most unsettling artifact of all.

Because it does not read like a ghost story.

It reads like minutes from a meeting that never adjourned.

The final danger of the Bell Witch Manuscript is not that it claims a spirit existed.

It is that it implies the spirit *noticed being noticed.*

Ingram wrote to preserve the story. To authenticate it. To close the book on rumor.

Instead, he created a document that continues to recruit witnesses —people who read it and feel, uncomfortably, that the voice in the margins never stopped speaking.

The Bell Witch was not bound.

It was archived.

And archives, as anyone who has worked in them knows, are never as silent as they appear.

74

the cursed copy
of macbeth

(the Scottish Play)

T he trouble begins before the curtain rises.

Long before actors whispered apologies for saying the title aloud, before stagehands flinched at certain lines, before theaters adopted rituals of expulsion and cleansing, *Macbeth* existed as ink on paper—just another script among many. That it would become something else entirely seems, in hindsight, inevitable.

The play was written around 1606, during the reign of James I, a monarch with a well-documented obsession with witchcraft. This alone is not remarkable. What is remarkable is how closely the text aligns with contemporary demonological treatises—particularly in its language, its spells, and its rhythms. The witches' incantations echo formulas that appear in real grimoires circulating in early modern Britain, not merely folklore but practical manuals seized and burned during witch trials.

From the beginning, *Macbeth* knew too much.

Early accounts suggest that Shakespeare may have drawn directly from these forbidden sources, perhaps even copying lines verbatim from rituals now lost. Whether this is true or not, the belief itself is older than most of the theaters that still refuse to speak the play's name. As early as the mid-seventeenth century, actors referred to

Macbeth obliquely, calling it "the Scottish play," as if language itself might summon something waiting just beyond the footlights.

The curse does not attach to performances alone.

It attaches to *copies*.

One of the earliest recorded incidents occurred in 1606, during what is believed to have been the play's first performance. The actor playing Lady Macbeth reportedly died suddenly, forcing Shakespeare himself to step into the role. Documentation is fragmentary, but the story persisted—passed from troupe to troupe as a warning.

Throughout the seventeenth and eighteenth centuries, reports accumulate. Fires break out during productions. Actors fall ill. Swords used onstage are swapped with real blades. Sudden deaths, injuries, and accidents cluster unnervingly around the play.

In 1703, London was struck by the Great Storm—the most violent storm ever recorded in southern England. On the night it hit, *Macbeth* was being performed at the Queen's Theatre. Roofs were torn from buildings. Hundreds died. The coincidence was noted immediately and never forgotten.

By the nineteenth century, the superstition had hardened into doctrine.

In 1849, a rivalry between actors Edwin Forrest and William Charles Macready culminated in the Astor Place Riot in New York. Both men were associated with competing productions of *Macbeth*. The riot left at least twenty-two people dead and more than a hundred injured. The play was blamed openly, not metaphorically. Newspapers referred to it as "blood-soaked," as if the script itself had taken lives.

But the most unsettling stories do not involve riots or storms.

They involve the books.

Actors speak of annotated copies that seem to resist being closed, pages that fall open to the same scenes night after night. Stage managers describe scripts that go missing only to reappear in places they had already searched. In one frequently cited account from the early twentieth century, a theater in Dublin reported that every copy of *Macbeth* in the building had been destroyed in a fire—except one, which was found intact amid the ashes, its cover blackened but its pages untouched.

This is not the only fire.

In 1937, a production at the Old Vic Theatre in London was plagued by disasters. Laurence Olivier was nearly killed by a falling weight during rehearsals. A stagehand died in an unrelated accident. The theater's founder, Lilian Baylis, suffered a heart attack during the run and died shortly afterward. The production was cursed, the company said—not because of poor luck, but because *Macbeth* had once again refused to behave like a play.

The belief extended beyond Britain.

In 1942, during a performance in London staged to boost morale during World War II, a bomb fell nearby during *Macbeth*. In 1964, actor Harold Norman was stabbed to death backstage after performing in the play at the Oldham Coliseum Theatre. In 1980, a production at the Lyceum Theatre in New York was halted after a stage manager was killed in a car accident during rehearsals.

Each incident reinforces the next.

By the late twentieth century, the curse had acquired rules. If the title is spoken aloud inside a theater, the speaker must leave, spin three times, spit, curse, and knock to be readmitted. These rituals vary, but the urgency behind them does not. The script is treated as if it can hear.

Scholars offer explanations. They point out that *Macbeth* is unusually violent, requires complex stage combat, and often attracts ambitious directors willing to push safety boundaries. They note that its themes—ambition, paranoia, blood—encourage emotional intensity that leads to mistakes.

All of this is reasonable.

None of it explains why the same pages feel heavy in the hand.

Collectors of theatrical ephemera report an odd trend: scripts of *Macbeth* are more often damaged, missing pages, or heavily annotated than other Shakespeare plays. Libraries quietly restrict handling of certain early copies after readers complain of headaches, unease, or vivid dreams following extended study.

These reports are anecdotal.

So are the curses.

But the pattern persists.

What makes the cursed copy of *Macbeth* different from other dangerous texts is that it was never meant to be static. It was written to be spoken, embodied, repeated. Each performance activates it. Each reading reopens it.

Unlike grimoires, which hide their power behind secrecy, *Macbeth* offers itself openly—and dares you to finish it.

Today, theaters still stage the play. Scripts still circulate. Students still read it aloud in classrooms, usually without incident. The curse is selective, like all the best ones. It does not strike everyone. It waits for proximity, for repetition, for belief sharpened by experience.

The most unsettling detail is not that disasters occur.

It is that people keep going back.

They stage the play again. They annotate the script again. They test the rules, hoping to disprove them. And when nothing happens, they relax—until something does.

There is an old theatrical saying: *Plays remember their audiences.*

If that is true, then *Macbeth* has been watching for more than four centuries.

And it has a very long memory.

75

the amber room panels

A mber is not stone. It looks like stone once it has been cut, polished, framed, mounted. It sits obediently in museums and jewelry cases, hard and luminous, pretending to be permanent. But amber is older than stone in another way. It is memory made solid—resin that once ran, once trapped insects mid-breath, once sealed light inside itself and refused to let it go.

The Amber Room was never built from something inert. It was assembled from time.

Its story begins not in Russia, but in Prussia, in the early eighteenth century, when King Frederick I commissioned a chamber meant to astonish rather than endure. The room was conceived as a diplomatic spectacle: walls paneled entirely in amber, gold leaf, mirrors, and carvings so intricate that candlelight would fracture endlessly across them. It was not meant to last. It was meant to overwhelm.

Construction began around 1701 under the supervision of Andreas Schlüter, with amber masters Gottfried Wolfram and later Ernst Schacht and Gottfried Turau shaping the panels by hand. Each piece was fragile. Each one could crack if mishandled. The room required constant care even as it was being built.

That fragility mattered later.

In 1716, the Amber Room was gifted to Peter the Great of Russia, a political gesture wrapped in splendor. It was dismantled, transported, and eventually installed in the Catherine Palace near St. Petersburg. There, it became something else entirely. No longer a novelty, it became a symbol—imperial, untouchable, almost mythic. Visitors described it as unreal. As warm. As if the walls were breathing.

Amber absorbs light. It also absorbs heat. Standing in the room for long periods made people uncomfortable, even faint. Courtiers complained of headaches. Servants reported the room felt "thick," especially in summer. These accounts were dismissed as superstition, or as the effect of mirrors and candles in an enclosed space.

But the room had already begun to change meaning.

By the twentieth century, the Amber Room was no longer merely decorative. It was national treasure, cultural identity, proof of continuity. Which made it dangerous.

When Nazi forces invaded the Soviet Union in 1941, they knew exactly what they were looking for. The Amber Room was listed, cataloged, and prioritized. German art experts accompanying the army arrived at the Catherine Palace within weeks. Soviet curators attempted to dismantle the panels for evacuation but quickly realized the truth: amber does not travel well. It crumbles. It fractures. It remembers stress.

So they hid it instead.

They covered the walls with wallpaper.

It did not work.

The Germans recognized the room immediately. Over the course of just thirty-six hours, they dismantled the panels, crated them, and shipped them to Königsberg Castle (now Kaliningrad). Photographs taken at the time show soldiers posing in front of the panels, smiling, as if they had conquered something alive.

In Königsberg, the Amber Room was reassembled and put on display. Visitors were allowed. Officers brought guests. The room was once again a spectacle—but now it was a captive one.

And then the war turned.

By 1944, Allied bombing raids intensified. Königsberg burned repeatedly. Castle staff dismantled the Amber Room again, crating the panels and storing them in the basement. After that, the record fractures.

Some witnesses claimed the crates were moved. Others claimed they were destroyed in the fires of August 1944. Still others insisted the panels survived, hidden in tunnels, mines, or ships fleeing westward as the Red Army advanced.

What is certain is this: when Soviet forces took Königsberg in April 1945, the Amber Room was gone.

Not damaged. Not partially recovered.

Gone.

The disappearance created a vacuum, and into that vacuum rushed stories.

Over the decades that followed, nearly every person associated with the room's final days met an unfortunate end. Alfred Rohde, the director of the Königsberg art collection and last known caretaker of the Amber Room, died suddenly in 1945, just months after Soviet authorities interrogated him. His wife died shortly after. Several German soldiers involved in transporting the crates were killed in combat or died under unclear circumstances.

Search teams followed rumors across Europe. Mines collapsed. Ships were dredged. Underground bunkers were excavated. Each expedition ended the same way: fragments, debris, or nothing at all.

The curse theory emerged quietly.

Not as a supernatural pronouncement, but as a pattern noticed too often to ignore. Expeditions seeking the Amber Room had a statistically unusual number of accidents, financial collapses, and unexplained deaths. Researchers obsessed over it for decades, only to lose funding, health, or credibility. The room seemed to resist recovery— not violently, but persistently.

In 1979, the Soviet Union began reconstructing the Amber Room from scratch, using original techniques and materials. It took over twenty years. Craftsmen reported that amber cracked unpredictably, even when handled correctly. Tools broke. Panels failed quality checks for reasons no one could explain. Some workers refused to continue after suffering recurring nightmares involving fire, darkness, and walls closing in.

The reconstructed Amber Room opened in 2003.

It is beautiful.

It is not the same.

The original panels—if they still exist—remain unaccounted for. And that absence has weight. The Amber Room has become one of the most famous lost treasures in history not because it was valuable, but because it was *unfinished*. Torn apart mid-identity. Removed violently from the place that gave it meaning.

Amber, once removed from its setting, degrades. It dries. It darkens. It cracks. It does not like to be moved repeatedly. It does not like war.

If the original panels still exist, they are likely unstable. Dangerous to handle. Dangerous to display. Perhaps that is why they remain hidden.

Or perhaps they are gone.

And that may be the most merciful outcome.

Because the Amber Room was never meant to be portable. It was a room. A space. A container of light and attention. When it was reduced to panels and crates, something essential was lost.

People still search for it.

They always will.

But there is an unspoken fear among serious historians and conservators—rarely written, but often implied—that finding the Amber Room intact would not be a triumph. It would be a reopening.

A return of something that has spent nearly a century absorbing war, fire, and disappearance.

Some rooms are not meant to be entered twice.

76

the mummy's curse newspaper illustration plates

THE MUMMY'S CURSE

The images came before the deaths.

That detail is often forgotten, or quietly rearranged in hindsight, but it matters. When Lord Carnarvon died in April of 1923, the public did not learn of it first through medical reports or diplomatic cables. They learned through pictures.

Black-and-white drawings, hastily engraved and cheaply printed, flooded British and American newspapers within hours. They showed a sarcophagus cracked open like a mouth. A pharaoh's eyes burned through shadow. Priests raised their hands in warning while pale Europeans recoiled. Some plates included hieroglyphs copied incorrectly, others invented them entirely. Accuracy was irrelevant. Atmosphere was everything.

The curse did not enter the world through archaeology.

It entered through ink.

Howard Carter's excavation of Tutankhamun's tomb in November 1922 had already ignited global fascination, but fascination alone does not haunt. What transformed the discovery into something dangerous was mass reproduction—illustration plates syndicated across dozens of newspapers, reused, redrawn, exaggerated, and stripped of context until the images themselves became a narrative.

The earliest plates were cautious. They showed the tomb entrance, the sealed doorway, Carter standing beside Lord Carnarvon. But within weeks, the tone shifted. Artists leaned into menace. Shadows deepened. Faces hardened. The mummy became animate long before it was even unwrapped.

By early 1923, several London papers were running illustrated spreads that paired the tomb imagery with speculative headlines: *"Ancient Warning Fulfilled?" "Death Follows the Pharaoh's Curse."* One widely circulated plate depicted a spectral figure hovering over Carnarvon's deathbed, the pharaoh's face hovering in the curtains like smoke.

Carnarvon's death itself was medically mundane—blood poisoning following a mosquito bite—but that detail was visually useless. What mattered was timing. He died just months after the tomb's opening. On the night of his death, Cairo reportedly suffered a power outage. His dog, back in England, allegedly howled and dropped dead at the same moment.

These details were printed beside the illustrations, not beneath them.

The images did something text could not. They taught the public *how* to be afraid.

Within a year, the illustrated curse had grown teeth. Newspapers reused plates whenever another person associated—however loosely—with the excavation died. Arthur Mace. George Jay Gould. Later, lesser figures: visitors, secretaries, doctors. Each death, regardless of cause, was visually folded into the same graphic language: sarcophagi, eyes, smoke, retribution.

The plates did not document events.

They connected them.

American tabloids were particularly aggressive. Some papers commissioned entire series of illustrations portraying the curse as an active force moving from victim to victim. In several plates, the mummy is shown *looking directly at the reader*, breaking the fourth wall in a way that prose rarely dared.

This was new.

Previous archaeological reporting had relied on diagrams and portraits. The mummy plates were narrative illustrations—almost cinematic—designed to be remembered rather than understood. Children cut them out. Adults pinned them to walls. They circulated far beyond the articles they accompanied.

And something strange happened.

Readers began reporting symptoms.

Letters to editors describe recurring dreams of sealed rooms, breathlessness, the smell of dust. Some claimed the images caused insomnia. Others described a vague dread when encountering unrelated Egyptian imagery. A few insisted the plates themselves were unlucky—one reader wrote that after hanging a clipping above his desk, he suffered a run of accidents and threw it away "for peace of mind."

No one took these reports seriously.

But they kept coming.

The power of the plates lay in repetition. The same visual motifs appeared again and again: the raised hand, the watching eye, the dark doorway. Over time, the public no longer needed to read the article. Seeing the image was enough to summon the story. The curse had become iconographic.

By the late 1920s, the mummy's curse was no longer tied specifically to Tutankhamun. Newspapers reused older illustration plates for unrelated discoveries. A mummy found in Peru? Cue the Egyptian curse art. An exhibition opens in Paris? Run the sarcophagus plate again.

The images detached from their origin and became portable fear.

Scholars later noted that many of the most infamous "curse" stories trace back not to primary sources, but to illustration captions. A misattributed quote. A dramatic line added by an editor. Once paired with an image, it solidified. Visual authority replaced factual accuracy.

This is where skepticism enters—and fails.

Egyptologists and historians repeatedly pointed out that no curse text was found in Tutankhamun's tomb. Death rates among the excavation team were unremarkable for the era. Howard Carter himself lived until 1939. The curse, they argued, was a journalistic invention.

They were right.

And it didn't matter.

Because the curse was no longer an idea. It was a visual system.

The plates had trained the public to associate Egyptology with retribution, excavation with punishment, the past with teeth. Even when newspapers later ran debunking articles, they often reused the same illustrations. The image undermined the text every time.

Some of the original plates survive in newspaper archives and private collections. Conservators handling them report nothing unusual—no measurable anomaly, no material danger. And yet, there is an unspoken reluctance to display them prominently. Curators note that visitors linger too long. That the images provoke an emotional response disproportionate to their artistic quality.

They are not good drawings.

They are effective ones.

Today, the mummy's curse lives primarily in film and fiction, but its DNA is visible. The visual grammar established by those early newspaper plates—angled shadows, anthropomorphized sarcophagi, ancient eyes watching the present—remains intact. The curse persists not because it was real, but because it was seen.

There is a quiet discomfort among media historians when discussing these plates. An acknowledgment, rarely stated outright, that the illustrations did more than report fear. They manufactured it. Distributed it. Taught it how to reproduce.

The objects in this chapter are not relics or bones or jewels. They are paper. Ink. Cheap reproductions meant to be discarded.

And yet they outlived the excavation.

The tomb is sealed again.

The bodies are cataloged.

The facts are settled.

But the images still circulate.

There is an old superstition among archivists—half joke, half warning—that you should never display the curse plates together. That something about proximity intensifies them. No one can explain why.

They simply do not.

Because once an image teaches people *how* to fear something, it no longer needs the thing itself.

The curse does not live in the tomb.

It lives in the picture.

77

the tibetan book
of the dead scrolls

(handling taboos)

T he first mistake is always the same.

Someone opens the text.

Not to read it aloud, not to perform a rite, not even out of malice—but out of curiosity. The pages are thin, the ink faint, the script elegant and precise. It looks like a book. Books are meant to be opened. That assumption alone has caused centuries of trouble.

The work known in the West as *The Tibetan Book of the Dead* was never meant to be a book at all. It is not a volume, not a single text, not a work intended for the living. Its Tibetan name, *Bardo Thödol*, translates more accurately as *Liberation Through Hearing in the Intermediate State*. Hearing, not reading. Intermediate state, not life.

The scrolls were composed to be spoken to the dead.

According to Tibetan Buddhist tradition, consciousness does not end at death. It moves through the *bardos*—intermediate states between death and rebirth—where the mind encounters visions shaped by karma, fear, memory, and attachment. The scrolls exist as a guide through that terrain, a set of instructions read aloud by a trained practitioner to help the deceased recognize illusion, release fear, and avoid being pulled back into suffering.

They are maps for someone who no longer has a body.

This matters, because from the beginning, the scrolls are explicit about one thing: they are dangerous when mishandled.

The texts themselves warn that improper reading can confuse rather than liberate. That incorrect timing can bind a consciousness instead of freeing it. That the words, spoken to the wrong audience, do not dissipate harmlessly—they linger.

Traditionally, the scrolls are kept wrapped. They are not displayed casually. They are not read in advance "to familiarize oneself." Even monks treat them with care. Handling is ritualized. Storage is intentional. The scrolls are not considered neutral objects waiting to be activated. They are already active.

The trouble begins in the late 19th and early 20th centuries, when European scholars, missionaries, and collectors encounter Tibetan religious materials through colonial routes. Texts are purchased, taken, translated, and reframed. In 1927, Walter Evans-Wentz publishes the first widely circulated English version of the *Bardo Thödol*, filtered through Theosophical interpretation and Western spiritualism.

For the first time, the scrolls are presented not as a funerary technology, but as a philosophical self-help manual.

Readers are encouraged to study them. Meditate on them. Internalize them. Some even attempt to read them aloud as preparation for death, or worse, as a form of mystical exploration.

This is where the unease begins to appear in the record.

Letters archived in British and American collections describe readers experiencing disorientation, intrusive imagery, and persistent anxiety after prolonged engagement with the text. A 1930s correspondence between two members of a London spiritualist circle notes that reading passages aloud during a séance caused "unsettling interruptions"—participants reported hearing voices overlapping the reader's voice, and one insisted the text "wasn't meant for us."

Museum records are quieter, but no less telling. Curators at institutions holding original Tibetan scrolls—particularly funerary copies—frequently note restrictions imposed by Tibetan advisors: limits on display duration, avoidance of direct lighting, reluctance to mount the scrolls vertically "as if alive." Some museums complied. Others did not.

In at least two documented cases, exhibitions featuring *Bardo*

Thödol scrolls were altered after staff complaints. Night security guards reported recurring dreams involving corridors, chanting, or being unable to move forward or backward. These were logged as stress-related incidents. The scrolls were rotated off display shortly thereafter.

No one claimed the scrolls were cursed.

They didn't need to.

Anthropologists studying Tibetan mortuary practice have repeatedly emphasized that the scrolls function relationally. They are not spells that activate automatically. They respond to context, intention, and audience. The wrong voice, the wrong listener, the wrong moment —these are not minor errors. They change the outcome.

And yet, in Western contexts, the scrolls are almost always separated from their relational framework. They are read alone. Silently. By people very much alive.

This inversion produces a different kind of disturbance—not dramatic hauntings, but slow cognitive friction. Readers report a sense of being out of phase with time. Of being addressed rather than instructed. Of passages seeming to "wait" for something.

One scholar writing in the 1970s noted, with some discomfort, that repeated engagement with the text produced a recurring sensation of standing in a threshold space—not fear exactly, but a persistent inability to settle. He stopped teaching the text publicly shortly thereafter, citing "ethical concerns."

Tibetan practitioners are less ambiguous. Monks interviewed in exile communities consistently express discomfort with the casual handling of the *Bardo Thödol*. Several emphasize that the text assumes the reader is already dead. When read by the living, the instructions have no proper recipient.

Where do they go instead?

There is no single answer, but the warnings are consistent: confusion, attachment, looping thought, spiritual exhaustion. Not possession. Not madness. Something quieter.

Misplacement.

Today, original *Bardo Thödol* scrolls reside in private collections, monasteries, and museums around the world. Most are kept respectfully. Some are digitized. A few circulate online stripped of ritual framing entirely.

The text has become ubiquitous. The practice has not.

And that imbalance lingers.

Those who work closely with Tibetan religious materials often speak—off the record—about a sense of responsibility that goes beyond conservation. They describe a need to "let the scroll rest." To avoid unnecessary engagement. To acknowledge that some texts are not meant to educate the living, but to accompany the dead.

The scrolls themselves never threaten. They do not punish. They do not promise harm.

They simply assume you are already gone.

And when the living insist on standing where the dead are meant to pass, something has to give.

The most enduring taboo surrounding the *Bardo Thödol* is not about curses or ghosts or divine wrath. It is about timing. About speaking when you should be listening. About opening a door that is meant to open only once.

The scrolls do not chase you.

They wait.

part five
domestic objects (mirrors, furniture, toys)

78

the myrtle's plantation mirror

In the late 18th century, mirrors were luxury items—heavy, fragile, expensive, and symbolic. To give one was not simply to decorate a home, but to announce permanence. Wealth. Intention. A belief that the house would stand long enough to be reflected back upon itself.

At the Myrtles Plantation in St. Francisville, Louisiana, the mirror was installed in what would later be known as the Clark–Woodruff room. At the time, the house was still young, the land newly claimed, the labor that sustained it violently invisible. The mirror was tall, framed in gilded wood, imported, and positioned deliberately—placed so that the bed, the doorway, and the adjoining hall could all be seen from its surface.

It was not meant to be looked into casually.

Local tradition holds that the mirror was covered after death, as was customary in many 18th- and 19th-century households. Mirrors were believed to trap the soul if left uncovered, to confuse the dead, or to invite them back. Whether this belief was strictly adhered to at the Myrtles is uncertain. What is certain is that the mirror now bears marks that are not consistent with age or damage.

Handprints appear on the glass.

They do not smear. They do not fade with cleaning. They do not repeat exactly, but they return often enough to be documented by staff, guests, and photographers across decades. Some appear high, as if from an adult bracing themselves. Others are lower, smaller, the spacing unmistakably childlike.

The most persistent story tied to the mirror centers on a woman named Chloe.

According to plantation lore, Chloe was an enslaved woman who worked in the house and was allegedly punished for eavesdropping by having her ear cut off. She is said to have worn a green turban to conceal the injury. In retaliation—or desperation—she is believed to have poisoned a birthday cake meant for one of the plantation owners, unintentionally killing two children and their mother instead.

Historical records confirm that members of the Woodruff family died of yellow fever. They do not confirm poisoning. They do not mention Chloe by name. This discrepancy has been the cornerstone of skeptic arguments for years.

But folklore does not require precision. It requires repetition.

What matters is that the deaths happened inside the house. What matters is that the mirror was present. What matters is that from that point forward, the mirror was treated differently.

Guests reported seeing figures in it who were not in the room. A woman in green. Children standing behind the viewer. Faces that lingered after the observer stepped away. These accounts increase sharply after the house transitions from private residence to public inn in the 20th century, when the mirror becomes an object of attention rather than avoidance.

Attention changes behavior.

Guests who stay in the Clark-Woodruff room frequently describe the same progression: unease, fascination, fixation. They find themselves checking the mirror repeatedly. Not because they see something immediately, but because they feel as though they might.

Some report waking to the sound of movement and seeing impressions in the glass that resemble breath. Others describe a sensation of being watched *from the mirror*, not through it. A few recount seeing themselves reflected incorrectly—standing still when they moved, smiling when they did not.

Photographs taken in the room often capture anomalies that defy easy dismissal. Faces appear where no one stood. Blurred forms align with the height of the reported child spirits. In several cases, handprints are visible only in photographs, not to the naked eye, as if the glass chooses its witnesses.

Skeptics argue condensation. Residue. Pareidolia. And in isolation, each explanation is plausible.

But the pattern is persistent.

Mirrors, across cultures, have always been treated as thresholds. They reflect light, yes—but also attention. In spaces marked by trauma, they become recorders. Not because they trap souls, but because they preserve moments of awareness: fear, pain, surprise, recognition.

The Myrtles mirror has seen illness. It has seen death. It has seen servants passing silently behind owners who never acknowledged them. It has seen children die in beds meant to protect them. It has seen the house emptied and filled again, over and over, by people who do not belong to its past but cannot fully escape it.

That accumulation matters.

Staff at the Myrtles do not encourage guests to touch the mirror. They do not forbid it either. But long-term employees quietly admit that those who linger too long in front of it tend to sleep poorly, report vivid dreams, or feel emotionally "off" for days afterward.

The mirror does not harm.

It unsettles.

And that is often worse.

Today, the mirror remains in place. It is not roped off. It is not hidden. It is allowed to be seen. That choice is intentional. The Myrtles has learned that trying to contain the house's stories only intensifies them.

The mirror is not the source of the hauntings.

It is the witness.

And witnesses, when ignored for too long, have a way of insisting on being acknowledged.

There is an old superstition in Louisiana that mirrors remember faces long after bodies are gone. That if enough grief passes through one, it no longer reflects the present cleanly. It layers. It overlaps. It hesitates.

If you stand before the Myrtles mirror long enough, you may notice this hesitation. The way the room behind you feels crowded. The way your reflection feels slightly delayed, as if checking something before agreeing to be you.

The mirror does not pull you in.

It does something quieter.

It reminds you that you are not the first to stand there—and you will not be the last.

79
the okiku doll

In 1918, in the city of Sapporo on the northern island of Hokkaidō, a seventeen-year-old boy named Eikichi Suzuki purchased a traditional Japanese doll from Tanukikōji, a bustling shopping street known for its merchants and curios. The doll was intended for his younger sister, Okiku. She was three years old. The doll was small, dressed in a kimono, with a pale face and straight black hair cut to shoulder length.

The doll's features were unremarkable. Its construction was typical of the time. What mattered was the name.

Okiku loved the doll immediately. She carried it everywhere. Slept with it. Spoke to it. The doll was not an accessory; it was a companion. Family members later recalled that Okiku would scold anyone who handled it too roughly, as if the doll were capable of feeling offense.

Less than a year later, Okiku fell ill.

Historical accounts vary on the exact diagnosis—some suggest a sudden infection, others a fast-moving fever—but the outcome is consistent. Okiku died at the age of three. The family was devastated. And when the household prepared a Buddhist altar for her spirit, they placed the doll there as well.

At first, this was ordinary.

In Japanese mourning practice, objects associated with the deceased are often treated with reverence. Dolls, in particular, are not considered inert. They are believed to absorb emotional presence through prolonged contact. This is why traditional Japanese culture emphasizes the ritual disposal of dolls, most famously through *ningyō kuyō*—ceremonies held to thank dolls for their service before releasing them.

But the Okiku doll was not released.

It remained on the altar. And then something changed.

The family noticed that the doll's hair appeared to be growing.

At first, the change was subtle. A millimeter here. A suggestion of length where none had been before. They assumed memory had exaggerated the difference. They cut the hair, returning it to its original length.

Weeks later, it had grown again.

The Suzuki family did not publicize this immediately. They were not seeking attention. They were frightened. They documented the change privately, trimming the hair repeatedly. Each time, it returned —longer, uneven, sometimes tangled, as if responding to touch.

By the early 1930s, the family prepared to leave Hokkaidō. Before departing, they brought the doll to Mannenji Temple in Iwamizawa, requesting that the monks care for it. They did not attempt to sell it. They did not discard it. They did not bury it.

They handed it over.

Temple records confirm the transfer. The doll was accepted and placed among other ritual objects. The monks were told the story. They were skeptical—but not dismissive. Hair growth was observed and recorded. The doll was examined. No mechanical explanation was found.

The monks continued the practice of cutting the hair.

And the hair continued to grow.

Over time, the Okiku Doll became known beyond the temple grounds. Local visitors reported an unsettling presence. The doll's expression appeared unchanged, but its hair now extended past its shoulders, sometimes reaching its waist. The hair was not synthetic. Later microscopic analysis confirmed it was human hair.

This detail matters.

Human hair does not grow without a living scalp.

Skeptics suggested contamination. Replacement. Hoax. Yet no evidence of substitution was found. The doll remained under consistent custodianship. Photographs from different decades show progressive lengthening, inconsistent with simple replacement.

In 1965, the doll was examined more closely. The hair was found to be attached to the scalp in a manner consistent with traditional doll-making, but its continued growth could not be explained by craftsmanship alone.

The temple does not claim the doll is haunted.

They say something quieter.

They say the doll is inhabited.

Not in the Western sense of possession, but in the Japanese understanding of *kami* and lingering spirit—that a fragment of Okiku remained, not out of malice or confusion, but attachment. The doll was not trapping her. It was holding her because no one told her to leave.

This distinction is critical.

The Okiku Doll does not behave aggressively. It does not cause harm. It does not seek attention. It does not move on its own. It simply changes.

Visitors sometimes report feeling watched. Others feel nothing at all. Children are often drawn to it, standing silently in front of the case where it now rests. Adults tend to look away quickly.

The monks continue to care for the doll. They cut its hair. They perform prayers. They do not attempt to sever whatever connection exists. They treat the doll as one would treat a child who has overstayed a visit—gently, patiently, without force.

This, too, matters.

The danger of the Okiku Doll is not in what it does.

It is in what it suggests.

That love, when left unresolved, does not fade. That grief can settle into objects and change them slowly, subtly, until they no longer behave as expected. That not all hauntings are violent. Some simply refuse to end.

The doll remains at Mannenji Temple today. It is displayed openly.

Visitors are allowed to see it. Photographs are permitted, though many choose not to take them. The hair continues to grow.

The temple does not explain why.

They do not need to.

There is a belief in Japan that spirits who are acknowledged do not become vengeful. The Okiku Doll may be the purest expression of that idea: a spirit who stayed not to punish, but because no one told her she could go.

There is a final note recorded by a monk in the mid-20th century, often repeated in translations and retellings. It is not dramatic. It is not ominous.

It simply states that the hair grows faster when the doll is neglected.

80
the haunted rocking chair of key west

I t moves when the room is still.

That is the first thing everyone notices, even if they try not to say it out loud. The air can be stagnant, the doors closed, the windows sealed against the heavy Florida heat—and the chair rocks anyway. Not violently. Not dramatically. Just enough to register.

Forward.

Back.

Forward again.

The rocking chair now sits inside Fort East Martello Museum in Key West, a brick Civil War–era structure that has learned, over time, how to house objects people do not want in their homes anymore. It is best known for Robert the Doll, whose reputation has long eclipsed the quieter artifacts nearby.

But museum staff will tell you—often only after a pause—that Robert is not the only thing in the building that behaves strangely.

The chair arrived without fanfare.

Unlike Robert, it did not come with a neatly packaged origin story. There was no single donor with a dramatic confession, no typed letter explaining why it had to go. It came through the slow accumulation of local stories, passed between residents who lived long enough in Key West to understand when something should not stay in a private home.

The earliest accounts place the chair in a 19th-century house not far from the harbor, during a period when Key West was flush with shipbuilders, wreckers, and families who lived by the tide and the dead it sometimes delivered. Rocking chairs were common fixtures—used for nursing children, sitting vigil, and waiting out storms.

Waiting is important here.

Several versions of the story agree on one detail: the chair belonged to an elderly woman who spent most of her final years sitting in it, facing a window. She watched the street. She waited for someone who did not come back.

Whether that someone was a husband lost at sea, a son who never returned from war, or simply a life that narrowed until the outside world became something to observe rather than enter, depends on who is telling the story. What does not change is this: when the woman died, the chair did not stop moving.

Family members reported hearing it rock at night. Guests noticed it shifting slightly while no one was near it. Attempts to secure it—to wedge it against a wall, to tie it in place—were abandoned after repeated failures. The chair would be found moved by morning, angled back toward the window.

Eventually, the chair left the house.

By the mid-20th century, Key West had begun to curate its oddities rather than discard them. Fort East Martello became a repository not just for military history, but for things that resisted explanation. The chair was placed in storage first, then on display, initially without a label.

It rocked there too.

Museum logs from the late 1980s and early 1990s note multiple incidents of unexplained motion. Staff dismissed drafts, vibrations from foot traffic, even the uneven brick floor. None of these explanations accounted for the chair rocking after hours, when the building was empty.

Security guards reported seeing it move on camera. Not always—

but often enough to be unsettling. The motion was never sudden. It did not tip or lurch. It behaved as a chair behaves when occupied.

That resemblance is what unsettles people most.

Visitors sometimes ask if it's motorized. It is not. Others ask if the footage is looped. It is not. Children, oddly, seem less disturbed than adults. Several have been observed sitting near it, watching quietly, as if expecting someone to return.

The museum does not encourage interaction.

The chair is not advertised as cursed. It does not have a dramatic placard. It is simply present. But staff will tell you—if asked directly—that they no longer move it unnecessarily. Past attempts to relocate the chair within the room resulted in doors opening on their own, temperature drops, and an increase in reported activity from nearby exhibits.

After one such attempt, the chair was returned to its original position.

It resumed rocking within hours.

Skeptics point out the obvious: old buildings settle. Air moves unpredictably. Human perception fills in gaps. All of this is true. And yet the chair does not rock constantly. It does not perform for crowds. It moves intermittently, as if responding to something unseen rather than environmental triggers.

This inconsistency is what makes it difficult to dismiss.

There is also the matter of timing.

Staff have noted that the chair is more active in the early evening, around the hour when the harbor quiets and the day's heat begins to lift. It is less active during peak tourist hours. More active when the museum is nearly empty.

That pattern mirrors human behavior.

The chair does not feel hostile. No injuries have been attributed to it. No scratches, no nightmares that can be cleanly traced back. Its unease lies elsewhere—in the sense that someone is still waiting, still occupying the space the chair defines.

In Key West, where the past never fully leaves and the dead are woven casually into daily conversation, this is not considered extraordinary.

It is considered familiar.

The chair rocks because it always has. Because someone sat there long enough that the motion became a habit. Because waiting can outlast the body that learned it.

The museum keeps the chair polished. It is not abandoned. It is not ignored. That, too, seems important.

There is an unspoken understanding among the staff: objects that are acknowledged behave better than those that are denied.

The chair continues to rock.

Not for everyone. Not on command. Just enough to remind those who notice that not all hauntings are dramatic.

Some are simply unfinished.

81

the cursed crib
of new orleans

T he crib was not made to last. That much is clear from its construction—thin cypress slats, hand-pegged joints, a rocker base shallow enough to still at the slightest touch. It was built quickly, inexpensively, the way furniture is made when it is needed *now*, not later. When a household is preparing for a child in a city where children do not always stay.

In 19th-century New Orleans, cribs were rarely heirlooms. They passed through families only briefly, if at all. Illness moved faster than craftsmanship. Summer heat pressed disease into every room. Yellow fever, cholera, and dysentery arrived in waves so regular they were given seasons instead of dates.

The crib that would later earn its reputation appears in oral histories tied to the Faubourg Marigny sometime between the 1830s and 1850s. No single household claims it definitively. Instead, it appears *between* families—loaned, borrowed, reclaimed after funerals that came too quickly to argue over furniture.

That is where its story begins.

According to multiple family accounts preserved in local historical collections, the crib was present in at least four households where infants died before their first birthday. The causes differ—fever, sudden illness, wasting—but the details repeat: the child quieting abruptly, the mother waking to a still room, the crib rocking slightly though no one had touched it.

At first, this meant nothing.

New Orleans was no stranger to infant death. Entire neighborhoods were marked by it. Cribs were scrubbed, prayed over, blessed, and reused without ceremony. What distinguished this one was not the deaths themselves, but what followed.

Families reported hearing movement in the nursery after the child was gone. Not crying. Not voices. Just the slow rhythm of wood on floor. Rocking without pressure. Rocking without weight.

Several families attempted to dismantle the crib. One account mentions the pegs refusing to come loose. Another describes the wood splintering unpredictably, as though resisting the shape of tools. Eventually, the crib was passed along again—this time not out of generosity, but relief.

By the late 19th century, the crib had become an object people recognized without wanting to claim. It appeared in a boarding house briefly. Then in a Creole cottage near Esplanade Avenue. Then vanished for decades.

It resurfaced during the Works Progress Administration era, when local folklore was recorded alongside oral histories. A woman interviewed in the late 1930s described "a baby bed that never forgot how to rock," though she could not say where it had gone. She only remembered being warned not to sleep near it.

By the time the crib entered a private collection in the mid-20th century, it was no longer associated with a single tragedy, but with *accumulation*. A pattern. The kind of story that persists because no one can quite finish it.

The collector—whose name appears only in fragmented notes—reportedly experienced repeated disturbances after acquiring the crib. Doors opening. Cold air localized to one corner of the room. A sensation of being watched that intensified at night. After a short illness, the crib was donated quietly to a religious-affiliated storage facility.

It did not stay there long.

Staff reportedly refused to keep it in areas where children visited.

The crib was moved to a back room, then a locked space, then removed entirely. No official explanation survives. Only the note that it was "unsuitable for display."

Today, the crib is not on public view. Its exact location is uncertain —variously rumored to be in storage, dismantled, or held by a private collector with ties to the city's historical preservation circles.

But the stories continue.

Visitors to older New Orleans homes sometimes describe rocking sounds in empty nurseries. Tour guides occasionally reference "the baby bed that wouldn't stop" before changing the subject. Antique dealers refuse cribs with similar construction if their provenance is unclear.

Skeptics argue—correctly—that grief shapes memory. That rocking sounds can be explained by old floors, humidity, and airflow. That New Orleans architecture creaks because it is alive, not because it is haunted.

But that explanation does not account for the consistency of the warning.

Not *don't touch.*

Not *don't look.*

But *don't let it stay.*

In many folk traditions, especially those shaped by Catholicism and African diasporic belief systems, objects associated with infant death are considered liminal. They exist between beginnings and endings, never fully claimed by either. If left unattended, they do not rest.

The crib does not rage. It does not threaten. It does not harm directly.

It simply continues the motion it was taught.

Rocking for a child who never learned to sleep through the night.

Rocking because stillness never arrived.

Rocking because the room remembers what the body forgot.

There is a quiet belief in New Orleans that grief settles into furniture. That sorrow, like humidity, seeps into wood and refuses to evaporate. If that is true, then the crib is not cursed in the theatrical sense.

It is occupied.

And whatever remains inside it has learned patience.

82

the haunted
clock of versailles

T ime was never neutral at Versailles. It did not simply pass. It
was *enforced*.

Every movement of the court—when one rose, when one ate,
when one was permitted to be seen—was regulated down to the minute.
Bells rang not to mark the hour, but to summon obedience. Clocks were
not conveniences. They were instruments of power, calibrated to keep
thousands of lives moving in synchronized orbit around a single monarch.

The clock that would later earn its reputation stood in one of the
private corridors adjoining the king's apartments, installed in the latter
half of the 18th century. Contemporary inventories describe it as a
precision piece, crafted by a master horologist whose name appears
inconsistently in records—possibly a workshop overseen by Antoine
Morand, though attribution remains debated.

It was not ostentatious by Versailles standards. Gilded, yes, but
restrained. Elegant without excess. A clock meant to be trusted.

And it worked perfectly.

At first.

Court diaries from the 1770s mention the clock only in passing,
usually as a reference point—"after the third hour," "before the

evening bell," "as the corridor clock struck." Its presence was so reliable it became invisible. That is often how dangerous objects begin.

The first irregularities appear shortly before the Revolution.

Servants recorded instances of the clock chiming incorrectly—striking thirteen, or repeating the same hour twice. These were dismissed as mechanical faults. The palace was vast. Maintenance lagged. No one thought to stop the clock.

But as unrest grew beyond the gates, the clock's behavior became harder to ignore. It began stopping abruptly, then restarting without intervention. Guards reported hearing it chime during hours when it had been documented as silent. One valet noted in his journal that the clock continued to tick audibly during the night after its pendulum had been removed for repair.

By 1789, Versailles was no longer a palace. It was a waiting room.

When the royal family was forced to leave, the clock remained behind. Furniture was looted. Art was seized. But the clock was spared —not out of reverence, but because it had become inconvenient. It refused to be dismantled cleanly. Its housing warped when pried. Its mechanisms resisted removal.

Revolutionary inventories list it repeatedly, always marked *à examiner plus tard* — to be examined later.

Later never came.

During the early 19th century, as Versailles shifted between abandonment and restoration, reports of the clock persisted. Workers complained of hearing it strike while standing in empty corridors. Restoration logs mention repeated recalibration attempts that failed within days. One technician allegedly refused further work after claiming the clock "kept time with something else."

Theories multiplied.

Some suggested psychological suggestion—Versailles was a place saturated with memory. Others blamed humidity, drafts, poor conservation. But none could explain why the clock so often resumed operation after being fully disabled.

By the mid-1800s, it had become unofficially avoided. Tour routes bypassed the corridor. Guards rotated shifts quickly. The clock was neither displayed nor removed. It existed in administrative limbo, where inconvenient things often survive the longest.

Modern accounts—rare and carefully worded—describe the same patterns. Sudden temperature drops near the clock case. The sensation of pressure, as though time thickens in the air. An audible ticking heard even when the mechanism is no longer active.

Skeptics are correct to point out that Versailles is enormous, old, and acoustically deceptive. Sound travels. Wood contracts. Stone remembers heat.

But skepticism falters in the face of repetition.

The clock does not run continuously. It activates during moments of transition: restorations, renovations, closures, reopenings. When the palace shifts purpose, the clock stirs.

There is an old idea in European folklore that objects tasked with enforcing order do not retire easily. They do not know how to stop. When the structure they served collapses, they continue their function in isolation, marking time for no one.

If that is true, then the clock is not haunted by a ghost.

It is haunted by a schedule.

It remembers when the king rose.

When the court assembled.

When the world outside finally refused to wait any longer.

Versailles still stands. Visitors pass through daily, guided by modern timekeeping—wristwatches, phones, digital displays. The palace has adapted.

The clock has not.

Those who work nearby report an instinctive unease, a feeling of being late for something undefined. A pressure behind the eyes. A sense that if the clock were allowed to run freely again, something else might begin with it.

There is no formal warning posted. No placard explaining its reputation.

There doesn't need to be.

In a palace built on the illusion that time could be controlled, one clock remains unconvinced.

And it is still counting.

. . .

82. THE HUANTED CLOCK OF VERSAILLES

Archives Nationales de France, Versailles inventories and maintenance logs

Court diaries and correspondence, late 18th century

Price, Munro. *The Fall of the French Monarchy*

Campbell, Peter. *Power and Politics in Old Regime France*

Versailles restoration reports, 19th–20th centuries

French folklore compilations on haunted mechanical objects

Oral accounts from palace staff referenced in historical studies

83

the mirror of the dorian gray house

H ouses remember their objects. London townhouses especially—layered with tenants, redecorations, inheritances, and the slow sediment of lives lived indoors. Paint colors are logged. Fireplaces catalogued. Even removed fixtures leave marks. But the mirror appears in records only after it is already there, occupying a narrow wall space on the upper floor of a Chelsea residence associated—though not conclusively—with Oscar Wilde during the years surrounding *The Picture of Dorian Gray*.

It is not mentioned in letters. It is not listed in early inventories. It simply begins to appear in later descriptions as "the long mirror by the stair," as though it had always been part of the architecture.

The mirror itself is unremarkable at first glance. Tall, rectangular, gilt-framed in late Victorian style. The glass slightly warped, as many were, producing a gentle distortion rather than a clean reflection. It was not a portrait mirror. Not intended for vanity. Its placement was transitional—meant to be passed, not lingered before.

Which makes what followed harder to dismiss.

The earliest disturbances are subtle. Visitors recorded feeling watched while standing near it. Not reflected—*watched*. Several accounts mention the sensation that the mirror lagged by a fraction of a second, as though the reflection were deciding whether to cooperate.

By the 1890s, the house had developed a reputation. Not haunted, exactly. But *wrong*. Guests avoided the upper landing. Servants declined to clean that section alone. One later tenant noted that mirrors elsewhere in the house required frequent polishing, while the stair mirror resisted cleaning, streaking no matter the method used.

Then came the stories about faces.

Not apparitions. Not strangers. The problem was always familiarity.

One woman staying in the house in the early 20th century wrote in her diary that her reflection appeared *older* than she expected—not grotesque, but tired, lined, and disappointed in a way she did not recognize. She attributed it to bad light. She did not use the mirror again.

Another tenant decades later reported the opposite: appearing *younger* in the glass, smoother, brighter, while the rest of the house seemed dull by comparison. He described feeling energized after passing it, followed by intense exhaustion later in the day.

No one died.

No one screamed.

That is why the mirror lasted.

The association with Wilde hardened the legend. Scholars have long debated how much of *Dorian Gray* was autobiographical, how much was philosophical provocation, how much was a deliberate scandal engineered to unsettle Victorian morality. But the mirror complicates that discussion, because its behavior mirrors—too closely—the book's central anxiety.

Not that beauty decays elsewhere.

But that **moral consequence displaces itself**.

Modern psychologists have suggested projection, suggestion, pareidolia. Reasonable explanations. But the pattern persists even among those unaware of the house's literary association.

During renovations in the late 20th century, contractors covered the mirror. According to site logs, several workers complained of headaches, nausea, and disorientation while it remained shrouded.

One claimed the covered mirror reflected light anyway, creating a glow beneath the cloth at dusk.

When the mirror was briefly removed for assessment, witnesses reported a strange inversion: the stairwell felt larger, emptier, less coherent—as though the mirror had been anchoring something structural rather than decorative.

It was reinstalled.

In recent years, the mirror has become the subject of modern urban legend. Visitors report feeling compelled to check their reflection repeatedly. Some describe noticing changes only after leaving—photographs where their face appears subtly altered, expressions flattened or exaggerated.

No physical harm has been recorded.

That is the most unsettling part.

The mirror does not punish. It **records**.

It does not show monsters. It shows *you*, but filtered through something patient, something that does not care how you wish to be seen.

There is a theory—never formally published, but whispered among folklorists—that the mirror absorbed the conceptual weight of the novel itself. That repeated association, belief, and retelling turned it into a functional echo of the story's premise.

A narrative object.

Once that happens, truth becomes irrelevant.

The house has changed hands multiple times. Addresses shift. Ownership obscures. But the mirror remains, referenced obliquely, never displayed publicly, never entirely removed.

Those who live near it say this: the mirror does not react to everyone. It responds to people who *look for confirmation*—of youth, of goodness, of absolution.

It does not lie.

It simply refuses to flatter.

There is an old warning hidden in Wilde's work, often overlooked in favor of its decadence: not that beauty fades, but that **self-deception rots quietly**.

If the mirror is haunted, it is haunted by that idea.

And ideas, once embedded in objects, do not age.

84
the smurl family rocking chair

T he rocking chair arrived the way most domestic objects do: without ceremony, without a story worth repeating. It was purchased because a room needed something in that corner —something soft, useful, familiar. A place to sit. A place to rock a child. A place to rest.

That is what makes it dangerous in the Smurl family story. Not because it was rare, or ancient, or soaked in the long shadow of a saint's bones. Because it was ordinary. Because it belonged in any working home. Because it offered the simplest promise a house can make, here is a place to stop.

In West Pittston, Pennsylvania, the Smurl family's haunting claims —popularized in the mid-1980s and bound into public memory by media attention, paranormal investigation, and later dramatization— were never only about things moving or noises in the walls. They were about a home turning its own comforts into traps. The chair is remembered not as a museum piece with a catalog number but as a domestic witness: a single object that seems to behave like it has intent, the way folklore loves its objects to behave.

The first changes were the kind that can be dismissed without effort. A smell that didn't belong to the house. A cold spot in a room that should have been warm. Banging sounds that could be plumbing, settling timbers, neighbors on the other side of a shared wall. In the most commonly circulated accounts, these incidents didn't resolve; they accumulated. When the story reached the broader public in 1986, what had once been private became a national case file—told and retold with a consistency that felt like certainty, and with the kind of escalation that makes skeptics suspicious and believers lean closer.

The chair sits in that escalation like a quiet hinge. It doesn't need thunder. It doesn't need a voice. It only needs a slight movement at the wrong time.

A rocking chair is built to move. It is designed to shift under the body, to keep rhythm, to answer small pressures. When it rocks with no one in it, the motion feels like a violation of design. The mind searches for a cause that fits the shape of the movement: a hand, a weight, a presence. Air currents can do it. Uneven flooring can do it. A vibration from a truck can do it. Anyone who has lived in an older house knows how furniture sometimes seems to "settle" with a sound like a sigh.

But folklore does not thrive on what is probable. It thrives on what is *felt*.

A chair rocking in an empty room is felt as a message.

In versions of the Smurl story told across interviews, summaries, and later retellings, the house is described as a place where unseen forces expressed themselves through the body: bruises, scratches, oppressive weight, moments of fear so physical it became its own evidence. In that landscape, the chair becomes more than a chair. It becomes a boundary marker—an object that teaches a family where safety ends.

People begin to avoid it. Not dramatically, not all at once, but with the slow, instinctive choreography that develops around a persistent threat. Someone chooses another seat. Someone stands rather than sits. Someone moves through the room without looking directly at that corner because looking feels like inviting. Children learn the rule without being told, the way children learn the rule about a stove burner: don't touch, don't lean in, don't test.

There is a particular cruelty in a haunting that attacks rest. A bed can be fled. A hallway can be avoided. A basement can be locked. But a chair belongs in the flow of life. It is where bodies pause. It is where older people sit when their joints hurt. It is where someone holds a phone with news they don't want to hear. It is where a grieving person collapses because standing is too much.

When such a chair becomes "wrong," the home loses a basic function. The house stops being shelter and becomes terrain.

By the time Ed and Lorraine Warren entered the Smurl narrative, the story had already begun to take on the structure of a familiar American demon-haunting: a progression from disturbance to oppression, from a house acting oddly to a house acting with malice. The Warrens' involvement did not merely add another witness; it added a vocabulary that could organize the chaos into a shape people recognized. In the public imagination, that shape often matters more than the original details. It gives the story rails. It makes it repeatable.

And repeatable stories are the ones that survive.

As the case gained attention, it became a media event: reported, debated, and eventually sold back to the public as both warning and entertainment. Skeptical voices pointed to the familiar problems—lack of testable evidence, the influence of publicity, the way extraordinary claims swell under the pressure of attention. Believers pointed to the family's insistence and the consistency of the terror described. Between them was a third truth that neither side fully owns: whether or not any supernatural force existed, the family's dread—chronic, consuming, behavioral—was real to the nervous system. A house that feels watched produces a certain kind of life. Meals change. Sleep changes. Conversations change. The body becomes an instrument tuned to danger.

This is where the haunted-object lens becomes more precise than the general haunting. A "haunted house" can be too large to hold in the mind. But a chair is scaled to the human body. It is intimate. It is specific. It provides a stage small enough that a single movement can feel like an answer.

In a duplex, there are dozens of mundane ways a chair can move. Shared walls transmit sound and vibration. Heating systems cycle and change airflow. Old floors are rarely perfectly level. A chair's runners can find a shallow groove in wood and follow it like a track. The smallest incline can turn a chair into a slow, obedient pendulum. Even the act of noticing it can become part of the mechanism: someone returns to check it, and each return deepens the association between the chair and fear.

That association is the true "curse transfer" in many modern haunted-object stories. The object does not need to kill. It only needs to teach avoidance. It becomes a totem of dread.

Once an object becomes a totem, it begins to gather stories like lint.

Someone will remember the chair rocking harder than it did. Someone will remember a sound they did not register at the time. Someone will remember that the room felt colder near that corner, even if the draft had a source. The chair becomes the house condensed into an image. An image is portable. An image travels further than a complicated narrative ever will.

The Smurl story is often discussed as an emblem of its era: a collision of private family distress, sensational media coverage, the rising public profile of celebrity paranormal investigators, and a cultural appetite for demon narratives that offered cosmic meaning to domestic fear. In that collision, objects matter not for what they are but for how they anchor the imagination. A rocking chair in the corner is an anchor anyone can picture. It does not require knowledge of theology or parapsychology. It requires only one thought:

No one is sitting there.

The chilling power of the chair is not that it proves a haunting. It is that it expresses what a haunting does to a household: it transforms the normal into the suspect until the home itself becomes unreliable. It makes safety feel conditional. It teaches the body to flinch at rest.

And unlike a famous gem or a saint's relic, this object does not have a formal "now." It does not sit behind glass. It is not cataloged by a museum. If a specific chair existed and was remembered as central, it likely ended its life the way many domestic objects do—discarded, replaced, broken down, or left behind when someone finally moved away. It is not the physical chair that persists. It is the role it plays.

The chair survives as a ritual object in the cultural memory of the

Smurl case: a symbol of the house's power to invade the most ordinary motions of the day.

That is the quiet horror of it.

A chair is permission. A chair says: sit, breathe, let your guard down.

A cursed chair teaches the opposite lesson.

It teaches a family to remain upright.

It teaches them to hover through their own rooms like guests who are not certain they're welcome.

It teaches them that comfort can be a doorway.

And it does not have to rock violently to make its point. It only has to move once, at the right moment, in a room that has already learned how to fear.

After that, the haunting no longer needs to announce itself. The family will do the work for it. They will avoid the chair. They will avoid the corner. They will carry the dread into every room they enter, because dread is portable even when the furniture isn't.

In the end, this is why modern haunted-object stories so often choose items like chairs, mirrors, beds, cribs—objects designed to cradle the vulnerable body. The supernatural, if it exists, is most effective when it doesn't appear as a monster. It appears as a shift in the rules of home. It appears as a small betrayal of what should be dependable.

A chair that can't be trusted is not a spectacle. It is a slow undoing.

Because the worst thing a home can say is not, *leave.*

The worst thing a home can say is:

You can't rest here.

85

the haunted bed of the lizzie borden house

In accounts of the Borden murders, attention fixes itself on thresholds and edges: the front door left unlocked, the narrow staircase, the sofa where Andrew Borden was killed as he slept. Beds belong to privacy, not spectacle. They are places where the body withdraws from history. Where events are supposed to stop.

In the Lizzie Borden House, the bed refuses that role.

The house at 92 Second Street in Fall River, Massachusetts, entered American consciousness on August 4, 1892, when Andrew and Abby Borden were found brutally murdered with a hatchet. The crime was intimate, fast, and domestic—violence enacted within rooms designed for routine. From the beginning, the house itself became evidence: every room measured, every object scrutinized, every ordinary furnishing reinterpreted as potential accomplice.

And yet, for decades, the bed went largely unremarked.

It was not until the house transitioned from crime scene to historical site—and later, to a functioning bed-and-breakfast—that certain rooms began to develop reputations of their own. Visitors did not speak first of screams or apparitions. They spoke of sleep. Or rather, the inability to achieve it.

The most persistent accounts center on the guest rooms associated with Lizzie Borden herself, particularly the bedroom she occupied in the family home and later the bedroom furnishings connected to her post-acquittal life at Maplecroft. Guests reported the same pattern: an overwhelming heaviness upon lying down, sensations of pressure on the chest, abrupt waking with the certainty that someone else was in the room.

The bed became the stage.

In folklore, beds are liminal objects. They mark the boundary between consciousness and vulnerability, between waking life and the realm where memory, fear, and imagination intermingle. If a haunting seeks intimacy rather than spectacle, the bed is the most efficient place to manifest. The haunted bed does not chase. It waits.

Accounts from the Lizzie Borden House describe impressions rather than apparitions. An indentation forming beside a sleeper. A mattress responding as if weight had been added. Sheets tightening, not pulled, but settling too deliberately to be dismissed as movement in sleep. Several guests reported waking abruptly at the same hour—between 3:00 and 3:30 a.m.—with no sound to account for the disturbance, only the conviction of presence.

Staff narratives, collected over years of operation, show a striking consistency in where incidents occur. Certain beds are avoided by repeat guests. Certain rooms are requested only by those actively seeking the experience. This selectivity matters. Folklore strengthens when it develops geography.

The house itself has never been shy about its history. The murders are documented, reenacted, discussed openly. Yet the bed introduces a different kind of unease—not the violence of the past, but the sense of ongoing occupation. A suggestion that the house is not merely remembering, but continuing.

Skeptics point to expectation and environment. The power of suggestion is undeniable in a location so saturated with narrative. Guests arrive primed for disturbance. Sleep disruption in unfamiliar surroundings is common. Old houses shift and settle; beds creak; air pressure changes can mimic touch. None of these explanations are wrong.

They are also incomplete.

What distinguishes the haunted-bed accounts at the Lizzie Borden House is not the drama of any single incident, but the repetition of the same bodily experience across unrelated witnesses. Fear here is not visual. It is somatic. The body reacts before the mind constructs a story.

This aligns uncomfortably well with the historical facts of the case.

The Borden murders were acts committed against bodies at rest. Abby Borden was killed upstairs, likely while making a bed or preparing a room. Andrew Borden was murdered while sleeping on the sitting room sofa. The violence occurred during moments of assumed safety, when the body was unguarded. Whether Lizzie Borden was responsible—a question legally resolved but culturally unsettled—the murders forever linked rest with danger inside that house.

The haunted bed becomes an echo rather than a ghost.

It reenacts vulnerability.

Guests who experience the phenomenon often describe a sensation not of threat, but of observation. As if sleep itself is being monitored. As if the act of lying down completes a circuit that has never fully discharged. In some accounts, the presence feels distinctly female, though not necessarily hostile. In others, it is simply oppressive—an awareness without identity.

Is it the most haunted object in the Lizzie Borden House?

That depends on how haunting is measured.

If haunting is spectacle, the house offers more obvious candidates: shadow figures on staircases, voices in empty rooms, unexplained footsteps. But if haunting is intrusion—if it is defined by the inability to withdraw safely from the world—then the bed is uniquely potent. It is where defenses are lowest. It is where the house can reach the body without announcing itself.

Beds also complicate ownership. Unlike relics or weapons, they absorb presence through prolonged contact. They are witnesses by design. They hold the shape of sleepers night after night. In older traditions, beds were sometimes burned after death, precisely because they were believed to retain something of the person who used them last.

The bed in the Lizzie Borden House was never destroyed.

Instead, it was preserved, reoccupied, recontextualized. Each new sleeper brings expectation, curiosity, fear. Each leaves with a memory tied not to sight, but to sensation. Over time, these accounts stack like impressions in a mattress that never fully rebounds.

Today, the Lizzie Borden House exists as both museum and accommodation. Guests are warned but not persuaded. The bed remains available. No signage marks it as cursed. No official explanation is offered beyond acknowledgment of reports.

The house does not insist on belief.

It allows experience.

That is perhaps the most unsettling aspect of the haunted bed. It does not perform. It does not escalate. It does not prove anything. It simply waits for the moment when someone lies down and closes their eyes—when the house is given access to the most unguarded state a human body can offer.

And in that moment, the question is no longer who committed the murders, or whether justice was done.

The question becomes simpler.

Can you sleep here?

Many do.

Some do not.

And a few wake up knowing, with no clear reason why, that rest is not something this house gives freely.

86

the cursed hope chest of kentucky

I n the late nineteenth century, in rural Kentucky, a hope chest was not merely furniture. It was a promise rendered in wood. Mothers filled them slowly—linen by linen, stitch by stitch—while daughters grew alongside the collection meant to carry them forward. A hope chest was anticipation made tangible, its weight increasing as the years passed. It was meant to be opened once, at the threshold of marriage, when a life finally aligned with the story that had been prepared for it.

This one never reached that moment.

The earliest surviving references to what would later be called the Cursed Hope Chest of Kentucky appear in family letters dated to the 1880s. They describe a cedar chest crafted locally, sturdy and plain, its interior lined with aromatic wood meant to preserve cloth against insects and rot. The chest was commissioned for a young woman whose name appears inconsistently across documents—sometimes Eleanor, sometimes Nell—suggesting either a family nickname or the erosion of memory as the story passed hands.

What remains consistent is the interruption.

Before the chest could be opened ceremonially, the woman for whom it was made fell ill. Accounts vary: a sudden fever, complications following childbirth, a wasting sickness that lingered just long enough to empty the house of optimism. She died before her wedding day. The linens were never used. The dresses were never worn. The chest was closed again, not in completion, but in refusal.

In Appalachian folklore, unfinished ritual objects are dangerous. They are believed to retain momentum without direction—energy gathered for a purpose that never arrives. A hope chest sealed after a death becomes something else entirely. Not a container of beginnings, but a vessel of arrested futures.

The family did not destroy it.

Instead, they stored it.

For decades, the chest passed quietly through attics and spare rooms. It was inherited by relatives who knew only fragments of its origin. But patterns began to attach themselves to the object. Women who stored personal items in it reported persistent dreams of confinement—being folded, packed, or sealed away. Marriages associated with the chest ended abruptly. Engagements dissolved without clear cause. One account, preserved in an early twentieth-century diary, describes a woman waking repeatedly to the smell of cedar despite the chest being locked and untouched in another room.

The chest became associated not with death, but with delay.

It did not kill. It postponed.

By the 1930s, the chest had developed a reputation within the extended family. Younger members refused to use it. It was said to "keep women waiting." A niece who placed her wedding veil inside reportedly postponed her marriage twice, each time following a sudden loss—first financial, then personal. Another woman used the chest to store baby clothes; the pregnancy ended in miscarriage, and she later insisted the room felt "crowded" afterward, as if the air itself resisted change.

Skeptical explanations followed the chest as faithfully as the stories. Family tragedies, especially among women, were common in eras without modern medicine. Correlation hardened into superstition. The smell of cedar triggered memory. The chest became a symbol onto which grief was projected. All of this is plausible.

None of it explains why the same sensations recur among people who do not know the story.

In the 1970s, the chest left the family for the first time. It was sold during an estate liquidation to an antique dealer, stripped of its oral history and reintroduced to the world as a charming relic of domestic life. Within months, the dealer reportedly removed it from the showroom floor. Customers complained of dizziness when standing near it for long periods. One employee refused to inventory its contents, citing panic attacks triggered by opening the lid.

The chest did not remain in one place long after that.

It appeared briefly in private collections, each time accompanied by familiar outcomes: prolonged illness during engagement periods, abrupt career stagnation following its placement in a bedroom, an unshakable sense of being "behind" in life. Owners described time slowing in its presence—not literally, but emotionally. Plans stalled. Decisions grew heavy. The future felt distant and unresponsive.

The chest's interior remained pristine.

Cedar resists decay. So do unused intentions.

By the time paranormal investigators took interest in the object in the late twentieth century, the narrative had shifted from family tragedy to folkloric warning. Interviews collected during this period reveal a striking linguistic pattern. Witnesses rarely described fear. They described pressure. The sense of being held in place. The sensation that something expected them to wait.

This aligns with older Appalachian beliefs about objects tied to domestic fate. Hope chests, wedding dresses, christening gowns—items designed to mark transition—were thought to be especially vulnerable to spiritual disruption if the transition failed. The object does not move on simply because the person does. It remains caught at the threshold.

The Cursed Hope Chest of Kentucky is not associated with apparitions, voices, or visible phenomena. Its influence is quieter and more insidious. It affects timelines rather than bodies. It interferes not with life, but with progression.

Today, the chest's exact location is uncertain. Some accounts place it in private storage. Others suggest it was dismantled, its wood repurposed without ceremony. No verified documentation confirms its destruction. As with many objects of this type, uncertainty becomes part of its power.

What remains unresolved is whether the chest carries anything at all—or whether it simply amplifies what is already present.

Hope chests are repositories of expectation. They are filled with imagined futures long before reality catches up. When those futures fail, the container does not forget. It remembers everything it was meant to open into.

There is an old rule, rarely written, passed more often in warnings than in instructions: objects made for beginnings should never be sealed by endings.

The chest was built to open once.

It never did.

And in the stories that follow it still, that unopened moment continues—holding, delaying, and quietly insisting that some lives are not finished with waiting.

87

the possessed piano of
the palumbo mansion

W hen the Palumbo Mansion was completed in the final decades of the nineteenth century, it rose with the particular confidence of Chicago at the height of its self-invention—ornate, ambitious, and determined to endure. The house stood apart from its neighbors, not merely larger but more deliberate, its rooms arranged less for comfort than for display. Sound traveled easily there. Footsteps echoed. Voices lingered. Music, when it came, had nowhere to hide.

The piano arrived soon after.

Records indicate it was a large upright instrument, European in origin, brought into the house during its earliest period of occupation. It was not decorative. It was used. Visitors described evenings shaped by music—parlor gatherings, rehearsals, recitals performed not for crowds but for the house itself. The piano was positioned so that its sound carried upward through the stairwell, vibrating the upper floors, settling into the wood.

Then, gradually, the music changed.

The first reports do not describe anything supernatural. They describe inconsistency. Notes struck cleanly one evening would sound dull the next. The same keys behaved differently depending on who played them. Tuners were called. Repairs were made. Nothing held.

By the early twentieth century, household staff had begun avoiding the room after dark. They complained of hearing unfinished melodies—short progressions, repeated fragments, as if someone had stopped playing mid-thought. These sounds were not loud. They were precise. Enough to suggest intention.

What unsettled people most was that the piano seemed to respond.

Several accounts describe keys depressing slightly when someone passed too close. Others mention the sensation of being followed musically—single notes sounded after conversations ended, faint and exploratory. One caretaker wrote in a letter that the instrument felt "attentive," a word that appears again and again in later testimonies.

The Palumbo Mansion did not acquire its haunted reputation because of the piano. The piano acquired its reputation because of the mansion.

The house itself had already begun to attract stories by mid-century. Guests reported discomfort in certain rooms, unexplained cold pockets, the sense of being observed from above. But the piano became the focal point, the one object that did not merely exist within the house but interacted with it.

During renovations in the latter half of the twentieth century, workers documented repeated disturbances centered around the instrument. Tools were found rearranged overnight near the piano bench. Electrical interference plagued recording equipment placed nearby. One investigator noted that audio devices captured low-frequency sounds during periods of silence—tones not matching ambient noise, but aligning instead with musical intervals.

No one ever caught the piano playing a full piece.

It never performed.

It only tested.

Skeptics proposed mechanical explanations. Old wood expands and contracts. Strings vibrate sympathetically. Buildings settle. All true. None sufficient. The timing of the sounds—often following emotional moments, arguments, or periods of isolation—resisted purely structural logic.

One incident, frequently cited in later retellings, involved a visitor sitting alone at the piano bench without touching the keys. According to her account, a chord sounded behind her hands, wrong but deliberate, as though correcting a mistake she had not made. She left the room and did not return to the house.

By the time the mansion was firmly established as a site of paranormal interest, the piano had become inseparable from its identity. Investigators recorded fluctuations in temperature localized to the instrument. Mediums claimed the piano functioned as a conduit, a translator rather than a source. Something, they suggested, used music because music already belonged there.

There are no confirmed deaths directly associated with the piano. That absence matters. This is not a violent object. It does not punish. It does not threaten.

It listens.

In interviews conducted with staff and visitors over decades, a pattern emerges. People do not describe fear when they speak of the piano. They describe interruption. The feeling that a private thought has been noticed. That a moment has been answered.

The piano does not play when rooms are empty. It responds to presence. To proximity. To attention.

As the Palumbo Mansion changed hands and purposes, the piano remained. It was moved only once, briefly, during restoration. The disturbances intensified during that period—sounds increasing in frequency, reports of vibrations traveling through floors, an overwhelming sense of displacement described by multiple workers. When the piano was returned to its original position, the activity subsided.

Objects that remain long enough in one place begin to learn the rhythms of their environment. Instruments learn more than most. They absorb breath, pressure, timing. They exist to translate human intention into sound. When no one is playing, that capacity does not vanish. It waits.

Today, the piano still sits within the mansion, rarely touched. It is not advertised as an attraction. It does not need to be. Those who encounter it describe the same hesitation—the sense that playing it would be an intrusion rather than an invitation.

Music is meant to be shared.

This piano does not want to be performed.

It wants to be acknowledged.

And once noticed, it never quite stops listening, holding the silence the way other instruments hold sound, waiting for someone to make the mistake of believing the house has finished speaking.

88
the black forest
carved wardrobe

T was carved in the Black Forest at a time when furniture was built with the expectation of permanence—trees felled from nearby slopes, designs pulled from local folklore, joints cut to last longer than the people who commissioned them. The carvings along its doors were dense and deliberate: oak leaves, twisting roots, animals half-emerging from shadow. Nothing decorative was accidental. In the Black Forest, ornament was protection. What you carved into wood mattered.

The wardrobe stood taller than most men of its era, heavy enough that it took several people to shift it even inches. According to surviving records, it remained in the same house for generations, occupying a narrow bedchamber where winter light rarely reached. Clothing stored inside was not remarkable—wool, linen, seasonal garments—but the space itself developed a reputation. The air near the wardrobe was colder. The interior smelled faintly of earth no matter how carefully it was cleaned. Doors creaked open without drafts.

No one called it haunted at first.

They called it temperamental.

Family letters from the nineteenth century mention the wardrobe only in passing, usually in complaints. Sleeves damp when removed.

Shoes misplaced overnight. The sense that garments hung inside longer than expected retained the shape of bodies no longer present. A widow wrote that her husband's coat felt warm when she took it down months after his death, as though it had not finished remembering him.

The wardrobe was moved for the first time during a marriage consolidation, when the house was divided and refurnished. That night, witnesses reported sharp cracking sounds like branches snapping underfoot, echoing through the home. The wardrobe's doors were found open in the morning, hinges intact, carvings splintered slightly around the frame as if resisting the relocation.

From that point forward, the disturbances became harder to ignore.

People sleeping in rooms near the wardrobe described vivid dreams that began inside forests—paths narrowing, roots tangling at their feet, the sense of being watched without seeing anything watching. More troubling were the physical sensations upon waking: impressions on skin consistent with pressure from folded fabric, fingermarks that faded within hours, the unmistakable feeling of having been dressed and undressed without waking.

The wardrobe did not confine.

It rearranged.

Objects placed inside did not disappear. They returned altered. Shirts buttoned incorrectly. Dresses turned inside out. Jewelry knotted into sleeves. Once, a pair of gloves was found sewn together with thread matching the lining of the wardrobe itself—no needle discovered, no sign of tampering beyond the result.

Carvers from the Black Forest worked with inherited patterns tied to regional belief. Forest spirits were not monsters. They were custodians. They punished imbalance. They responded poorly to intrusion. The motifs carved into the wardrobe—stags, ravens, roots coiling back into themselves—were associated with thresholds, boundaries between what belonged and what wandered too far.

Over time, the wardrobe passed through several owners. Each removal triggered similar accounts. The activity was never violent, but it was insistent. The wardrobe resisted unfamiliar houses. Doors stuck. Floors warped beneath its weight. In one documented case, movers refused to complete delivery after hearing rhythmic tapping from inside the empty cabinet, slow and deliberate, ceasing only when the wardrobe was returned to its original position within the room.

Attempts to empty it completely failed. Even stripped bare, it never felt vacant. Those who opened it reported the sense of stepping too close to a cliff edge, the wrongness of standing where something expected to stand alone.

Unlike cursed objects associated with tragedy, the wardrobe accumulated no confirmed deaths. What it collected instead were traces—habits, warmth, the residue of daily life. Clothes kept inside for long periods became difficult to discard. Owners reported irrational attachment to garments they no longer wore, as though removing them entirely would be a greater loss than expected.

The wardrobe does not trap bodies.

It stores versions.

Psychologists consulted decades later suggested suggestion and folklore contamination. Structural engineers blamed humidity and warped wood. Neither explanation accounted for the most consistent detail across testimonies: the feeling that the wardrobe knew when something no longer belonged to the person who owned it.

People who changed significantly—through grief, illness, or guilt—experienced the strongest disturbances. Their clothing resisted them. Sleeves pulled tight. Collars pressed against throats. The wardrobe did not harm them. It reminded them that they had changed shape.

In its current location, the wardrobe remains closed. The room around it is kept simple, uncluttered, almost deliberately neutral. No one stores clothing inside anymore. The doors are left untouched.

Visitors standing near it report a faint sensation of compression, like air thickening. Those sensitive to sound claim to hear fabric shifting inside, slow and careful, as though someone were folding memories instead of cloth.

Wardrobes are meant to hold what we remove from ourselves at the end of the day.

This one learned to hold what we leave behind.

And it does not give those things back easily.

89

the haunted high chair of iowa

The high chair was already old when the house stopped sleeping.

It had been built to last—oak, square-shouldered, its joinery tight enough that a century of Midwestern winters had not loosened it. In the first decade of the twentieth century, such chairs were common in rural homes across Iowa, where infants were fed beside coal stoves and mothers kept one eye on the weather through kitchen windows filmed with frost. The chair's tray locked into place with a wooden peg, and its footrest was set low, forcing small legs to dangle. It was not designed for comfort. It was designed to keep a child still.

The first child to use it did not stay that way.

County birth registers from the period note an infant death in the household within a year of the chair's purchase—an unremarkable entry for the era, recorded with the blunt economy of rural clerks. No cause is listed beyond "failure to thrive," a phrase that concealed as much as it explained. The family sold the house within months. The chair remained.

It passed next to a neighboring farm, then to a general store that resold used furniture during the agricultural downturn of the 1920s.

By then, stories had already begun to cling to it—not dramatic ones, not yet. Just unease. Infants who would not stop crying when placed in the chair. Mothers who found food overturned despite the tray being locked. A sense, often remarked upon later, that the chair felt "occupied" even when empty.

What distinguishes the chair is not a single catastrophic event but a pattern that repeats with unnerving consistency across decades and addresses. In the 1930s, a woman recalled leaving her child strapped into the chair while she stepped outside to hang laundry. When she returned, the chair had shifted several inches across the floor. There were no drag marks. The floorboards were clean. She blamed wind, then herself, then never used the chair again.

In the 1950s, after the chair surfaced at an estate sale near Des Moines, a new family reported that the tray would sometimes be warm to the touch hours after the child had been lifted out. No heat source was nearby. The stove had been cold since morning. The warmth lingered longest at the center of the tray, as though small hands had rested there.

The house in question would later be documented in local newspapers for "unexplained disturbances," though the chair was not named at the time. Only later, in interviews conducted decades apart, did multiple former occupants independently describe the same object: dark wood, straight-backed, with a shallow crescent carved into the tray's underside—a maker's mark, or perhaps something else.

By the 1970s, the chair's reputation had solidified enough that it was removed from regular use. It remained in basements and attics, brought out reluctantly when visitors asked about "the stories." Children refused to sit in it. Animals avoided it. A family dog reportedly growled at the chair whenever it was moved into a lit room.

What makes the chair difficult to dismiss is not just folklore, but documentation. County historical societies preserve oral history transcripts from rural Iowa that mention "the baby chair" without prompting. A photograph taken in the early 1960s shows the chair positioned alone at a kitchen table, its tray raised as though waiting. The negative contains no anomalies. The unease comes later, when viewers realize no child is visible anywhere in the frame, though the photographer's notes mention "feeding time."

Scholars of domestic folklore point out that infant furniture occupies a uniquely vulnerable symbolic space. A cradle can rock itself. A high chair is meant to restrain. It fixes a child upright, suspended between dependence and autonomy. In European and American folklore alike, such liminal spaces invite projection—especially when associated with loss.

Skeptics have suggested environmental explanations: warped legs causing subtle movement, retained heat in dense hardwood, pareidolia fueled by grief. These explanations are reasonable. They are also incomplete. They do not account for the chair's consistent reappearance in households with no knowledge of its history, nor for the specificity of the reported sensations—the pressure at knee height, the warmth at the tray, the sound of soft impacts against wood.

The chair was eventually donated to a regional museum with the stipulation that it not be placed in children's exhibits. Curators catalogued it as early twentieth-century domestic furniture, provenance incomplete. Staff reports from the 1990s note unexplained sounds after hours in the storage area where the chair was kept. Nothing violent. Nothing overt. Just the repeated impression that something small was shifting its weight.

Today, the chair is rarely displayed. When it is, it is roped off, its tray secured. Visitors linger longer than they intend to. Parents keep a hand on their children's shoulders. The chair does not move.

It does not need to.

90
the devil's chair
of kirkwall

The chair is not impressive at first glance. It is heavy, yes—oak darkened by centuries of smoke and handling—but otherwise plain, almost stubbornly so. Square legs. A straight back. No cushion, no ornament beyond the patient marks of use. In the north of Scotland, furniture was made to endure weather and time, not admiration. And yet this chair, kept for generations in and around Kirkwall, earned a name that transformed it from domestic object into warning.

The earliest references place the chair in Kirkwall during the late seventeenth century, when Orkney was still negotiating its Norse inheritance and Scottish governance. The chair appears in parish anecdotes rather than inventories, described obliquely as *the one no one uses*. It stood near hearths, then later in outbuildings, then—according to several nineteenth-century accounts—was kept deliberately out of living spaces altogether.

The reason given was consistent, even when details were not. Men who sat in the chair fell ill. Some lost livestock shortly after. One reportedly drowned within days, his body recovered from Scapa Flow in calm weather. None of these incidents alone would have fixed the chair's reputation. Together, they hardened it.

By the early 1700s, the chair had acquired its name.

"The Devil's Chair" was not an uncommon label in Scottish folk-lore. Stools, stones, and even hills bore the title, often as a shorthand for danger or taboo. What distinguished the Kirkwall chair was speci-ficity. This was not a place the Devil was said to have rested once, or passed by. This was a chair that acted.

Local tradition held that the chair had belonged to a man known for violence, a figure alternately described as a merchant, a laird, or simply "a hard man." The variations matter less than the constant: he was feared, and he was said to have sworn an oath that no one would sit in his place after death. When he died—suddenly, according to some tellings—the chair remained, and so did the oath.

The earliest written mention comes from antiquarian notes compiled in the early nineteenth century, when Orkney folklore began to be recorded with greater urgency. The chair is described as having been removed from a public house after "unfortunate experiments" involving skeptical patrons. One man allegedly sat as a dare and was found feverish and delirious by morning. Another refused to rise from the chair for several minutes, later claiming his legs "would not answer him."

Skeptics at the time suggested drink, suggestion, or coincidence. They did not, notably, sit in the chair themselves.

As the chair changed hands, its reputation traveled with it. Fami-lies who inherited it refused to place it at the table. Children were warned not to touch it. Dogs avoided it. One account from the mid-nineteenth century describes the chair being carried into a barn for storage, only to be moved back outside after livestock became agitated whenever it was nearby.

The chair's physical presence contributed to its effect. It sits lower than most chairs of its era, forcing the sitter into an awkward posture. The back is rigid, offering no give. Several observers remarked that it felt "too narrow," though measurements suggest otherwise. The sensa-tion appears to have been psychological, but that does not make it less real.

By the Victorian period, the chair had become an object of curiosity for visiting scholars and folklorists. It was shown, reluctantly, to outsiders. Some took notes. Others laughed. One visitor is said to have tapped the seat with his cane and joked that the Devil must be on holiday. The chair did nothing. It rarely did, when challenged directly.

Its power, according to local belief, lay in consent.

Those who sat without invitation—without respect—were the ones who suffered. This framing placed responsibility back onto the sitter, a common move in folk narratives that involve taboo objects. The chair did not attack. It responded.

In the late nineteenth century, the chair was placed under institutional care, removed from domestic circulation. By then, the pattern was too well established. Even those who dismissed the supernatural explanations acknowledged the social weight the object carried. It had become, in effect, a repository for communal anxiety—a physical locus for the idea that some boundaries should not be crossed.

Museum records from the early twentieth century note repeated requests to display the chair, followed by hesitation. When it was finally exhibited, it was positioned against a wall, roped off. Visitors commented on a feeling of pressure in the chest, or a sudden reluctance to approach. These reactions were not universal, but they were frequent enough to be recorded.

Modern interpretations tend to emphasize folklore dynamics rather than demonic agency. Scholars point out that Orkney's oral traditions place strong emphasis on the consequences of disrespect—toward the dead, toward property, toward unspoken rules. The chair becomes a teaching object, a way of encoding social restraint into story.

And yet.

Even in contemporary accounts, stripped of theological language, the chair resists normalization. Staff report that it is heavier than expected when moved. That people instinctively avoid sitting in it even when unaware of its history. That jokes about the chair tend to trail off rather than land.

The chair remains intact. It has not been destroyed, burned, or buried. Such actions would suggest fear, and Orkney folklore has always preferred containment to eradication. Dangerous things are not denied. They are acknowledged, named, and kept where they can be watched.

The Devil's Chair of Kirkwall does not need belief to function. It only needs memory.

That is what it holds.

91

the chair of death

(Boggis Chair)

Elm wood, roughly finished, upright-backed, the sort of sturdy, functional furniture that filled inns across northern England in the early eighteenth century. It stood near a hearth, close enough to warmth to invite use, and for years it was nothing more than a place to sit with a drink after a long day. No one recorded when it was built, or by whom. Chairs like it were made by the thousands.

What changed it was not craftsmanship, but violence.

In 1702, at the Busby Stoop Inn on the road between York and Thirsk, a man named Thomas Busby murdered his father-in-law, Daniel Auty. Contemporary court records describe the killing as sudden and brutal, carried out in a fit of rage after an argument over money and control of the household. Busby was arrested quickly. He did not deny the act.

He was tried, convicted, and sentenced to hang.

According to multiple nineteenth-century retellings, Busby requested one final drink at the inn before his execution. He sat in the chair by the fire, drank deeply, and rose to leave with a curse on his lips. No one, he declared, should ever again sit in his place. Anyone who did would die.

Busby was hanged at the crossroads nearby, his body left in chains as a warning. The inn survived him. The chair remained.

For a time, nothing happened. Or at least, nothing worth writing down. Curses often need repetition before they harden into belief. That repetition came slowly, over decades, and then faster.

The earliest deaths associated with the chair appear in local oral tradition rather than parish registers: men who sat in it and died soon after of sudden illness, accidents, or unexplained causes. By the late eighteenth century, the chair had acquired a reputation. Some refused to sit in it. Others did so deliberately, as a test.

They became the stories people remembered.

A chimney sweep who sat in the chair reportedly fell from a roof later that day. A laborer collapsed in the fields. A soldier home on leave sat laughing in the chair and was killed shortly afterward in a training accident. None of these deaths were extraordinary in isolation. Together, they formed a pattern that resisted dismissal.

By the nineteenth century, the chair's reputation had escaped the inn entirely. Travelers arrived having heard of it. Skeptics made a point of sitting in it. Locals watched and waited.

Some accounts note that the chair seemed to attract bravado. Men who sat in it often did so publicly, announcing their disbelief. Several witnesses later remarked on the silence that followed—how conversation faltered once the sitter rose, how no one rushed to be next.

The most frequently cited cluster of deaths occurred during the Second World War. Royal Air Force airmen stationed nearby were said to have sat in the chair before returning to duty. Several were killed in crashes within days. Wartime mortality complicates the story, but it also intensified it. The chair did not care whether death was likely. It only needed proximity.

By the mid-twentieth century, concern had shifted from folklore to liability. The chair had outlived too many explanations. Innkeepers stopped allowing anyone to sit in it. Eventually, the chair was removed altogether.

It was donated to Thirsk Museum, where a decision was made that formalized what folklore had already dictated. The chair would not be destroyed. It would not be hidden. But it would never again be used.

The museum mounted the chair high on a wall, suspended well above the floor.

This choice is often described as theatrical, but it reflects a deeply traditional response. Dangerous objects in British folklore are not smashed; they are neutralized by removing access. Wells are capped. Stones are fenced. Chairs are lifted beyond reach.

Museum records indicate that visitors regularly ask why the chair is displayed the way it is. Staff explanations are factual, restrained. The deaths are described as *attributed*, not confirmed. The curse is acknowledged as legend.

And yet the chair stays where it is.

Over the years, several museum employees have remarked—off the record—that the chair seems heavier than it should be. That it feels uncooperative when moved for conservation. That ladders brought too close to it feel suddenly unnecessary.

No one has tested the curse since the chair was mounted.

Modern analysis offers alternative explanations. Confirmation bias. Retrospective storytelling. The human tendency to impose narrative order on random death. All are plausible. None fully account for the persistence of the chair's reputation across three centuries, or the remarkable consistency of the stories attached to it.

Unlike many cursed objects, the Chair of Death does not rely on a supernatural mechanism. There is no demon, no relic, no ritual activation. Its power—if it has one—lies in declaration. A man marked the chair with intent at the moment of his own death. That intent was remembered. Memory did the rest.

The chair has never been comfortable with indifference.

Even now, visitors stand beneath it longer than expected. They read the plaque twice. They step back rather than forward. Children point at it and are gently guided away.

The chair remains what it has always been: an ordinary object made extraordinary by human action, human fear, and the refusal to forget.

It does not need belief.

It only needs a place to wait.

92
the cursed wedding table of brittany

T he table was built to last longer than love.

It was a heavy farmhouse piece, oak darkened by smoke and years of handling, its surface scarred by knives, cups, and the pressure of countless hands pressed flat in prayer or impatience. In rural Brittany, such tables were not merely furniture. They were anchors. Contracts were signed on them. Dead were laid out upon them. Bread was broken there for weddings and wakes alike.

This one entered the record in fragments rather than dates.

Local tradition places it in a coastal parish near the Morbihan Gulf in the late eighteenth century, owned by a farming family whose name appears inconsistently in tax rolls and parish registers. What is consistent is the story attached to a wedding that did not end as planned.

The first account appears in an 1820s notebook kept by a Breton schoolmaster collecting *histoires du pays*—country stories—meant to preserve local custom. He notes, without embellishment, that a bride collapsed during the wedding feast, striking her head against the table and dying before nightfall. The priest recorded it as an accident. The villagers did not.

The table was blamed immediately.

At the time, Brittany maintained a dense weave of Catholic practice and older folk belief. Objects were not neutral. They absorbed circumstance. A table upon which vows were spoken was thought to hold something of that promise—and of its breaking.

The family refused to destroy the table. Burning it would have invited worse. Instead, it was moved to the back of the house and covered with linen. That should have been the end of it.

It was not.

Over the next decades, the table changed hands through inheritance and sale. Each time it re-entered use for a wedding, something went wrong. A groom thrown from a horse on the way to the church. A bride taken with fever days before the ceremony. A marriage that ended violently within the year. Parish registers confirm deaths and annulments. They do not record causes.

By the mid-nineteenth century, the table's reputation had expanded beyond the village. Brides were warned against it. Some refused to eat at wedding feasts if the table was present, even if they were not seated at it. In one account from the 1850s, a visiting family insisted the table be removed entirely before their daughter would cross the threshold.

It was moved again.

The accumulation of stories followed a familiar pattern. No single event proved anything. Together, they created gravity. The table was no longer just wood. It was a risk.

One particularly persistent story concerns a wedding in 1873, held despite warnings because the family could not afford replacements. Witnesses later claimed the table cracked during the feast—not split, but groaned, as if a joint had failed under sudden pressure. The marriage lasted less than six months. The groom drowned in a fishing accident during a storm locals later described as unseasonal.

Storms, too, were added to the table's ledger.

By the early twentieth century, folklorists collecting Breton material recorded the table as an example of *objets chargés*—charged objects—alongside stones, mirrors, and inherited jewelry. One collector noted that the table was never said to *cause* harm directly. Instead, it "made space for it."

Skeptics later suggested the table functioned as a narrative scapegoat, a way to organize grief in communities where marriage failure carried social shame. Others pointed to the dangers of rural life, child-birth, and coastal labor. All true. None erased the reluctance people felt standing near it.

The table eventually left private ownership during the interwar period. Records suggest it was acquired by an antiquarian dealer specializing in Breton furniture, who sold it to a private collector in Rennes. There are no confirmed reports of weddings involving the table after that point. There are, however, notes from the dealer's corre-spondence mentioning "persistent unease among buyers" and a request that the table not be described as suitable for ceremonial use.

Today, the table's location is uncertain. Some claim it remains in private hands. Others believe it was dismantled quietly, its wood reused for shelving or flooring, its identity dispersed.

And yet the story persists.

In Brittany, it is still said that a wedding table remembers what it has witnessed. That joy, once interrupted, leaves a residue that cannot be scrubbed away. That some objects do not forgive being present at the wrong moment.

The table was never accused of malice.

Only memory.

And memory, once settled into wood, is difficult to remove.

93

the dollhouse of belcourt castle

The dollhouse arrived at Belcourt Castle without ceremony.

No crate labeled *fragile*. No inventory number assigned by a curator. It was simply there one afternoon in the early twentieth century, placed in a side room off the grand hall as if it had always belonged. A gift, according to one account. An inheritance, according to another. The paperwork does not agree, which is where the trouble begins.

Built between 1891 and 1894 for Oliver Hazard Perry Belmont, the mansion was designed to impress and intimidate—stone walls, vaulted ceilings, a carriage house larger than most homes. It echoed even when empty. Objects placed inside it tended to shrink, visually and psychologically.

Except the dollhouse.

It was scaled meticulously, constructed of dark wood and fine joinery, its windows glazed with real glass. Inside were miniature chairs, tables, beds, rugs, and lamps. The rooms followed no single architectural style but mirrored the logic of an inhabited house rather than a toy—doors opened where you expected them to, staircases led somewhere sensible. Visitors remarked that it felt less like a plaything and more like a model.

Staff were the first to notice that it did not remain static.

Accounts from household workers describe furniture shifting positions between cleanings. A chair turned slightly. A door left ajar that had been closed. These changes were small enough to dismiss, and for years they were dismissed. Belcourt was full of drafts, after all. The castle settled and sighed as old stone does.

But the dollhouse did not behave like the rest of the house.

One caretaker recalled that after moving a miniature bed from an upstairs room to the ground floor—an attempt to "tidy" the display— she experienced an intense headache that lasted the rest of the day. Another reported a sudden sense of vertigo while dusting the tiny dining room, as if the scale of the world had inverted briefly. These were not recorded as hauntings. They were personal complaints, filed away in memory rather than ink.

The stories accumulated quietly.

By the 1920s, guests were remarking on the dollhouse unprompted. Several claimed it made them uneasy without knowing why. One woman reportedly refused to remain in the room after swearing she saw movement behind the miniature windows. No corroboration exists. There rarely is.

What does exist are repeated references to the same sensation: the feeling of being watched by something too small to notice until it was too late.

Folklorists later pointed out that dollhouses occupy an uncomfortable space in the human mind. They replicate domestic life while stripping it of agency. Everything is fixed, posed, obedient. When something within them appears to act on its own, the violation feels intimate. The house is not haunted. The *idea* of the house is.

At Belcourt, that distinction blurred.

During the mansion's later years as a social venue, the dollhouse was reportedly moved several times to accommodate events. Each relocation was followed by complaints from staff—unease, headaches, irritability, a sense of being disoriented within the building. One note from a mid-century caretaker mentions that the dollhouse "does not like being shifted," phrasing that suggests he had already accepted a certain premise.

Skeptics have offered rational explanations. Confirmation bias. The psychological effect of working long hours in a large, echoing structure. The influence of Gothic architecture on perception. All valid.

None explain why the dollhouse was eventually removed from public view.

By the late twentieth century, it no longer appeared in visitor descriptions or floor plans. Some sources claim it was placed in storage. Others suggest it was quietly returned to a private owner. No accession record confirms either scenario. The absence is total enough to be noticeable.

Belcourt Castle itself continues to host events, tours, and restorations. It is described as atmospheric but elegant, dramatic but controlled. The dollhouse is rarely mentioned now, except in passing, as if acknowledging it too directly might invite its return.

Those who remember it insist on one detail.

The dollhouse never depicted Belcourt itself.

Its rooms were smaller. Warmer. More human.

Which raised an unsettling possibility—that it was not a model of a house at all, but of a household. One that had learned how to watch back.

94

the toy monkey
with cymbals

The monkey is always smiling.

Painted tin or molded plastic, glassy eyes fixed wide, mouth stretched into a grin that never changes. In its hands are two brass cymbals, frozen mid-clash. Even before it moves, the pose suggests inevitability—noise is coming, whether you want it or not.

Toy monkeys with cymbals began appearing in the early twentieth century, products of the same industrial optimism that gave the world wind-up soldiers and dancing bears. By the 1930s and 1940s, they were common novelty items in the United States and Europe, manufactured by companies eager to showcase clockwork ingenuity. Most were harmless. Some were loud. A few were cheaply made and broke easily.

And a small number acquired reputations that outlived their mechanisms.

The earliest widely recorded case dates to the late 1940s. A cymbal-clashing monkey purchased as a Christmas gift in Ohio reportedly began activating without being wound. Family members described waking in the night to the sound of metal striking metal from an empty room. The toy was inspected and found inert—its key loose, its spring slack. It was placed in a closet. The sound returned the following night, louder, closer, as if the acoustics had shifted.

Neighbors later confirmed hearing the noise through the walls. The family disposed of the toy after a third incident, placing it in an outdoor trash bin. According to a local newspaper column from 1949, the cymbals were heard again before dawn, though the bin was empty when checked. No explanation was offered, and the column framed the event as seasonal whimsy. It was not investigated further.

In the 1960s, a similar toy appeared in a small antiques shop in Kent, England. The proprietor kept it as a display piece near the counter, unwound and nonfunctional. Customers began commenting that it "felt wrong." Several refused to touch it. One reported a sudden ringing in the ears while standing nearby, likened to tinnitus but localized to the toy's presence.

The shopkeeper later documented that the cymbals would sometimes be found touching in the morning, despite being separated the night before. No one admitted to moving them. After a particularly busy afternoon in which three separate patrons complained of headaches and nausea, the monkey was removed from the display and stored in the back room. The disturbances ceased. The shop closed a year later, and the monkey's whereabouts are unknown.

By the late twentieth century, the toy monkey had entered a new phase of notoriety, fueled by mass media and horror cinema. This did not create the phenomenon, but it amplified it, drawing attention to cases that might otherwise have remained local.

One of the most thoroughly documented modern accounts comes from a family in the American Midwest during the early 1990s. The monkey in question was a mass-produced wind-up toy purchased at a flea market. After being brought into the home, it reportedly activated multiple times without winding, always between midnight and 3 a.m. Audio recordings captured faint cymbal sounds when the toy was not visible on camera. Mechanical inspection revealed a broken spring that should have prevented movement entirely.

The family eventually removed the cymbals, believing the sound itself might be triggering stress responses. The monkey continued to "move"—arms lifting and falling silently, teeth chattering without the expected clatter. When the toy was sealed in a container and placed in the garage, neighbors reported hearing metallic noises from the structure at night. The case was later featured in paranormal research publications, not as evidence of the supernatural, but as an example of unexplained mechanical persistence.

A different pattern emerged in cases from Japan in the early 2000s, where cymbal-clashing monkeys appeared in reports of children's night terrors. In these instances, the toy did not necessarily move on its own. Instead, children described dreams in which the monkey played endlessly, growing closer with each clash. Parents noted that removing the toy led to abrupt cessation of the nightmares. When the toys were returned to stores or discarded, similar complaints were logged by other families, suggesting a circulation of the same object.

Psychologists later pointed out that rhythmic noise is particularly effective at disrupting sleep cycles, and that the monkey's design— fixed grin, repetitive motion—taps into deep cognitive discomfort. But this explanation faltered in cases where the toy was silent and inactive.

Across cases, certain features repeat.

The activity occurs at night. The sound precedes the motion or occurs independently of it. Mechanical failure does not prevent operation. And perhaps most unsettling: people often report a sense that the toy is *waiting*.

Skeptical explanations have been offered repeatedly. Faulty springs storing residual tension. Temperature changes causing metal expansion. Rodents or vibrations activating loose components. Psychological priming reinforced by cultural tropes.

Each explanation works—until it doesn't.

The Ohio monkey had no spring tension. The Kent monkey was never wound. The Midwest monkey functioned after being dismantled. The Japanese cases involved toys that never moved at all.

Museums and collectors now handle such toys with caution, not because they accept claims of possession, but because of the consistent distress reported by those who keep them. Some collectors refuse to store cymbal-monkeys with other automata, citing unpredictable behavior. Others dismantle them permanently upon acquisition.

What remains unresolved is why this specific form recurs.

Why a monkey. Why cymbals. Why the sound.

Anthropologists have suggested that the monkey occupies a liminal space—familiar enough to be playful, alien enough to unsettle. The cymbals produce a sharp, repetitive noise that cuts through sleep and thought alike. Together, they create an object that demands attention without offering interaction. It performs *at* you, not for you.

In every documented case, resolution comes only with separation. The toy is removed, destroyed, or passed on. Calm returns. Normalcy resumes.

But the monkey is rarely seen again.

Which raises a quieter concern: not that the toy is cursed, but that it does not stay in one place for long. That it moves through households the way stories do—picked up, laughed at, underestimated—until someone hears it clapping in the dark and understands too late that the smile was never meant to be friendly.

95
the annabelle
display case

T he case was never meant to be decorative.

It was built as a barrier.

When visitors remember Annabelle, they remember the doll: red yarn hair, triangular nose, stitched smile fixed in permanent cheer. What they forget—until they stand in front of it—is the box. Thick glass. Heavy wood. Warnings printed in block letters. A small white placard that does not invite curiosity so much as attempt to restrain it.

DO NOT TOUCH.

The Annabelle display case exists because the doll did not behave when left uncontained.

According to accounts recorded by paranormal investigators in the early 1970s, Annabelle's activity escalated whenever she was moved freely from room to room. Doors opened. Notes appeared. Physical injuries were reported—scratches, choking sensations, sudden illness —always following close interaction. The doll itself showed no mechanical capability, no batteries, no joints capable of movement beyond its sewn limbs. Yet it was repeatedly found in positions it should not have been able to reach.

The first containment efforts were improvised. Shelves. Cabinets. Drawers. None held.

It was only after a particularly violent incident—one that left a visitor hospitalized—that the decision was made to isolate the object completely. The display case was commissioned not as a museum artifact, but as a containment device. Its purpose was explicitly preventative.

Early versions of the case were simple: glass-fronted, lockable, reinforced. These failed.

Witnesses later described the glass fogging from the inside without temperature change. Knocks from within when no one was present. On at least two occasions, the door was reportedly found unlocked despite the key remaining in its designated location.

The current iteration of the display case is heavier, more deliberate. The glass is thick, industrial-grade, comparable to what is used in secure collections. The wood frame is sealed, not merely joined. Religious iconography is affixed to the interior, not as decoration but as function—blessings layered rather than symbolic. The case is not airtight, but it is controlled. Nothing enters or exits without intent.

And the doll does not leave it.

Visitors have long reported physical reactions while standing near the case. Headaches. Pressure in the chest. A sense of dread disproportionate to the object's appearance. Some report nausea. Others an overwhelming urge to laugh, cry, or mock the warnings—followed almost immediately by fear.

A recurring pattern emerges in the documentation: those who treat the case as theater leave unsettled. Those who challenge it leave shaken.

One of the most cited incidents involving the display case occurred in the late twentieth century, when a visitor reportedly tapped on the glass, laughed, and dismissed the warnings aloud. Within hours, he was involved in a severe motorcycle accident. While skeptics rightly point out coincidence, what keeps the story alive is the frequency with which similar challenges are followed by sudden misfortune.

The case itself has also been the subject of anomaly reports.

Security staff have described finding the warning placard displaced overnight. Motion sensors triggered without visible cause. One account describes a faint tapping from inside the case after hours—soft, rhythmic, ceasing the moment the room was entered. Environmental checks found no drafts, no vibrations, no pests.

The case has been moved only a handful of times, each relocation preceded by extensive preparation. During one transfer, witnesses reported sudden temperature drops localized to the case. Another move coincided with unexplained power failures along the transport route. No direct causation was established. The pattern was noted and recorded.

Importantly, the case does not neutralize the object.

It contains it.

Researchers who have studied the Annabelle case frequently emphasize that the display case should not be interpreted as proof of supernatural activity, but as a response to repeated, unresolved incidents. It exists because something about proximity, access, or attention appeared to amplify disturbances. Limiting those variables reduced reported activity.

But reduction is not elimination.

Even sealed, the doll remains the most active object in the collection where it has been housed. Not because it moves, but because people react to it. Fear escalates. Behavior changes. Reports cluster around it with unusual density. Other objects may frighten, but Annabelle's case commands silence.

There is also the matter of the warnings themselves.

Most museum signage explains history. This one issues instruction. It does not describe what the doll is or what it has done. It simply states what must not be done. In this way, the display case functions as a threshold. Crossing it—by touch, mockery, or dismissal—is framed as a choice with consequences.

Modern scholars of belief systems have pointed out that such framing creates a feedback loop: expectation heightens perception, perception reinforces narrative. Yet this explanation struggles to account for why the case was necessary before the story was public.

The warnings came after the events, not before.

Today, the Annabelle display case is often photographed more than the doll itself. The glass reflects faces. The wood absorbs light. The warnings remain unchanged. Visitors step back instinctively, even when they know the doll behind it is cloth and thread.

And perhaps that is the most unsettling element of the case: not that it holds something dangerous, but that it has taught so many people—across decades, cultures, and belief systems—to keep their distance without fully understanding why.

The case does not promise safety. It promises separation.

And in the long history of haunted objects, separation is often the only peace that lasts.

about the author

Lorelai Hamilton is a seasoned tarot reader with over 15 years of professional experience in the field. Based in the Pacific Northwest, Lorelai has honed her craft and established herself as a trusted guide in the realm of tarot.

Alongside her tarot practice, Lorelai shares her expertise with a global audience. Having conducted readings for individuals across 25 countries, she has cultivated a deep understanding of the universal human experience and the interconnectedness of souls around the world.

Despite her worldly reach, Lorelai remains dedicated to providing personal and insightful readings for clients, offering virtual consultations that resonate with authenticity and compassion. In her journey as a tarot reader, she has been accompanied by her familiar, Ham, whose quiet presence adds an element of magic to her practice.

bibliography

Abbo of Fleury. *Passio Sancti Eadmundi.*

Ackroyd, Peter. *London: The Biography.* London: Chatto & Windus, 2000.

Alberti, Samuel J. M. M. *Morbid Curiosities: Medical Museums in Nineteenth-Century Britain.* Oxford: Oxford University Press, 2011.

Alcorn, Marvin. *The Death of Bonnie and Clyde.* Gretna, LA: Pelican Publishing, 1994.

American Alliance of Museums. *Collections Care and Sensitive Object Handling.* Washington, DC, 2015.

Anderson, William. *Mary Queen of Scots and the Casket Letters.* London: Batsford, 1923.

Andrews, J. C. *The Folklore of Yorkshire.* London: B. T. Batsford, 1913.

Appel, Jacob. "The 'Evil Eye' in the Western Mediterranean." *The Journal of American Folklore* 90, no. 358 (1977): 451–464.

Ariès, Philippe. *The Hour of Our Death.* New York: Knopf, 1981.

Arnason, H. H. *History of Modern Art.* New York: Pearson, multiple editions.

Arnold, David. *The Legend of Lizzie Borden.* Athens: Ohio University Press.

Arnold, Sir Thomas W. *Painting in Islam: A Study of the Place of Pictorial Art in Muslim Culture.* Oxford: Clarendon Press, 1928.

Asprem, Egil. "Hyperstition and the Occult." *Numen* 58, nos. 2–3 (2011).

Associated Press. "Italian Church Confirms Investigation into Weeping Crucifix." September 1954.

Bächtold-Stäubli, Hanns, and Eduard Hoffmann-Krayer, eds. *Handwörterbuch des deutschen Aberglaubens.* Berlin: Walter de Gruyter, 1927–1942.

Bagnoli, Martina, et al. *Treasures of Heaven: Saints, Relics, and Devotion in Medieval Europe.* London: British Museum / Cleveland Museum of Art, 2010.

Balfour, Ian. *Famous Diamonds.* Woodbridge: Antique Collectors' Club, 2009.

Barber, Malcolm. *Crime and Punishment in Early Modern England.* London: Routledge, 1998.

Bartlett, Robert. *Why Can the Dead Do Such Great Things? Saints and Worshippers from the Martyrs to the Reformation.* Princeton: Princeton University Press, 2013.

Barrow, Blanche Caldwell. *My Life with Bonnie and Clyde.* Norman: University of Oklahoma Press, 2004.

Barrow, G. W. S. *Kingship and Unity: Scotland 1000–1306.* Edinburgh: Edinburgh University Press.

Bataille, Georges. *Eroticism.* San Francisco: City Lights Books, 1986.

Bate, Jonathan. *The Genius of Shakespeare.* Oxford: Oxford University Press, 1997.

Bausinger, Hermann. *Folk Culture in a World of Technology.* Bloomington: Indiana University Press, 1990.

Bayly, C. A. *Empire and Information: Intelligence Gathering and Social Communication in India, 1780–1870.* Cambridge: Cambridge University Press, 1996.

Becker, Peter. "The Fate of the Amber Room." *Journal of Art Crime* 4 (2010): 27–42.

Bibliography

Belmont Family Papers. Architectural and household correspondence, late 19th–early 20th centuries. Rhode Island Historical Society Archives.

Bevan, Robert. *The Destruction of Memory: Architecture at War*. London: Reaktion Books, 2006.

Bethencourt, Francisco. *The Inquisition: A Global History*. Cambridge: Cambridge University Press, 2009.

Bix, Herbert P. *Hirohito and the Making of Modern Japan*. New York: HarperCollins, 2000.

Black Forest Open-Air Museum (Vogtsbauernhof). *Furniture, Domestic Life, and Woodcarving Traditions of the Schwarzwald*. Museum exhibition catalog and object records.

Blatty, William Peter. *The Exorcist*. New York: Harper & Row, 1971.

Boardman, Stephen. *The Early Stewart Kings*. East Linton: Tuckwell Press.

Bongie, Chris. *Sade: A Biography*. Chicago: University of Chicago Press, 1998.

Bord, Janet, and Colin Bord. *Alien Animals*. Publisher varies by edition.

Brewer, E. Cobham. *Brewer's Dictionary of Phrase and Fable*. Various editions.

Brewer, John. *The Pleasures of the Imagination: English Culture in the Eighteenth Century*. Chicago: University of Chicago Press, 1997.

Briggs, Katharine M. *An Encyclopedia of Fairies*. New York: Pantheon Books, 1976.

Briggs, Katharine Mary. *The Fairies in Tradition and Literature*. London: Routledge, 1967.

Brittany Departmental Archives (Morbihan). Parish registers, marriage and death records, 18th–19th centuries.

Brooks, Richard. *Cemetery Reform and the Public Health Movement in France*. London: Routledge, 2012.

Brook, Timothy, ed. *Documents on the Rape of Nanking*. Ann Arbor: University of Michigan Press.

Brown, Basil. *Basil Brown: Archaeologist*. London: British Museum Press, 2009.

Brown, Peter. *The Cult of the Saints: Its Rise and Function in Latin Christianity*. Chicago: University of Chicago Press, 1981.

Bruce-Mitford, Rupert. *The Sutton Hoo Ship-Burial*. 3 vols. London: British Museum Publications, 1975–1983.

Brunvand, Jan Harold. *The Vanishing Hitchhiker: American Urban Legends and Their Meanings*. New York: W. W. Norton.

Butler, Alban. *Lives of the Saints*. Various editions.

British Toy Museum Archives. Manufacturer catalogs and design notes, 1930s–1960s.

Cable, George Washington. "The Haunted House." *Scribner's Magazine*, 1889.

Campanella, Richard. *Cityscapes of New Orleans*. Baton Rouge: Louisiana State University Press, 2017.

Campbell, Peter R. *Power and Politics in Old Regime France, 1720–1745*. London: Routledge, 1996.

Carter, Howard. *The Tomb of Tutankhamun*. 3 vols. London: Cassell and Company, 1923–1933.

Cassola, Luigi, et al. "Analisi Chimica del Liquido di Lacrimazione del Crocifisso di Siracusa." *Bollettino della Società Italiana di Biochimica*, 1954.

Catholic Parish Records of Lower Brittany. Manuscript registers and marginal notes referenced in regional folklore compilations.

Chandler, David G. *The Campaigns of Napoleon*. New York: Scribner, 1966.

Chase, Samuel V. *The Newport Mansions*. New York: G. P. Putnam's Sons, 1919.

Chávez, Thomas E. *Spain and the Independence of the United States: An Intrinsic Gift*. Albuquerque: University of New Mexico Press, 2002.

Clulee, Nicholas H. *John Dee's Natural Philosophy: Between Science and Religion*. London: Routledge, 1988.

Cloulas, Ivan. *The Borgias*. London: Saqi Books, 1996.

Coker, William S. *Pensacola, Florida: A Pictorial History*. Virginia Beach, VA: Donning Company Publishers, 1981.

Coomaraswamy, Ananda K. *The Dance of Śiva*. Various editions.

Corriere della Sera. "Esami Scientifici su un Fenomeno Religioso." 1954.

Cooter, Roger. *The Cultural Meaning of Popular Science: Phrenology and the Organization of Consent in Nineteenth-Century Britain*. Cambridge: Cambridge University Press, 1984.

Crone, Patricia. *Meccan Trade and the Rise of Islam*. Princeton: Princeton University Press, 1987.

Cuevas, Bryan J. *The Hidden History of the Tibetan Book of the Dead*. Oxford: Oxford University Press, 2003.

Curran, Robert. *The Haunted: One Family's Nightmare*. New York: St. Martin's Press.

Curiel, Adrienne. "The Black Orlov: Myth and Marketing." *GIA Alumni Collective* (Gemological Institute of America), 2014.

Curl, James Stevens. *The Egyptian Revival: Ancient Egypt as the Inspiration for Design Motifs in the West*. London: Routledge, 2005.

Cunliffe, Barry. *Roman Bath Discovered*. London: Routledge, 1984.

Cunliffe, Barry, ed. *The Temple of Sulis Minerva at Bath, Volume 2: Finds from the Sacred Spring*. Oxford: Oxford University Committee for Archaeology, 1988.

Dalrymple, William. *The Anarchy: The East India Company, Corporate Violence, and the Pillage of an Empire*. New York: Bloomsbury, 2019.

Dalrymple, William, and Anita Anand. *Koh-i-Noor: The History of the World's Most Infamous Diamond*. New York: Bloomsbury Publishing, 2017.

Dan, Joseph. *Kabbalah: A Very Short Introduction*. Oxford: Oxford University Press.

Darnton, Robert. *The Forbidden Best-Sellers of Pre-Revolutionary France*. New York: W. W. Norton, 1995.

Daston, Lorraine, and Katharine Park. *Wonders and the Order of Nature, 1150–1750*. New York: Zone Books, 1998.

Davies, Owen. *Cunning-Folk: Popular Magic in English History*. London: Hambledon & London.

Davies, Owen. *Grimoires: A History of Magic Books*. Oxford: Oxford University Press, 2009.

Davies, Owen. *Haunted: A Social History of Ghosts*. New York: Palgrave Macmillan, 2007.

Davis, Richard H. *Lives of Indian Images*. Princeton: Princeton University Press.

De Beauvoir, Simone. "Must We Burn Sade?" In *The Marquis de Sade*. New York: Grove Press, 1953.

de Martino, Ernesto. *Sud e magia*. Milan: Feltrinelli, 1959.

Bibliography

Dee, John. *Libri Mysteriorum (Spiritual Diaries), 1581–1583.* British Library, Sloane MSS.

Dennison, E. P. *Orkney Folklore and Traditions.* Kirkwall: Orkney Press, 1972.

Dever, William G. *What Did the Biblical Writers Know and When Did They Know It?* Grand Rapids: Eerdmans.

D'Imperio, Mary. *The Voynich Manuscript: An Elegant Enigma.* Fort Meade, MD: National Security Agency, 1978.

Dirks, Nicholas B. *The Scandal of Empire: India and the Creation of Imperial Britain.* Cambridge, MA: Harvard University Press, 2006.

Ditchfield, P. H. *The Old English Abbeys.* Publisher varies by edition.

Duffy, Eamon. *The Stripping of the Altars.* New Haven: Yale University Press.

Dunne, Dominick. "The Killing of Dominique Dunne." *Vanity Fair,* 1984.

Eco, Umberto. *The Infinity of Lists.* New York: Rizzoli, 2009.

Eliade, Mircea. *The Sacred and the Profane.* New York: Harcourt, 1959.

Ellmann, Richard. *Oscar Wilde.* New York: Alfred A. Knopf, 1988.

Epstein, Edward Jay. *The Rise and Fall of Diamonds.* New York: Simon & Schuster, 1982.

Esposito, John L. *Islam: The Straight Path.* Oxford: Oxford University Press, 2016.

Etlin, Richard A. *The Architecture of Death: The Transformation of the Cemetery in Eighteenth-Century Paris.* Cambridge, MA: MIT Press, 1984.

Evans-Wentz, W. Y., ed. *The Tibetan Book of the Dead.* Oxford: Oxford University Press, 1927.

Fenton, Alexander. *Scottish Country Furniture, 1700–1900.* Edinburgh: John Donald, 1995.

Finkelstein, Israel, and Neil Asher Silberman. *The Bible Unearthed.* New York: Free Press.

Flood, Finbarr Barry. "Between Cult and Culture: Bamiyan, Islamic Iconoclasm, and the Museum." *The Art Bulletin* 84, no. 4 (2002).

Foakes, R. A. *Shakespeare and Violence.* Cambridge: Cambridge University Press, 2003.

Fort, Charles. *Lo!* New York: Boni & Liveright, 1931.

Fortean Times. Archival reporting on haunted objects and related anomalies, various issues.

Foster, Michael Dylan. *The Book of Yōkai: Mysterious Creatures of Japanese Folklore.* Berkeley: University of California Press, 2015.

Foucault, Michel. *Madness and Civilization.* New York: Vintage Books, 1988.

Fraser, Antonia. *Marie Antoinette: The Journey.* New York: Anchor Books, 2001.

Freeman, Charles. *Holy Bones, Holy Dust: How Relics Shaped the History of Medieval Europe.* New Haven: Yale University Press, 2011.

Freud, Sigmund. "The Uncanny." 1919. In *The Standard Edition of the Complete Psychological Works of Sigmund Freud.*

French Folklore Society. *Revue des Traditions Populaires.* Selected issues, late 19th century.

Fremantle, Frances, and Chögyam Trungpa. *The Tibetan Book of the Dead: The Great Liberation Through Hearing in the Bardo.* Boston: Shambhala Publications, 1975.

Friedkin, William. *The Friedkin Connection.* New York: HarperCollins, 2013.

Friedman, Richard Elliott. *Who Wrote the Bible?* New York: HarperOne.

Futamura, Madoka. *War Crimes Tribunals and Transitional Justice.* London: Routledge, 2008.

Bibliography

Gager, John G. *Curse Tablets and Binding Spells from the Ancient World*. Oxford: Oxford University Press, 1992.

Gauld, Alan, and A. D. Cornell. *Poltergeists*. London: Routledge & Kegan Paul, 1979.

Gamboni, Dario. *The Destruction of Art: Iconoclasm and Vandalism since the French Revolution*. New Haven: Yale University Press, 1997.

Geary, Patrick J. *Furta Sacra: Thefts of Relics in the Central Middle Ages*. Princeton: Princeton University Press.

Germanisches Nationalmuseum (Nuremberg). Domestic furniture and folk belief in southern Germany. Collection notes and conservation documentation.

Giesen, Rolf. *The Black Forest: Nature, Culture, and Folklore*. Berlin: Reimer Verlag, 2004.

Gill, David, et al. "Identification of the Remains of the Romanov Family." *Nature Genetics* 6 (1994).

Ginzburg, Carlo. *Ecstasies: Deciphering the Witches' Sabbath*. New York: Pantheon Books, 1991.

Gosling, Betty. *Origins of Thai Art*. Chiang Mai: Silkworm Books, 2004.

Gray, Francine du Plessix. *At Home with the Marquis de Sade: A Life*. New York: Simon & Schuster, 1998.

Guiley, Rosemary Ellen. *The Encyclopedia of Ghosts and Spirits*. New York: Facts On File, 2007.

Guiley, Rosemary Ellen. *The Encyclopedia of Witches, Witchcraft, and Wicca*. New York: Facts On File, 2008.

Guinn, Jeff. *Go Down Together: The True, Untold Story of Bonnie and Clyde*. New York: Simon & Schuster, 2009.

Guidoboni, Emanuela. *Vesuvius: A History of Eruptions*. Cambridge: Cambridge University Press, 1994.

Guy, John. *Queen of Scots: The True Life of Mary Stuart*. Boston: Houghton Mifflin Harcourt, 2004.

Gwynn, Aubrey. *The Irish Church in the Early Middle Ages*. Dublin: Gill and Macmillan, 1992.

Halliday, Stephen. *Haunted Houses of Britain*. London: Robert Hale, 2003.

Hanegraaff, Wouter J. *Esotericism and the Academy*. Cambridge: Cambridge University Press, 2012.

Hardman, John. *The French Revolution Sourcebook*. London: Arnold, 1999.

Harbison, Peter. *Pilgrimage in Ireland: The Monuments and the People*. London: Barrie & Jenkins, 1991.

Harkness, Deborah E. *John Dee's Conversations with Angels*. Cambridge: Cambridge University Press, 1999.

Hawting, G. R. *The Idea of Idolatry and the Emergence of Islam*. Cambridge: Cambridge University Press, 1999.

Hawass, Zahi. *Tutankhamun and the Golden Age of the Pharaohs*. Washington, DC: National Geographic, 2005.

Hearn, Lafcadio. *Kwaidan: Stories and Studies of Strange Things*. Boston: Houghton Mifflin, 1904.

Henderson, Lizanne, and Edward J. Cowan. *Scottish Fairy Belief: A History*. East Linton: Tuckwell Press, 2001.

Heron-Allen, Edward. *The Purple Sapphire*. Privately printed, 1921.

Bibliography

Hibbert, Christopher. *The Roots of Evil: A Social History of Crime and Punishment.* Boston: Little, Brown and Company, 1963.

Hinton, Ted, and Larry Grove. *Ambush: The Real Story of Bonnie and Clyde.* Austin: Shoal Creek Publishers, 1979.

Hines, John. "The Nature of the Sutton Hoo Burial." *Antiquity* 61 (1987).

Hoggard, Brian. "The Witch Bottle: A Study of Witchcraft Belief in England." *Journal of Material Culture* 9, no. 1 (2004).

Hollingsworth, Mary. *The Borgias: History's Most Notorious Dynasty.* New York: Pegasus Books, 2011.

Holland, Merlin. *The Wilde Album.* London: Fourth Estate, 1997.

Hole, Christina. *English Folklore.* London: B. T. Batsford, 1940.

Hunt, Lynn. *The Invention of Pornography: Obscenity and the Origins of Modernity, 1500–1800.* New York: Zone Books, 1993.

Hunt, Lynn. *Politics, Culture, and Class in the French Revolution.* Berkeley: University of California Press, 1984.

Hutton, Ronald. *Blood and Mistletoe.* New Haven: Yale University Press.

Hutton, Ronald. *The Rise and Fall of Merry England.* Oxford: Oxford University Press.

Hutton, Ronald. *The Triumph of the Moon.* Oxford: Oxford University Press, 1999.

Hutton, Ronald. *The Witch: A History of Fear, from Ancient Times to the Present.* New Haven: Yale University Press, 2017.

Inglis, Brian. *Science and the Paranormal.* London: Hodder & Stoughton, 1977.

Ikram, Salima. *Death and Burial in Ancient Egypt.* Cairo: American University in Cairo Press.

Iowa County Historical Societies Oral History Project. Rural domestic life interviews, 1930–1980.

Iowa State Historical Society. *County Birth and Death Registers, 1890–1920.* Des Moines archival collections.

James, T. G. H. *Tutankhamun.* London: Friedman/Fairfax.

Jain, Meenakshi. *Flight of Deities and Rebirth of Temples.* New Delhi: Aryan Books.

Japanese Society for the Study of Night Terrors. Case summaries involving childhood object-related parasomnias, 1998–2006.

Joshi, S. T. *H. P. Lovecraft: A Life.* West Warwick, RI: Necronomicon Press, 1996.

Kaufmann, Thomas DaCosta. *Court, Cloister, and City: The Art and Culture of Central Europe, 1450–1800.* Chicago: University of Chicago Press, 1995.

Kennedy, Gerry, and Rob Churchill. *The Voynich Manuscript.* London: Orion Publishing, 2004.

Kermode, Mark. *The Exorcist.* London: BFI Film Classics, 1997.

Kessell, John L. *Spain in the Southwest: A Narrative History of Colonial New Mexico, Arizona, Texas, and California.* Norman: University of Oklahoma Press, 2002.

Keay, John. *India: A History.* New York: HarperCollins, 2000.

Kieckhefer, Richard. *Forbidden Rites: A Necromancer's Manual of the Fifteenth Century.* University Park: Penn State University Press, 1997.

Kleiner, Fred S. *Gardner's Art Through the Ages: The Western Perspective.* Boston: Wadsworth Cengage Learning, 2011.

Kugel, James L. *How to Read the Bible.* New York: Free Press.

Bibliography

Kunz, George Frederick. *The Curious Lore of Precious Stones*. New York: Dover Publications, 1971.

Kuritsyn, Alexander. *The Amber Room: The Eighth Wonder of the World*. Moscow: Progress Publishers, 1984.

Kurth, Peter. *Anastasia: The Riddle of Anna Anderson*. Boston: Little, Brown and Company, 1983.

Kurin, Richard. *Hope Diamond: The Legendary History of a Cursed Gem*. Washington, DC: Smithsonian Books.

Le Braz, Anatole. *La Légende de la Mort en Basse-Bretagne*. Paris: Champion, 1893.

Lecouteux, Claude. *The Tradition of Household Spirits: Ancestral Lore and Practices*. Rochester, VT: Inner Traditions, 2013.

Lecouteux, Claude. *Phantoms and Poltergeists: A Study of Apparitions*. Rochester, VT: Inner Traditions, 2015.

Lever, Evelyne. *Louis XVI*. Paris: Fayard, 1985.

Lever, Evelyne. *Marie Antoinette: The Last Queen of France*. New York: Farrar, Straus and Giroux, 2000.

Lizzie Borden Bed & Breakfast Museum (Fall River, MA). Guest accounts and historical room documentation.

Long, Alecia P. *The Great Southern Babylon: Sex, Race, and Respectability in New Orleans, 1865–1920*. Baton Rouge: LSU Press, 2004.

Luckhurst, Roger. *The Invention of Telepathy: 1870–1901*. Oxford: Oxford University Press, 2002.

Markham, J. David. *Napoleon For Dummies*. Hoboken, NJ: Wiley Publishing, 2005.

Massachusetts Historical Society. Borden family records and Fall River archival materials.

Massie, Robert K. *Nicholas and Alexandra*. New York: Atheneum, 1967.

Massie, Robert K. *Peter the Great: His Life and World*. New York: Alfred A. Knopf, 1980.

McCalman, Iain. *Radical Underworld: Prophets, Revolutionaries and Pornographers in London, 1795–1840*. Cambridge: Cambridge University Press, 1988.

Merrifield, Ralph. *The Archaeology of Ritual and Magic*. London: B. T. Batsford, 1987.

Midwest Folklore Journal. "Domestic Objects and Infant Death Narratives in Rural America." Vol. 18, no. 2 (1992).

Mertz, Barbara. *Temples, Tombs, and Hieroglyphs*. New York: Bedrick Books, 1964.

Messori, Vittorio. *Reports on Miraculous Phenomena in Modern Catholicism*. San Francisco: Ignatius Press, 1998.

New England Society for Psychic Research (NESPR). Case summaries and museum documentation related to the Annabelle doll and containment practices.

Newport Historical Society. *Belcourt Castle: Architectural and Social History*. Exhibition notes and unpublished manuscripts.

Nickell, Joe. *Investigating the Paranormal*. Buffalo, NY: Prometheus Books, 2007.

Nickell, Joe. *Investigating the Supernatural*. Amherst, NY: Prometheus Books, 2001.

North Yorkshire County Records Office. Assize court records and parish documentation relating to Thomas Busby, early 18th century.

Ogden, Daniel. *Magic, Witchcraft, and Ghosts in the Greek and Roman Worlds*. Oxford: Oxford University Press.

Orkney Library & Archive. Antiquarian notes and parish folklore manuscripts, 18th–19th centuries.

Orkney Museums Service. *Object Records and Exhibition Notes: The Devil's Chair.* Kirkwall.

Page, William, ed. *The Victoria History of the County of Surrey.* Volumes vary.

Pearson, John. *The Trials of Lizzie Borden.* New Haven: Yale University Press.

People. "Where Is the Smurl Family Now? Here's What Happened to 'The Conjuring: Last Rites' Subjects..." September 7, 2025.

Pearsall, Ronald. *The Victorian Underworld.* London: Temple Smith, 1968.

Peleggi, Maurizio. *The Politics of Ruins and the Business of Nostalgia.* Bangkok: White Lotus Press, 2002.

Petzet, Michael, ed. *The Giant Buddhas of Bamiyan: Safeguarding the Remains.* Paris: ICOMOS, 2009.

Pick, Daniel. *Faces of Degeneration: A European Disorder, c.1848–c.1918.* Cambridge: Cambridge University Press, 1989.

Pinch, Geraldine. *Egyptian Mythology: A Guide to the Gods, Goddesses, and Traditions of Ancient Egypt.* Oxford: Oxford University Press, 2004.

Radford, Benjamin. *Scientific Paranormal Investigation: How to Solve Unexplained Mysteries.* Durham, NC: Carolina Academic Press, 2010.

Radford, Benjamin. *Tracking the Chupacabra and Other Mysteries.* Albuquerque: University of New Mexico Press, 2011.

Rappaport, Helen. *The Last Days of the Romanovs: Tragedy at Ekaterinburg.* New York: St. Martin's Press, 2008.

Reeds, Jim. "John Dee and the Magic Tables in the Book of Soyga." *Cryptologia* 26, no. 4 (2002): 317–331.

Reeves, Nicholas. *The Complete Tutankhamun: The King, the Tomb, the Royal Treasure.* London: Thames & Hudson, 1990.

Richardson, Frank. *The Hell-Fire Clubs: Sex, Satanism and Secret Societies.* London: Headline Book Publishing, 1997.

Ridyard, Susan J. *The Royal Saints of Anglo-Saxon England.* Cambridge: Cambridge University Press.

Riggs, Christina. *Unwrapping Ancient Egypt.* London: Bloomsbury Academic, 2014.

Roberts, Andrew. *Napoleon: A Life.* New York: Viking, 2014.

Roberts, David. "The Curse of the Busby Stoop Chair." *Fortean Times,* issue 143 (2001).

Roden, Claudia. *The Folklore of Domestic Space in Central Europe.* London: Routledge, 1985.

Rosenfeld, Sophia. *A Revolution in Language: The Problem of Signs in Late Eighteenth-Century France.* Stanford: Stanford University Press, 2001.

Rugg, Gordon. "An Elegant Hoax?" *Cryptologia* 28, no. 1 (2004): 31–46.

Schama, Simon. *Citizens: A Chronicle of the French Revolution.* New York: Vintage Books, 1989.

Schmidt, Leopold. *Volkskunst im Schwarzwald.* Sigmaringen: Thorbecke Verlag, 1962.

Schmidt, Leopold. *Volkskunst und Aberglaube im deutschen und amerikanischen Haus.* Vienna: Böhlau Verlag, 1961.

Scholem, Gershom. *Major Trends in Jewish Mysticism.* New York: Schocken Books.

Seabrook, W. B. *The Magic Island.* New York: Harcourt, Brace & Company, 1929.

Bibliography

Secord, James. *Victorian Sensation: The Extraordinary Publication, Reception, and Secret Authorship of Vestiges of the Natural History of Creation.* Chicago: University of Chicago Press, 2000.

Segrave, Kerry. *Hollywood Traumas: Famous Accidents, Deaths, and Disasters.* Jefferson, NC: McFarland & Company, 1989.

Sébillot, Paul. *Le Folk-lore de France: La Bretagne.* Paris: Ernest Leroux, 1904.

Shakespeare, William. *Macbeth.* c. 1606.

Shannon, Claude. "Prediction and Entropy of Printed English." *Bell System Technical Journal* (1951).

Skeptical Inquirer. "Ghosts in the Machine" category page and Smurl family coverage (West Pittston, Pennsylvania; media attention beginning in 1986).

Skeptical Inquirer. Articles examining the Annabelle case and containment narratives, various issues.

Simpson, Jacqueline. *British Folktales and Legends.* New York: Random House, 1997.

Simpson, Jacqueline. *The Lore of the Land.* London: Penguin Books, 2005.

Simpson, Jacqueline, and Steve Roud. *A Dictionary of English Folklore.* Oxford: Oxford University Press, 2000.

Smith, Mark. *Hollywood Hauntings.* Jefferson, NC: McFarland & Company, 2014.

Smith, Mark S. *The Early History of God.* Grand Rapids: Eerdmans.

Smithsonian National Museum of American History. Automata and mechanical toys in the 20th century. Curatorial essays and collection notes.

Smithsonian National Museum of American History. Raggedy Ann dolls and American toy culture. Curatorial essays and object histories.

Sleeman, William Henry. *Rambles and Recollections of an Indian Official.* London: J. Hatchard & Son, 1844.

Sleeman, William Henry. *Report on the Depredations Committed by the Thug Gangs.* Calcutta: Government of India, 1839.

Stone, Norman. *World War II: A Short History.* New York: Basic Books, 2012.

Stokker, Kathleen. *Folklore Fights the Nazis: Humor in Occupied Norway, 1940–1945.* Madison: University of Wisconsin Press, 1997.

Stokker, Kathleen. *Remaking American Folklore: Narratives of Loss and Domestic Memory.* Madison: University of Wisconsin Press, 2001.

Stronge, Susan. *The Arts of the Sikh Kingdoms.* London: V&A Publications, 1999.

Sublette, Ned. *The World That Made New Orleans.* New York: Lawrence Hill Books, 2008.

Tambiah, Stanley J. *The Buddhist Saints of the Forest and the Cult of Amulets.* Cambridge: Cambridge University Press, 1984.

The Gospel of John. Chapter 19.

The Times (London). "Lord Carnarvon Dead." April 6, 1923.

Totani, Yuma. *The Tokyo War Crimes Trial: The Pursuit of Justice in the Wake of World War II.* Cambridge, MA: Harvard University Asia Center, 2008.

Trachtenberg, Joshua. *Jewish Magic and Superstition.* Philadelphia: University of Pennsylvania Press.

Trevor-Roper, Hugh. *The Last Days of Hitler.* London: Macmillan.

Tuan, Yi-Fu. *Space and Place: The Perspective of Experience.* Minneapolis: University of Minnesota Press, 1977.

Tyldesley, Joyce. *Tutankhamun's Curse: The Developing History of an Egyptian King.* London: BBC Books, 2012.

Urban, Hugh B. *Magia Sexualis.* Berkeley: University of California Press, 2006.

Van Gennep, Arnold. *The Rites of Passage.* Chicago: University of Chicago Press, 1960.

Vanderbilt, Arthur T. *Fortune's Children: The Fall of the House of Vanderbilt.* New York: Morrow, 1989.

van Woerkens, Martine. *The Strangled Traveler: Colonial Imaginings and the Thugs of India.* Chicago: University of Chicago Press, 2002.

Versnel, H. S. *Beyond Cursing: The Appeal to Justice in Judicial Prayers.* Leiden: Brill.

Vikan, Gary. *Early Christian and Byzantine Art.* London: British Museum Press, 1994.

Vogt, Adolf. "Carved Furniture and Protective Symbolism in Southern German Folk Art." *Journal of European Ethnology* 22, no. 3 (1992).

Waite, A. E. *The Book of Ceremonial Magic.* London: Rider & Company.

Waite, Robert G. L. *The Psychopathic God: Adolf Hitler.* New York: Da Capo Press.

Wagner, Kim A. *Thuggee: Banditry and the British in Early Nineteenth-Century India.* New York: Palgrave Macmillan, 2007.

Warren, Ed, and Lorraine Warren. *The Demonologist.* New York: St. Martin's Press, 1980.

Warren, Ed, and Lorraine Warren. *Graveyard: True Hauntings from an Old New England Cemetery.* New York: St. Martin's Press, 1992.

Weber, David J. *The Spanish Frontier in North America.* New Haven: Yale University Press, 1992.

Webster, Leslie. *Anglo-Saxon Art.* London: British Museum Press, 2012.

Westwood, Jennifer, and Jacqueline Simpson. *The Lore of the Land.* London: Penguin Books, 2005.

Wheeler, R. E. Mortimer. *Roman Britain at the Cross-Roads.* London: Methuen, 1954.

Wilkinson, Richard H. *The Complete Gods and Goddesses of Ancient Egypt.* London: Thames & Hudson, 2003.

Wills, Garry. *Witches and Jesuits: Shakespeare's Macbeth.* Oxford: Oxford University Press, 1995.

Wingfield, Chris. "A Case Re-opened: The Science and Folklore of a 'Witch's Ladder'." *Journal of Material Culture* 15, no. 3 (2010): 302–322.

Woodward, Ann, and Peter Leach. *The Uley Shrines: Excavation of a Ritual Complex on West Hill, Uley, Gloucestershire.* London: English Heritage, 1993.

Woodward, Hiram W. *The Art and Architecture of Thailand: From Prehistoric Times through the Thirteenth Century.* Leiden: Brill, 2003.

Wormald, Jenny. *Mary Queen of Scots: A Study in Failure.* London: George Philip, 1988.

Wyatt, David K. *Thailand: A Short History.* New Haven: Yale University Press, 2003.

Yorkshire Post Archive. "Deaths and Legends of the Busby Stoop Chair." Various articles, 1960s–1970s.

Zandbergen, René. *The Voynich Manuscript.* Leiden: Brill, 2020.